THE
ABOLITIONIST
AND THE SPY

THE ABOLITIONIST AND THE SPY

*A Father, a Son, and
Their Battle for the Union*

KEN LIZZIO

THE COUNTRYMAN PRESS

A Division of W. W. Norton & Company

Independent Publishers Since 1923

We welcome your comments and suggestions. Please contact

Editor
The Countryman Press
500 Fifth Avenue
New York, NY 10110
or e-mail countrymanpress@wwnorton.com

For information about permission to reproduce selections from this book, write to
Permissions, The Countryman Press, 500 Fifth Avenue, New York, NY 10110

For information about special discounts for bulk purchases, please contact
W. W. Norton Special Sales at specialsales@wwnorton.com or 800-233-4830

Manufacturing by LSC Harrisonburg

The Countryman Press

www.countrymanpress.com

A division of W. W. Norton & Company, Inc.
500 Fifth Avenue, New York, NY 10110

www.wwnorton.com

978-1-68268-471-9 (pbk.)

10 9 8 7 6 5 4 3 2 1

CONTENTS

PREFACE

ON A BITTERLY COLD EVENING IN JANUARY 1862, A brash young seaman in the Union Navy named Spencer Kellogg Brown paced uneasily aboard the gunboat *Essex*. Hunched against the cold, he strode back and forth across the deck, debating the wisdom of a bold plan he wished to propose to the ship's captain. It was a risky gambit, and each time a niggling doubt arose, he had to remind himself that he had received an important assignment once before by impressing his commanding officer with his pluck and daring.

The previous August, while serving as a private in the Union's western army under General Nathaniel Lyon, the nineteen-year-old had led a body of scouts to identify rebel strength and positions. He had so impressed Lyon's successor, General John C. Frémont, that Frémont had tasked him with recruiting the Lyon Legion, a body of Union scouts attached to the 24th Missouri Volunteer Infantry. Frémont himself had given Spencer the assignment with the promise of a captain's commission. But when Frémont issued an emancipation edict that freed slaves in his district, an angry President Lincoln relieved the impulsive general of his command for insubordination. With Frémont's dismissal, both Spencer's mission and his promotion had evaporated. Feeling the army had reneged on its commitment, Spencer cast about for a new opportunity, one where he could show his mettle and advance quickly through the ranks. He chose the Union Navy in the belief it would be the deciding factor in the war.

When the Civil War broke out, both sides recognized the importance of controlling the country's major rivers. Not only did they offer a swift means of moving men and matériel, they were vital arteries for the Confederate economy. At the outset of the war, Union General Winfield Scott proposed a sweeping plan aimed at dividing the Confederacy in two. Dubbed the Anaconda Plan, it consisted of blockading Southern ports and gaining control of the Mississippi River. Control the Mississippi, Scott believed, and you would strangle the Confederacy.

Even though the Union had taken control of large swaths of the Mississippi, one Confederate battery had proved particularly resistant to attack: the batteries at Columbus, Kentucky. The batteries had been constructed the previous September by General Leonidas Polk, who saw Columbus as a highly strategic position from which to thwart any advance of Union troops. Known as the Fighting Bishop for having been a clergyman prior to the war, Polk had fortified the river bluffs and had drawn a massive chain of foot-long links clear across the river to Belmont, Missouri, to block Union gunboats and supply ships from passing. With Union boats stymied above Columbus, Polk proudly declared his fortified riverine garrison the Gibraltar of the West.

In November, Frémont ordered General Ulysses S. Grant to take Belmont. Descending by riverboat from Cairo, Illinois, with three thousand men, Grant landed above the town and took the Confederates by surprise, seizing hundreds of prisoners and driving off several infantry regiments. But the Confederates quickly counterattacked, eventually pushing Grant back, thanks to a thunderous barrage of artillery fire from Polk's batteries. The *pièce de résistance* of Polk's artillery was a fifteen-thousand-pound howitzer, the Lady Polk, named after the good general's wife.

Two months later, while the *Essex* was docked at Cairo, the ship's commander, Captain William D. Porter, received word that several enemy vessels were towing a large floating battery upriver from Columbus. In a thick early morning fog, Porter quickly disembarked, accompanied by the gunboat *St. Louis.* Four miles north of Columbus, he engaged the enemy at Lucas Bend. Thanks to Porter's foresight in modifying what was originally a timberclad gunboat into a heavily armed ironclad—and without official authorization—Porter was able to force three Confederate gunboats to retreat to Polk's iron batteries.[1] Protected as they were by Polk's batteries, Porter was unable to pursue the ships. Frustrated, he returned to Cairo to reprovision.

The son of the distinguished Commodore David D. Porter, and a highly capable navy commander in his own right, Captain Porter had found no solution to the Confederate conundrum at Columbus. Now nearly two weeks after the Battle of Lucas Bend, Spencer Kellogg Brown was traipsing the deck of the *Essex,* pondering whether to share his idea for cracking Polk's impregnable fortress at Columbus with the commander. Gathering his courage, he marched up to the deckhouse and asked Captain R. K. Riley, the Executive Officer, permission to speak with Porter in private.

Seeing the lanky youth standing furtively at the door, Porter ejected Riley from the room and shouted, "Come in, young man. Speak quick!" Clearing his throat nervously, Spencer said, "I'd like to volunteer my services, sir, as a spy."[2] His plan, he explained, was to cross over to Columbus with a shipmate, Trussel, and pose as deserters so they could map Polk's river batteries. As Porter listened in silence, Spencer laid out the details of his dangerous scheme. Porter then asked a few questions, answers to which Spencer had already thought out. Impressed with the plan, Porter approved. The time allotted for their absence would be ten days.

The next day the tug attending the *Essex* took Spencer and Trussel up to Cairo to make preparations. In Spencer's pocket were leave of absence papers and a pair of irons he intended to have twisted apart to bolster his ruse. He also had nearly a hundred dollars given to him by his shipmates for purchases. At noon, having satisfactorily acquitted their business, the two enjoyed a tasty meal of fried Mississippi Gulf oysters. After spending a leisurely afternoon at billiards, they got back to the *Essex* around dark. At the ship's cashier, Spencer deposited seven and a half dollars, and, keeping three dollars in specie, took a receipt that he gave to a friend to keep. He then left word to wake him and his comrade at half past two in the morning. When they awoke it was so cold that they put on an extra layer of clothing. They then dropped into a skiff and began their mock escape. In the darkness they drifted downriver toward an uncertain fate. When they had gone some distance from the ship, they could hear the mournful bell of the *Essex* sounding three o'clock. After just thirty minutes on the water, the two boys were shivering and began moving vigorously to stay warm. When they tried to muffle the oars with handkerchiefs, the water froze the cloth hard as rocks, rendering them useless. Spencer then had his comrade place the irons on his wrists but quickly removed them on account of the intense cold, deciding to wait until they were within sight of Columbus before putting them on. After two hours on the water, they came across the Confederate ship, the CSS *Grampus,* anchored in the river, but they went unnoticed. As the lights of Columbus came into sight, they conducted a last-minute search for any letters or papers in their possession they had neglected to destroy. At dawn they finally reached the city where the rebel steamer *Charm* was docked. When their hails to the men on board failed to bring any answer, they climbed on board. Once on deck, they succeeded in catching someone's attention and announced they were deserters from the North. Immediately, they were escorted to General Polk.

At just nineteen years of age, Spencer had become a Union spy.

Just what had motivated a young sailor, a boy really, to volunteer for such a dangerous mission? He was acutely aware that captured spies were routinely executed, often without so much as a trial. Was it overweening ambition? A youthful thirst for swashbuckling adventure? Or an impassioned abolitionist's abhorrence of slavery? It was most likely all of these. Whatever the motive, the trajectory of his life had been set in motion long before he was born—by his father Orville in a place called the Burned-Over District—a vast area that stretched from western New England to Ohio—at a time called the Second Great Awakening. The religious fervor born of that time and place would make abolitionists of both. Each would fight in a war against slavery, one for Kansas, the other for the Union.

Only one would survive.

PART I

THE ABOLITIONIST: ORVILLE BROWN IN BLEEDING KANSAS

★ ★ ★ ★

Chapter One

A GREAT AWAKENING

"Will You not revive us again, that your people may rejoice in You."
—Psalm 85:6

IF EVER THERE WAS A MAN WHO WAS A PRODUCT OF his times, it was Orville Chester Brown. The only son of Ephraim and Philomela Brown first saw the light amid the rolling hills of Litchfield, New York, on February 25, 1811. Litchfield was then a rural hamlet, and Orville's early schooling took place in a covered wagon run by a stern disciplinarian named Lyman Scott. By his own admission, Orville was an unruly lad whom Scott routinely punished with whippings and other forms of abuse, much to the amusement of his classmates. When he was eight, his parents moved from the house Ephraim's father had built to a smaller one. In the process Orville was transferred, to his great relief, to another school.

Orville came of age during an unusual period of intellectual and religious ferment in an America occasioned by the uncertainty of the times. The young republic had only recently cast off the shackles of British domination to embark on its grand "experiment in freedom." Yet Britain continued to harass its former colony, arming Indians on the frontier, seizing American ships, and impressing seamen. Provoked to the breaking point, the United States once again declared war against Britain in 1812, in a conflict sometimes called the Second War of Independence. The war went badly for the young nation as one failure followed another. Andrew Jackson finally snatched triumph from the jaws of defeat with his decisive triumph over the British at the Battle of New Orleans in 1815.

No sooner had America's independence finally been secured when it was followed by a revolution of another sort, the Industrial Revolution. The shift from an agricultural economy to an industrial economy wrought profound social dislocations. People who migrated to cities in search of factory jobs found crowded living conditions and worked long hours in oppressive sweat shops. As the standard of living rose, the population swelled from four million in 1790 to over eighteen million by 1840.

With society in such rapid flux, it is not surprising that many people turned to religion for stability and comfort. As early as the 1790s, strange prophets had begun to appear in New England, prescribing everything for man's salvation from vegetarianism to the wearing of distinctive clothing like bearskin tunics with leather girdles.[1] As Yankees drifted westward, the religious enthusiasm spread. By 1800 a religious revival was underway throughout the country called the Second Great Awakening (the first was in the 1740s).

Viewed from our largely secular times, it is hard to appreciate the sweeping scale and emotional intensity of the Second Great Awakening. It was nothing less than a complete cultural upheaval in American life, akin to the counterculture revolution of the 1960s. It lasted nearly fifty years and led to the conversion of millions—the majority of them women. The revival started as a Protestant movement, and by the 1820s, Congregational, Baptist, Calvinist, Presbyterian, and Methodist denominations were all swept up in the frenzy.

It was a decidedly different, more emotional style of religion Americans turned to. In reaction to the dehumanizing effects of the Industrial Age, a new emphasis was placed on human feelings and emotion over cold reason in man's search for truth and happiness. Suffering souls had only to hear God's call and open themselves to his divine mercy and forgiveness in order to be saved. The romantic impulse spawned a great flowering of intellectual and literary activity that sought to extol the beauty of nature and the value of the individual. Best known were the Transcendentalists, a group of New England writers like Henry David Thoreau and Ralph W. Emerson, who rejected the old Puritan notion of a sinful man being punished by a wrathful deity, emphasizing man's inherent goodness and divinity instead.

All over the country in churches and meeting houses, evangelical preachers called listeners to repent in order to be saved from the fires of hell. On the frontier, where no buildings could accommodate the massive crowds, camp meetings were held in the open air with tents for lodging. In 1801 at one camp revival in Cane Ridge, Kentucky, estimates of attendees ranged from an astonishing ten to twenty-five thousand. Spurred by the impassioned oratory of rural preachers, listeners indulged in orgies of emotional behavior. Some were moved to tears and cried out for mercy, while others, convinced they were possessed by the devil, howled liked rabid dogs. Some swooned in awe at the beatific outpouring of the Holy Spirit. Frances Trollope, a British traveler, witnessed one such revival in Indiana as two preachers exhorted the fold to "come to Jesus":

And now in every part of the church a movement was perceptible, slight at first, but by degrees becoming more decided. Young girls arose, and sat down, and rose again; and then the pews opened, and several came tottering out, their hands clasped, their heads hanging on their bosoms, and every limb trembling, and still the hymn went on; but as the poor creatures approached the rail their sobs and groans became audible. They seated themselves on the "anxious benches;" the hymn ceased, and two of the three priests walked down from the tribune, and going, one to the right, and the other to the left, began whispering to the poor tremblers seated there. These whispers were inaudible to us, but the sobs and groans increased to a frightful excess. Young creatures, with features pale and distorted, fell on their knees on the pavement, and soon sunk forward on their faces; the most violent cries and shrieks followed, while from time to time a voice was heard in convulsive accents, exclaiming, "Oh Lord! Oh Lord Jesus! Help me, Jesus!" and the like.... Violent hysterics and convulsions seized many of them, and when the tumult was at the highest, the priest who remained above again gave out a hymn, as if to drown it.... One young girl, apparently not more than fourteen, was supported in the arms of another, some years older; her face was pale as death; her eyes wide open, and perfectly devoid of meaning; her chin and bosom wet with slaver; she had every appearance of idiotism. I saw a priest approach her; he took her delicate hands, "Jesus is with her! Bless the Lord!" he said, and passed on.[2]

The awakening was particularly intense from western New England across upstate New York to Ohio, an area that came to be known as the Burned-Over District, an allusion to the spiritual fire that scorched the souls of the converted.[3] So intense was the religiosity in the Burned-Over District that it spawned entirely new movements, such as the Mormonism of Joseph Smith, who claimed in a vision to have been guided by two spirits to a buried set of golden religious plates. Existing movements, such as Mother Ann Lee's Shakers, were drawn to the region's religious passion and established colonies there.

By 1825 the religious excitement—some might say hysteria—reached a climax that lasted twelve years. So many people converted to Evangelical Protestantism that it seemed to confirm the Bible's prediction of the unanimity of belief that would precede the coming of Christ and the establishment of God's Kingdom on earth. Most vocal of the chiliastic proponents was William Miller, a former sheriff who turned to religion after seeing his comrades die in battle during the War of 1812. After converting to the Baptist faith, he immersed himself in the Bible. Eventually, Miller came to the conclusion that every prophecy in the holy book was literal and accurate.[4] On the basis of Daniel's vision of the ram, the he-goat, and the little horn, in which there is mention of twenty-three hundred days, Miller made an elaborate calculation which, he thought, proved that the millennium would end in the year 1843.

In the 1830s Miller began preaching the Second Coming at revivals in the Burned-Over District and New England. Moved by Miller's dramatic biblical imagery, over fifty thousand people converted to Millerism, believing the end of the world was at hand and would usher in heaven on earth, the return of Christ, and the Day of Judgment. Another one million Americans were "skeptically expectant."[5] Behind the wild conviction were the economic dislocations wrought by the economic depression of 1837 and a comet that appeared nightly on the horizon between February 28 and April 1, 1843. Some despairing souls committed suicide rather than face the Day of Judgment.[6] State lunatic asylums took in many driven mad by fears of the world's imminent end. According to historian Alice Tyler:

In Portsmouth, New Hampshire, a Millerite in voluminous
white robes climbed a tree, tried to fly when he thought the
fatal hour was near, fell, and broke his neck. A Massachusetts
farmer cut his wife's throat because she refused to be converted
to Millerism, and a despairing mother poisoned herself and all
her children. The editor of a New Bedford paper described the
somewhat amusing anguish of a mechanic whom he had seen
kneeling in the snow with a Millerite pamphlet in each hand,
praying and blaspheming alternately in a "most piteous man-
ner." In Wilkes-Barre, Pennsylvania, a storekeeper requested
the sheriff to give all his goods to anyone who would take them
away, and in New York another merchant offered to give a pair
of shoes to anyone who needed them, since "he had no further
use for them."[7]

But when 1843 passed without event, Miller was under popular pressure to come up with a new date. He revised his forecast
repeatedly, finally settling on October 23, 1844, as the day when
the world would come to an end. In anticipation of the event, many
began to divest their belongings and abandon worldly occupations.
Even voting in elections that fall was light as temporal matters had
taken a back seat to eternal verities for many. One Philadelphia
tailor hung a sign outside his shop that read, "This shop is closed
in honor of the King of Kings, who will appear about the 23rd of
October 1844. Get ready friends, to crown the Lord of all."[8] But
when life continued after October 23, die-hard Millerites concluded an error had simply been made in calculating the correct
date. Or perhaps the Lord was simply testing his followers. Others
returned to groups espousing less extreme beliefs.

At the epicenter of all this religious frenzy was the town of
Litchfield, New York, where Orville's early life unfolded. By the

time he was fourteen years old, he was already "much occupied with my duty to God," and he began attending revivals in the area.[9] At the Presbyterian church in Cranes Corner, he listened to the emotional orations of itinerant revivalist Jedidiah Burchard whenever he came to town. A former haberdasher, traveling actor, and circus rider, Burchard was converted after attending a revival in Oneida, New York, held by the greatest orator of his day, Charles Grandison Finney.[10] A former lawyer, Finney had converted to Presbyterianism in Oneida County in 1821 after reading the Scriptures. Soon after his conversion, he began preaching in little frontier towns in the Burned-Over District. Unlike other orators, Finney paced up and down the aisles arguing, as historian Whitney Cross observed, in a deliberate, persuasive manner like a lawyer before a jury. Some say he was tall, while others say he was short. Whatever his stature, all agreed he made a powerful impression. He rarely wrote down his sermons in advance, delivering them extemporaneously "through the power of God." With large, flashing electric blue eyes, Finney seemed to cast a spell over listeners as he exhorted them to "be holy and not rest satisfied until they are as perfect as God." But it wasn't enough for sinners merely to repent to find salvation; they needed to work toward their own moral perfection and that of society as well. Among the many social ills Finney railed against were alcohol and prostitution. But of all of man's moral afflictions, the greatest was slavery. It was "a national sin" that could only be atoned by the complete emancipation of slaves.[11]

In the summer of 1825 a rash of spectacular revivals broke out in Oneida County, just north of Litchfield. In Boonville, Whitestown, Western, Rome, Mount Vernon, and a dozen other towns, revivals took place in churches and private homes, where preachers exhorted the fold to open their hearts to Jesus. Finney, who was by now much sought after as a preacher, gave two sermons in Utica, one of which Orville attended.[12] In a booming voice, Finney depicted the horrors of the fiery pit and the condition of the damned. With a raised fist he demanded his listeners repent forthwith and be saved. He then went among the crowd. Even though they were strangers, by fixing his eyes on each individual for a few seconds, he read the exact state of their mind and congratulated them on their conversion. So moved was Orville by Finney's powerful oration that he then and there committed to take part in temperance and anti-slavery activities. Of the two, the war against slavery would come to define the long trajectory of his life. For Orville, the persistence of slavery in a nation founded on liberty was a contradiction too disturbing and unjust to ignore. Liberty, he felt, was blind to color and applied to all. Just as the American colonies had combined armed resistance to British oppression with a reliance on the guiding hand of Divine Providence, he, too, would take up arms against pro-slavery men to rid the American soil of those "noxious weeds . . . in the body politic."[13]

Such high-minded ideals, however, would have to take a back seat to more pressing matters at home. While working as an apprentice mason in 1828, Orville was called home when his father suddenly came down with pleurisy. He arrived in time to see him die. With his mother lame since childhood and four sisters ranging in age from two to nineteen to look after, he was forced to stay and work the family farm. The following spring he cleared, plowed, and planted two acres of corn that he fenced with fieldstone. But two acres was insufficient to feed six mouths. To make ends meet, Orville worked on neighbors' farms cutting hay or building mill dams for which he earned a bushel of corn or fifty cents in cash a day. After laboring all day, he would walk seven miles home to look after his own farm and care for his eldest sister, who was dying of consumption. Orville had to carry her from room to room to eat, bathe, and dress. In winter, he wove heavy baskets and sold them for a dollar each to the coal workers at the Paris Iron Foundry in Oneida. With the money he made he paid his sister's medical bills and, eventually, her funeral expenses.

After his sister's death the family moved a few miles east to Cranes Corner, where he became a carriage boy in Utica for Asahel Seward and William Williams, publishers of educational and religious books and one of the city newspapers. Williams was an elder in the Presbyterian church, which regularly held revivals at his home. During one such revival, Orville found himself on his knees next to Williams's eldest son, Wells, who, moved by the emotion of the event, decided to consecrate himself to God.[14] Wells and his brother Frederick would later serve as missionaries for the American Board of Commissioners for Foreign Missions in China and Persia.

Orville may have had a similar vocation in mind when, soon after, he enrolled in the Oneida Institute in nearby Whitestown under Seward's patronage. A Presbyterian evangelical training school, the institute was founded in 1827 by the evangelical preacher and abolitionist George Washington Gale, just after the wave of Presbyterian revivals that swept Oneida County. The Oneida Presbytery donated $2,000 to launch the school and a hundred-acre farm was bought with money raised from a long list of donors. A graduate of the Union Theological Seminary, Gale believed that religion and education should go hand in hand; he disapproved of Thomas Jefferson's secular philosophy of education enshrined in the University of Virginia. While Oneida's mission was to educate young men for the gospel ministry, young men of good character were also received as students. The curriculum included courses in theology, Latin, Hebrew, and Greek. The school would quickly become the hub of Western abolitionism.

Initially, a few dozen students were accepted. In return for room and board, students worked three hours a day on a forty-acre farm that produced oats, corn, potatoes, onions, beans, cider, and hay. Gale had a Calvinistic conviction that farm labor promoted mental as well as physical health. Students worked for two hours at dawn and one hour in the afternoon after studies. Orville's job was to take the vegetables each morning to the market four miles away in Utica, a job which earned him the moniker Onion Grubber. Two instructors, one of whom was Gale, received a half dollar weekly and a share in any profits from the farm. Oddly, Orville thought Gale "a feeble old man" and was probably glad when the latter left for Illinois.*[15]

In 1832 a cholera epidemic that had swept London the previous year struck New York. Most people who had the means fled home and business (Charles Grandison Finney contracted it but recovered). When the disease hit Utica, Gale closed the academy's doors. Practically the only ones remaining in the terror-stricken city were the sick and dying—and Orville. Walking about the abandoned town one evening, he came upon an afflicted young woman, who, as the sun set, closed her eyes for the last time "in the sleep of death."[16] The Sewards, who had remained behind in Cranes Corner, eventually gave Orville the use of their horse, and he left town until November when the epidemic had passed.

In spring he once again withdrew from school—this time for unspecified health reasons, possibly asthma. His destination: the shoals of Newfoundland, whose hot and cold springs were believed at the time to be salubrious. He and two other students found work on a forty-five-ton schooner fishing for cod in the rich, deep

---

* Gale would later found Knox College in the eponymous town of Galesburg, Illinois.

waters of the Grand Banks. To catch fish, each man used two one-thousand-foot lines and four-pound sinkers and two hooks baited with pickled clams. Once caught, the fish livers were extracted and tossed into a large cask lashed to the mast to make cod liver oil. The meat of the fish was salted in the holds of the vessel until reaching shore where the crew dried the fish in the sun on makeshift stands of brush. Despite occasional bouts of seasickness, Orville later said his time at the Grand Banks was the most enjoyable of his life, and the money he earned fishing was icing on the cake.

In the winter of 1833, Orville returned to Oneida, but at the end of the semester he was once again itching for adventure. The new president of the school, abolitionist Beriah Green, advised him to go to Sag Harbor on Long Island, New York. In May 1834 he signed on with three other Oneida students with the whaling ship *Ann,* bound for the Atlantic near the Azores islands. This sojourn was decidedly unlike the more benign cod fishing. Orville found the whaling business terrifying. Most of the seventeen whales they caught on his maiden voyage were between seventy and ninety feet in length, and when harpooned they came flailing wildly alongside the ship where a single stroke of their massive flukes could instantly crush a man. Indeed, one time a whale's fluke struck the boat, sending a man overboard.

When the season closed, they docked at Jamestown Harbor on the island of Saint Helena, a regular port of call in the South Atlantic for ships of the East India Company. Touring Jamestown, Orville came across several employees of the company, "venerable old Chinamen who, in their immensely broad brimmed hats, moved around with the cold-marked precision of machinery apparently without nerves, feelings, or emotions."[17] He also visited Napoleon's first burial site on Saint Helena. From Jamestown a gentle southeast trade wind bore them along the equator for sixteen hundred miles to the Gulf Stream, which lifted them back to Sag Harbor exactly one year after departing. In all he logged thirty thousand miles on the *Ann,* a marvelous adventure he would write about late in life for a New York newspaper in a series called "Leaves from The Book of Memory."[18]

Upon his return he opened his own dry goods store in Whitesboro, New York. On cold winter evenings he would ride to Utica to listen to now famous debates on colonization and slavery between his old rector Beriah Green and Joshua N. Danforth. A graduate of Princeton Theological Seminary, Danforth advocated repatriating American blacks to Africa, a policy known as recolonization. For eleven successive weekday evenings, the "contest of giants" raged on, drawing large audiences.[19] Although Green claimed to have won, a group of Uticans vexed by Green's attack on the colonization scheme later marched through the streets in protest and hanged him in effigy.

In the fall of 1835, Orville made one final attempt to finish his education at Oneida. But when spring came he turned his back on school once and for all, taking a job as a clerk in a dry goods store in Utica for Spencer Kellogg & Sons. The move proved fortuitous for the budding abolitionist. For on October 21, 1835, at a Baptist church on Bleecker Street in Utica, Oneida County abolitionists held a state convention to unite the forty-two local anti-slavery societies under a single umbrella, the New York Anti-Slavery Society, committed to ending slavery nationwide as New York had done in 1827. The convention was organized by Beriah Green. In the hope of rousing wide support, Green had persuaded wealthy businessman Gerrit Smith to attend. (Smith would later use his vast fortune to support abolition causes.) Orville, who was still looking for a way to pursue his abolitionist ambitions, decided to attend.

Anticipating trouble from anti-abolitionists, Green convened the meeting at 9:00 AM, an hour earlier than announced. By then an angry pro-slavery mob led by Oneida County Judge Chester Hayden and US Representative Samuel Beardsley had materialized and pelted them with eggs, shouting, "Break down the doors! Damn the fanatics."[20] Undeterred, Green pressed on with the meeting. Attendees were about to adopt the Society's constitution when the mob, consisting of some of the leading men in town, rushed the podium. As they attempted to steal the minutes of the meeting, the convention secretary, E. A. Wetmore, held the papers high above his head. In a bizarre twist, one of the leaders of the mob was Wetmore's son who, fearing for his father's safety, persuaded him to turn over the papers to him for safekeeping.[21] *

Foiled by the demonstrators, Gerrit Smith suggested they continue the meeting at his elegant home in Peterboro, twenty-seven miles away. As the attendees, cut and bruised, spilled out of the church and into Fayette Square, the still furious mob continued to harass and hoot them. By happenstance, Orville, who was unharmed, jumped into a carriage carrying Lewis Tappan, New York's preeminent abolitionist and one of the framers of the convention's constitution. Six years later Tappan would win freedom for the illegally enslaved Africans of the ship *Amistad*.

As they were embarking, an amusing incident occurred in front of the Franklin House on the square. Two Quakers had just left their meeting house and climbed into their carriage to go for a ride in the country. As they drew their reins to start, several in the mob grabbed on to their wheels and refused to let them depart. One of the Quakers calmly and politely asked the men to let go of the

---

* The local press applauded the mob's actions in disrupting Smith's convention.

wheels and "we will from your town be gone and do our work without thine aid."²² Holding even more firmly to the wheels, the men now began to hurl epithets at the two implacable Quakers. Soon a crowd appeared to watch the scene. Once again the Quakers asked the men to remove their hands from the wheels. Upon the third request that went unheeded, the driver gave the word and his horse reared, knocking all the men to the ground in a tumbled heap. Before riding off, the Quakers momentarily halted to observe the men on the ground and bid "fare thee well" to the crowd.²³

In the morning the guests arrived at Smith's home in a driving rain, having been hounded en route by the previous day's hecklers and at their hotels the night before. By noon the sky had cleared and the house was humming with over three hundred delegates. During the convention, Smith rose to give an eerily prophetic speech in support of abolitionists' rights:

> *It is not to be disguised, that a war has broken out between the North and the South. Political and commercial men are industriously striving to restore peace: but the peace, which they would affect is superficial, false, and temporary. True, permanent peace can never be restored, until slavery, the occasion of the war, has ceased. The sword, which is now drawn, will never be returned to its scabbard, until victory, entire decisive victory, is ours or theirs; not, until that broad and deep and damning stain on our country's escutcheon is clean washed out—that plague spot on our country's honor gone forever; or, until slavery has riveted anew her present chains, and brought our heads also to bow beneath her withering power. It is idle— it is criminal, to hope for the restoration of the peace, on any other condition.*²⁴

It was the most rousing speech of the convention in language that, not surprisingly, was peppered with frequent and emotional references to the Bible. Among the two dozen resolutions adopted was one formally establishing the New York Anti-Slavery Society and a commitment to raise $30,000 for its operation. William Jay became its president and Spencer Kellogg its secretary. The Presbyterian Church of Utica would serve as temporary headquarters for the Society. Thus began a grassroots abolition movement that would last until the Civil War. Although Orville had pledged himself to the cause of abolition, it would be a year before he would join the Society. He also signed a temperance pledge in 1836, the same year the American Temperance Union adopted a teetotalism pledge as part of its mission.

In March of 1837, Orville married Mary Ann Cozzens. By now he was managing the Kellogg dry goods store outright. Once again, his health began to flag, this time from overwork. He decided to seek a cure in another sea voyage. He got as far as Boston when an onset of "bilious fever" (possibly hepatitis) kept him from departing. Returning to Utica, he began attending anti-slavery lectures at the newly built Mechanics Hall. Two years later in April 1839 their first child Cordelia Gould "Kitty" was born.

Soon after, Orville sold the store and used the $2,600 profit to open a new, larger dry goods store in Utica. The day after opening, the store burned to the ground. It was the first in a strange series of sudden reversals that would occur throughout his life. With the insurance money he opened another store in Belleville on April 1, 1840, and bought a beautiful stone house on the banks of North Sandy Creek. Two years later, on a warm August day, their first son, Spencer Kellogg (named for Orville's former boss and secretary of the Anti-Slavery Society) was born. He was followed by a second son, James "Rocky" Rockwell. Another daughter and son were born later, but both died in infancy.

As a toddler, Spencer was small and slender with a delicate constitution, traits clearly inherited from his parents. He had a nervous, uneasy disposition, and his restlessness required extra attention from his mother until he learned to walk.[25] Early on, however, he showed signs of intellectual precocity such that his mother felt he was destined for an unusual life. When he was nine months old, while his mother rocked him to sleep, he could already sing the tune of "Ortonville," a religious hymn composed by a Utica choir director.[26] His aptitude and interest in music would only increase with the years. He had a fine voice and learned to play several musical instruments "almost intuitively," according to his mother.[27] His parents would later give him a violin, which he never went without.

In Belleville, Orville's social reform activity increased. He frequently hosted lectures of the New York Tract Society, which distributed Christian literature promoting abolition and temperance. Of greater consequence, he became a station agent on the Underground Railroad. Since the late seventeenth century, New York had been a major destination for fugitive slaves seeking to flee to Canada. Belleville's proximity to the border made it one of a number of transit points for those headed there. On their clandestine journey north, slaves received temporary shelter from free black farmers living on the fringes of New Amsterdam before they moved on to Indian nations or Canada.[28] When New York finally abolished slavery in 1827, the number of slaves fleeing southern states to New York surged. By the 1840s slaves were passing through on a daily basis.

In the wake of the Second Great Awakening, several anti-slavery organizations sprang up to provide legal and other assistance to fugitive slaves. These organizations tended to be run by white abolitionists who, like Orville, were either Protestant evangelicals or radical Quakers. One anti-slave group, the New York Committee of Vigilance, founded in 1835, actively helped fugitives to places of safety. Although clandestine transit was not its main activity, by 1840 the Committee had helped some eight hundred fugitives escape to freedom. The overwhelming majority of runaways were from Maryland and Virginia, the most famous of whom was Frederick Bailey who, upon arrival in New York City in 1838, changed his name to Frederick Douglass. In his flight to freedom, Douglass had received aid from David Ruggles, one of the founders of the Committee. Gradually, as more and more local abolition organizations appeared, they formed an "interlocking series of local networks" through which fugitive slaves passed.[29] By 1842 this patchwork system was being referred to as the Underground Railroad.

As a link in the clandestine chain, Orville provided runaway slaves shelter and assisted their onward passage to Canada. Many, if not most, of those he assisted came by way of Syracuse, which was on the direct line for fugitives passing from Virginia through Pennsylvania on what Orville called the Great Central Underground Railroad.[30] The Syracuse station was run by the Reverend Samuel J. May, a reformer and pastor of the city's Unitarian Church of the Messiah and uncle of the novelist Louisa May Alcott. During his life, the Reverend May assisted some seventeen hundred fugitives to escape to Canada.[31] Eighty miles to the south in Peterboro, Gerrit Smith operated a station along the Underground Railroad, and Orville's station was most likely linked to Smith's. Other stations operated in Oneida County in Rome, Utica, Paris, Remsen, Steuben, Boonville, Clinton, Camden, New Hartford, Clayville, and Whitestown.

As an agent, Orville Brown communicated with other agents

in a secret language abolitionists called the grapevine telegraph.[32] Each local network had its own system of signs, cat calls, and passwords. The hoot owl was a common, if unimaginative, nighttime call. Most fugitives were men, and they usually traveled by foot or on horseback; the only passport one needed was the name of the next station agent. One Ohio Quaker transported fugitives in a large wagon he called The Liberator.

The route to Belleville was anything but straight. It followed a meandering path so as to elude slave hunters and avoid unsympathetic localities. While moving from station to station, fugitives often used a disguise such as carrying farm implements. They were also hidden in false bottoms of wagons. While laying over, slaves were hidden in churches, secret rooms, or cellars in houses and barns.[33] From Orville's house, fugitives usually went north to Watertown and then on to Cape Vincent, where they crossed the Saint Lawrence River into Canada.

In the spring of 1848 Orville's health faltered once again and his doctor advised "the sea cure." He sold his store and moved the family to Saratoga Springs, New York, for the summer. The following year he moved to New York City where he took a job as a salesman in a drugstore. There he had three more children born to him, Freddy, Fanny, and one who died in infancy.

Seven-year-old Spencer flourished in the rich cultural environment of the big city. In the public libraries he read Shakespeare and could soon recite many of his plays by heart. He also became an avid reader of history and delighted in epic tales of war and heroism. By age eleven he was reading the Bible, which would be an endless source of inspiration for him the rest of his life. He also read the historical novels of Sir Walter Scott and James Fenimore Cooper. Scott's works in particular imbued him with chivalrous ideas prevalent in the literature of the South of men bidding goodbye to their "ladye loves" before "going off to the warres."[34] At the schoolyard, while his friends played, he could often be found alone, poring over one of Scott's novels, a book of history, or the Holy Book. He would continue reading into the evening while lying stretched out on the parlor carpet propped up on his elbows. Only when ordered to bed would he finally stop, and even then reluctantly. He sometimes sought out other texts to substantiate certain religious ideas and doctrines, which he transcribed on foolscap and tucked within the pages of his Bible. After he read the Holy Book in its entirety, his father, fulfilling a promise he had made, allowed Spencer to purchase his own at the Bible House on Nassau Street in Lower Manhattan. The boy returned with a large, heavy violin instead.

Spencer was also a writer. In addition to keeping a daily journal he penned essays on such topics as rules of speaking ("Don't speak an opinion that you can't substantiate") and behavior ("In the company of inferiors be willing to teach"), light verse, and short stories.[35] For one so young, he was forever cognizant of doing and saying the right thing, above all trying to understand what the right thing was.

When Spencer was twelve years old, Orville sent him, Rocky, and Kitty to a Methodist boarding school in the village of Charlotteville in central New York. The boys had been there only a few months when a fire swept the seven-hundred-bed dormitory, consuming all their clothing and books. Miraculously Spencer's precious violin survived the inferno. Spencer's roommate, an older student named Britton, found Spencer wandering alone in the woods, dazed and dispirited. He took him to a store to purchase some clothing. Spencer never forgot the generosity and moral support Britton showed him. In the wake of the conflagration, new buildings were improvised and school continued. Years later, when languishing in a Confederate prison in Jackson, Mississippi, Spencer would recall the kind assistance his schoolmate had rendered.

All this time, poor health continued to dog Orville, aggravated by the city's cold winters and the damp basements in which he sometimes worked. As his wife had long suffered from chronic bronchitis, in 1854 they decided to pack up and move—to the drier climes of the Midwestern prairie. He chose Kansas Territory as his destination because, as the devout abolitionist put it, "the Kansas question was up."[36]

Chapter Two
A GREAT NATIONAL TRANSACTION

"If I went West, I think I would go to Kansas."
—Abraham Lincoln

UNTIL IT WAS ORGANIZED AS A TERRITORY IN MAY of 1854, Kansas had been as far from the national consciousness as Timbuktu. President Thomas Jefferson had acquired the area as part of the Louisiana Purchase in 1803. Soon after, he dispatched Lieutenant Zebulon Pike to explore his new acquisition. Traveling the length and breadth of the treeless Great Plains, Pike offered the glum appraisal that the entire region was a semiarid wasteland unfit for white habitation or cultivation, a land fit only for savages and wild beasts. Subsequent explorers confirmed Pike's findings and the plains came to be disparaged as the Great American Desert. By 1830, Kansas was being used to resettle Indians from the East under the Indian Removal Act. Over two dozen Eastern tribes including the Delaware, Ottawa, Potawatomi, Sac, and Fox were settled there, some forcibly. Yet for whites it remained merely a place to cross to get somewhere else: for Kearny's soldiers marching to New Mexico during the Mexican War, for California gold rushers, and for Mormons fleeing persecution to only their God knew where. By the time Orville Brown set out for Kansas in October of 1854, there were at most eight hundred whites in the entire Territory, mostly military personnel at Fort Leavenworth, trappers, traders, and a smattering of missionaries.

That year, however, Kansas became the focus of national attention in a long-running dispute between North and South. While the dispute involved many issues—territorial government, public lands, Indian policy, and the choice of a route or routes for railroads to the Pacific—none was as incendiary or consequential to the Territory's future as slavery.

Sectional differences over slavery grew out of the Northwest Ordinance of 1787, which had established a procedure for managing and creating new states in the Territory south and west of the Great Lakes. Because the ordinance prohibited slavery in the Northwest Territory, it had the practical effect of making the Ohio River the boundary between free and slave territories west of the Appalachians. As new states applied for statehood, an attempt was made to maintain an equal number of free and slave states in the North and South—and hence voting parity in the US Senate.

Over the years, as new states were admitted to the Union, the balance of power between North and South swung to and fro. In 1820, Missouri was admitted as a slave state as a condition for admitting Maine, keeping a balance at twelve each. The Missouri Compromise, as it was called, also prohibited slavery north of the thirty-six degrees, thirty minutes parallel (essentially north of present-day Oklahoma) in the old Louisiana Purchase lands. With the admission of Arkansas to the Union in 1836, the South had thirteen slave states to the twelve free ones in the North. The admission of Texas and Florida in 1845 briefly gave the South a four-seat advantage in the Senate. Two years later, the admission of Iowa and Wisconsin again evened things up at fifteen each.

Then in 1850, California applied for admission as a free state. By now the South had run out of Territory into which to expand. But Kentucky senator Henry Clay—a stalwart defender of the hallowed institution of slavery—proposed a way around this restriction by introducing a compromise. In effect, the deal allowed California to be admitted as a free state in return for several concessions to the South, one of which was that the disposition of slavery in the newly acquired territories of New Mexico and Utah be determined by "squatter" or popular sovereignty. It also required escaped slaves to be returned to their masters. Although a Fugitive Slave Act had been in existence since the 1790s, the new Fugitive Slave Act of 1850 established stiff penalties for Northern citizens and officials who did not cooperate.

For a time, it appeared as if this Compromise of 1850 to the Fugitive Slave Act had finally eliminated slavery as a political issue between North and South, as those who had shepherded the bill through Congress had hoped. To show their appreciation, the Whigs even helped elect the Democratic pro-slavery candidate Franklin Pierce during the presidential election of 1852.

On December 4, 1853, however, the controversy reopened like a festering wound when Senator Augustus C. Dodge of Iowa introduced a bill providing for the establishment of a territorial government for Nebraska, a measure unsuccessfully tabled in the previous session. Behind the legislation was Iowa's hope that by organizing Nebraska, a planned transcontinental railroad would cross Iowa and open the state to white settlement.[1] Dodge's bill made no mention of slavery and, it was assumed, would leave the Missouri Compromise in force. When the bill arrived on the desk of Senator Stephen A. Douglas, chairman of the important Committee on Territories, he must have been pleasantly surprised, for the Illinois senator had long been a champion of westward expansion as a means of spreading freedom and civilization to all corners of the continent. Twice before, Douglas had tabled a bill to organize a free Nebraska Territory, only to face staunch opposition from Southern senators. He had even invested heavily in land around Chicago and Superior City, Michigan, in anticipation that a railroad would eventually pass through one of those cities to territories west of the Mississippi.

But so long as the Missouri Compromise, barring slavery north of the thirty-six degrees, thirty minutes parallel, remained in effect, Douglas knew he had little chance of gaining Southern approval. Many Southern congressmen were states' rights advocates who believed the federal government had no power to regulate slavery in the territories. Nor did they believe the government had the right to defer the issue to the territories, for that would mean the federal government was delegating an authority it did not itself possess. Individuals, they argued, should have the right to travel freely into the territories and take with them any property they wished—including their most valuable possession, slaves. The only power Congress might confer upon territorial governments was the power, indeed the obligation, to protect slave owners in their property rights.[2] As far as Southerners were concerned, the Missouri Compromise was simply unconstitutional, and it begged to be repealed to protect Southern rights.

By contrast, not one Northern senator subscribed to the principle of states' rights. Congress, they maintained, had the authority both to regulate slavery in the territories and to delegate that authority to a territorial legislature. Transferring the question of slavery to territorial legislatures was not an option, as it would simply have been passing the buck.[3]

Douglas was thus caught on the horns of a dilemma. To repeal the Missouri Compromise would "raise a hell of a storm," as he put it, for the legislation had been hammered out with great difficulty and was essentially regarded as inviolable.[4] Douglas himself acknowledged this, remarking in 1849 that the Missouri law had become "canonized in the hearts of the American people as a sacred thing which no ruthless hand would even be reckless enough to disturb."[5]

With such polarization over the issue, it was therefore not surprising that, when Douglas reported Dodge's bill on January 4, he made no mention of the Missouri Compromise or the status of slavery in the Nebraska Territory. In the words of the bill: "When admitted as a State or States, the said Territory, or any portion of the same, shall be received into the Union, with or without slavery, as their constitution may prescribe at the time of admission." In sidestepping the issue of slavery, Douglas may well have been testing the political winds to find a way through the impasse. But the bill contained a glaring contradiction: It allowed for admission of Kanas as a slave state while at the same time prohibiting slaveholders from establishing themselves in the Territory prior to voting.

The Southern response to Douglas's bill came swift and blunt. The coarse, hard-drinking, Missouri senator David R. Atchison told him flatly the bill would not get Southern support. Atchison later declared he would rather "sink in hell" before he turned over the Territory to free-soilers.[6] When Douglas reported a revised bill on January 4, he gamely attempted to remove the Missouri Compromise restriction by altering the Nebraska boundary. But Southern senators demanded nothing less than repeal. Privately, they began pressuring Douglas for more concessions when, on January 16, 1854, Kentucky senator Archibald Dixon proposed an amendment explicitly repealing the Missouri Compromise. At first, Douglas demurred. But during a cordial carriage ride around Washington, Dixon was able to persuade him that repeal was the only logical course of action. While Dixon was massaging Douglas, Iowa senators, concerned that the center of population would likely fall to the south of Iowa if Nebraska were organized as a single Territory, recommended that Congress divide it into two territories—Nebraska and Kansas—along the fortieth parallel.

A week later Douglas reported a revised bill, proposing the creation of two territories divided along the fortieth parallel, each state having squatter sovereignty. The bill also declared the Missouri Compromise "inoperative," artfully avoiding use of the explosive word "repeal." Evoking the principle of popular sovereignty, the bill stated that "all questions pertaining to Slavery in the territories and in the new States to be formed are to be left to the decision of the people residing therein, through their appropriate representatives."[7]

The creation of two territories instead of one was perceived throughout Congress as a major step toward compromise. On one hand, it greatly increased Kansas's chances of becoming a slave state.[8] Kansas lay directly west of pro-slave Missouri, and Missourians could, it was presumed, cross over in sufficient numbers early on to establish slavery firmly in the state. On the other hand, Nebraska, lying just west of free Iowa, could expect to become a free state. Not surprisingly, both Iowa and Missouri supported the bill. Ergo, a degree of parity between North and South might once again be assured.[9]

Unlike Iowa, however, Missouri would go to great lengths to ensure its territorial neighbor became a slave state, feeling that if it failed to do so, the entire institution would be in jeopardy not only in its own state but all across the South. The roots of slavery in Missouri ran deep. In the early 1700s, French miners first used slaves to mine silver and lead in the region. The French regulated slavery through the decree *Le Code Noir,* which sought to establish humane treatment for blacks.[10] The Code stipulated that slaves could not be forced to work on holidays or the Sabbath, nor could they be tortured or killed. Such rules were hard to enforce and most slave owners applied the Code as they saw fit. During the Spanish interregnum from 1762 to 1803, African slaves were widely used in agriculture, which served to reinforce the institution. When the United States acquired the region in 1803 under the Louisiana Purchase, slavery was continued. But it wasn't until Missouri applied for statehood in 1818 that Congress finally got around to addressing the practice. After two years of deliberation, Congress passed the Missouri Compromise, sanctioning slavery in the state. The law encouraged slaveholders from other Southern states to emigrate, and in the ensuing decade the population more than doubled. Most slaveholders in Missouri, however, were not large plantation owners like those in the Deep South but small-scale farmers who cultivated tobacco and hemp with a handful of slaves. With the opening of the Oregon and Santa Fe Trails, still more slaves were brought to Independence and St. Joseph to work as outfitters, blacksmiths, and servants for migrating families. Although the slave system had not yet penetrated Kansas to any degree, Fort Leavenworth was already a pro-slave town, as many of the Fort's employees owned slaves or, in the case of some officers, rented them from Missouri.

When formal debate on Douglas's bill began on January 30, an angry cry of opposition arose from free-soilers in Congress. Senators William H. Seward and Charles Sumner charged Douglas with wanton betrayal in proposing what was essentially an abrogation of the Missouri law. In the House, Salmon P. Chase and two other members published an editorial in which they attacked the bill as "a gross violation of a sacred pledge, as a criminal betrayal of precious rights, as part and parcel of an atrocious plot."[11] That sacred pledge, they argued, was that the North had agreed to admit Missouri to the Union in return for the South's agreement that there would be no further slave states in the Louisiana Purchase above the thirty-six degrees, thirty minutes parallel. Now the South was pushing for outright repeal of the law.

In reply, the South accused the North of hypocrisy, pointing out it had never considered the Missouri Compromise a sacred compact but had been forced to accept it to prevent Missouri from becoming a free state by a numerically superior North. Furthermore, the South had generously accepted California as a free state even though it had never gone through the territorial stage. And with little prospect for agriculture in New Mexico and Utah, Southerners were unlikely to ever get slavery into those territories, despite the popular sovereignty principle that had been applied there. The South felt it had made sundry other concessions to the North, such that the repeal of the Missouri Compromise was simply the restoration of its constitutional right to extend slavery into the territories.

The entire debate underscored the fact that Congress had never established a single solution for determining slavery in the territories. In Missouri it was granted in return for establishment of a geographical boundary. In Utah and New Mexico it was to be determined by popular sovereignty, while in California it was a states' rights issue. With no single solution to slavery in the territories, the Douglas bill sparked a flurry of maneuvering in closed committee meetings and rushed caucuses to carve out a bill palatable to both sides. Negotiations went on for weeks.

If debate over the bill in Congress was fierce, popular reaction was even fiercer. In the Northern cities, demonstrations broke out protesting the bill as a Southern betrayal of the Missouri Compromise. In New England, over three thousand clergymen signed a statement to the Senate protesting the Kansas-Nebraska bill "as a great moral wrong, as a breach of faith, and . . . as a measure full of danger to the peace and even existence of our beloved Union."[12] Similar protests from clergymen in other Northern states poured into Congress. A flurry of pro-abolition newspapers warned that Kansas and Nebraska would both become slave states if the bill passed.

Yet Douglas, known as the Little Giant for his diminutive size and political forcefulness, deftly fended off the barrage of opposition. At midnight on March 3, 1854, just before the Senate vote, he rose to the floor and delivered a stirring defense of the bill that lasted five and a half hours. When he finished at 5:30 AM, the vote was taken. It passed handily by thirty-seven ayes to fourteen nays.

Even though the bill had yet to pass the House, abolitionists had already deciphered the writing on the wall. Just a few hours after the bill passed the Senate, a group of abolitionists led by Massachusetts legislator Eli Thayer met in Boston and formed the Massachusetts Emigrant Aid Company. Organized as a joint stock venture, the company aimed to facilitate a mass emigration of free-soilers to thwart implantation of slavery in Kansas while providing businessmen a chance to invest in the state's growth. All that spring and summer, the bushy-bearded Thayer stumped the state to sell stock in his company, pledging to bring Yankee mechanical ingenuity to keep Kansas free. "Set [Kansas] to sawing tough gnarled oak," he declared, "and its song with be 'Never a slave state! Never a slave state!'"[13] Something of a blowhard, Thayer claimed he would sell five million dollars of stock in his company. He also spoke wildly of turning his imagined armies into free slaves throughout the South at the rate of one state per year. In the end, however, few were willing to invest in the venture, put off by Thayer's grandiose claims and wanton profit motive. Indeed, Thayer seemed more interested in implanting capitalism in the Territory than in waging a moral crusade against slavery.[14]

Only a modest investment by wealthy Massachusetts philanthropist Amos A. Lawrence saved it from going under.* To remove any suspicion of profit motive in the company's mission, the following year Lawrence reorganized it as a private venture under the title of the New England Emigrant Aid Company.

Despite falling far short of its financial goal, the company nonetheless managed to attract several other committed abolitionists who were destined to play important roles in the fight for a free Kansas. Edward Everett Hale was a Unitarian minister from Worchester, Massachusetts, who had signed the March petition to Congress. Several years earlier Hale had anticipated Thayer's scheme by proposing free labor emigration as a way of preventing Texas from becoming a slave state. Now he would help Thayer set his plan in motion. Charles Robinson, who had studied at Amherst before becoming a Massachusetts physician, would head the first of Thayer's colonies to Kansas and become the state's first governor.

As Thayer was stumping in Massachusetts, after a continuous thirteen-hour debate, the Kansas-Nebraska Act passed the House on May 30, 1854. The final vote had been 113 ayes to 100 nays, revealing, as one historian noted, "the deep sectional divisions the bill had created."[15] (Congressman Gerrit Smith, the New York abolitionist who had since been elected to the House, had led the opposition.) That same day, in an editorial in the *New-York Tribune*, editor Horace Greeley, an avid moral supporter of Thayer's venture, captured Northern sentiments even as he prophesied the future:

> *The revolution is accomplished and Slavery is King! How long shall this monarch reign? This is now the question for the*

---

* Indeed, Thayer would purchase only $400 in stock yet draw a hefty $10,000 in commissions.

*Northern people to answer. Their representatives have crowned
the new potentate, and the people alone can depose him. If we
were a few steps further advanced in the drama, he could only
be hurled from his seat through a bloody contest.*[16]

Four days after its passage in the House, President Franklin
Pierce signed the bill into law. In effect, the old Missouri Compromise was now dead. Henceforth, slavery in the new territories would be determined by popular sovereignty. In the months
preceding passage of the bill, the Delaware, Kickapoo, Otoe, and
other tribes living in Kansas within two hundred miles of the
Missouri border were invited to Washington to "renegotiate"
their treaties. Overnight, millions of acres of fertile land in eastern Kansas were thrown open for white settlement. With Kansas
nearly devoid of settlers, the race was now on between free-soilers
and pro-slavers as to who would get to the prairie first. "Come on
then Gentlemen of the Slave States," William Seward declared
shortly after the bill had passed the House. "Since there is no
escaping your challenge, I accept it in behalf of the cause of freedom. We will engage in competition for the virgin soil of Kansas,
and God give the victory to the side which is stronger in numbers
as it is in right."[17]

On July 17, 1854, Thayer's first company of twenty-nine emigrants departed Boston by wagon. A large crowd lined the streets
for several blocks to cheer them on and pledge moral support from
home. As they proceeded west through the Burned-Over District,
Bible societies and abolitionist groups turned out in large numbers
along the road to cheer the emigrant party on. These emigrants
were no ordinary pioneers but viewed themselves as moral crusad-
ers marching to do battle against a great evil. Thayer called it "the
first organized physical resistance to the power of slavery that this

country has ever seen."[18] Along the way, they jubilantly sang poet John Greenleaf Whittier's "Kansas Emigrant Song" to the tune of "Auld Lang Syne":

> *We cross the prairies as of old*
> *Our fathers crossed the sea;*
> *To make the West, as they the East,*
> *The homestead of the free*

Southern newspapers, weighing in favor of Missouri, were quick to denounce Thayer and his righteous band of emigrants. The *Lynchburg Republican* threatened:

> *The Worcester Spy announces that the first band of emigrants for Kansas under the charge of the Emigrant Aid Company, will start from Boston on the 17th inst. We wish them the utmost success their hearts can desire in getting there, for the hardy pioneers of Kansas will doubtless have tar and feathers prepared in abundance for their reception. . . . Slavery has been kept out of the Territories by Congressional enactments, but has never failed to carry the day and firmly establish itself upon new Territories when allowed to enter.*[19]

Others periodicals attempted to deter Thayer's emigrants with threats of bowie knives, revolvers, and "hemp" (viz., hanging). *De Bow's Review* offered a 200 dollar reward for the capture and delivery of Thayer into the hands of Missouri settlers. So many threats in editorials of southern journals were levelled at Thayer that he remarked sardonically that it would be "easy to fill a volume with them."[20]

Thayer's companies of free-soilers were, in fact, inconsequentially small—the first company was twenty-nine strong, followed by a company of sixty-seven a month later. But when Southerners read Horace Greeley's sympathetic account in the *New-York Daily Tribune,* claiming Thayer had $5 million and was preparing to launch twenty thousand rabid abolitionists toward the state, they became alarmed. Missourians regarded Northern emigrants as interlopers, "an army of Hessians" interfering in the South's affairs.

Nor was simply Kansas at stake. There was the added fear that a free Kansas would become a safe haven for fugitive slaves. Missouri had some eighty-seven thousand slaves worth $30 million, and some had already escaped across the state's eastern and western borders to freedom in Illinois and Iowa. In part for this reason, Senator Atchison declared that to have a free state as Missouri's western neighbor would spell disaster and he urged Missourians to hasten to Kansas to secure it as a slave state for the South. The *Democratic Platform* of Liberty, Missouri, echoed the sentiment, advising readers to rush to Kansas with muskets in hand.[21]

For their part, free-soilers disparaged their Missouri counterparts as Border Ruffians, dirty and uncouth frontiersmen easily given to fighting and hard drinking. *New York Times* correspondent William Phillips, who made no secret of his sympathies for the free-soil cause, might well have been speaking for all Northerners when he wrote:

> *Most of them have been over the plains several times,—if they have not been over the probability is, they have served through the war in Mexico, or seen a "deal of trouble in Texas;" or, at least, run up and down the Missouri River often enough to catch imitative inspiration from the catfish aristocracy, and penetrate the sublime mysteries of euchre or poker. . . . Imagine a fellow, tall, slim but athletic, with yellow complexion, hairy faced, with a dirty flannel shirt, or red, or blue, or green, a pair*

of common-place, but dark-colored pants, tucked into an uncertain altitude by a leather belt, in which a dirty-handled bowie-knife is stuck rather ostentatiously, an eye slightly whiskey-red, and teeth the color of a walnut. Such is your border ruffian of the lowest type.[22]

In early May, Missourians began crossing into eastern Kansas in small numbers to stake claims on land still owned by the Omaha Indians. Often the claim was little more than a posted warning sign, a rectangle of logs, or a name etched into a tree. In summer they returned home, some to wait for their land to appreciate, others to emigrate.[23] When the Kansas-Nebraska Act passed, Missouri politicians crossed into Kansas to meet with Missouri squatters. At one of several such meetings held in June at Salt Creek near Fort Leavenworth, the first squatters' association was formed. It passed a resolution recognizing the institution of slavery in the Territory and denying abolitionists any right to settle there.

All that summer and fall David Atchison stumped the state with his aide Benjamin F. Stringfellow urging Missourians to take up residence in Kansas. In town after town, the two held rallies in which they portrayed Thayer's men as "the sum and filth of the Northern cities; sent here as hired servants, to do the will of others; not to give their own free suffrage."[24] At one rally in Weston on July 29, Missourians formed the Platte County Self-Defensive Association with the objective of settling Kansas with pro-slave men. The association, which attracted a thousand members, resolved "whenever called upon, hold itself in readiness to arrest and remove any and all emigrants who go there [Kansas] under the auspices of the Northern Emigrant Aid Societies."[25] The association's password was "Kan," and its moniker a skein of bleached hemp tied in the buttonhole of the coat. A month later the association tried a former Iowa sheriff, Thomas Minnard, with abolitionism. He was sentenced to fifty lashes and sent packing.

Soon after, Stringfellow, his brother John, and Atchison began organizing more secretive and aggressive Blue Lodges (pro-slavery societies) along the border with Kansas. Blue Lodges were composed of tough men who had been trappers and traders on the frontier and had fought in the Indian wars. Its members, who also wore a piece of hemp in their lapels, operated clandestinely, and used secret handshakes and the password "sound on the goose" to communicate. In the wake of the Blue Lodges, other secret societies sprang up along the border, such as the Sons of the South, Social Band, and Friends Society, all committed to affording one another protection and boycotting abolitionists' businesses.[26]

Despite calls for Missourians to migrate, few actually did. For those seeking cheap land, there was still an abundance of it in Missouri, which had only ten persons per square mile. Also, slave owners were reluctant to settle in Kansas for fear of losing their slaves should a free state eventuate.[27] Even Stringfellow, for all his shrill demagoguery, preferred to orchestrate activities from the comfort of his hometown of Weston, a contradiction not lost on some observers. At one rally in Lexington, Stringfellow cried out, "We must have settlers. We must have men to live on the land—voters. And Kansas, gentlemen, is a land of infinite promise, a land of opportunity." As Stringfellow was extolling the benefits of living in Kansas, a large man with a tobacco-stained beard rose and spat demonstrably, saying, "If this here Kansas is such a daggone dreadful nice place to live in, why ain't you a-livin there?"[28]

In late July the first contingent of Thayer's men arrived. Upon seeing the harsh conditions of the prairie, nearly half the emigrants returned home and denounced Thayer for deceiving them.

The remainder he led to a site between the Wakarusa and Kansas Rivers in the Kaw River Valley. Even though a handful of people had already settled there, he and Charles Branscomb proceeded to found the town of Lawrence, in honor of the company's treasurer and benefactor, Amos Adams Lawrence. The little band pitched tents and began building their homes.[*] Missourians noticed their arrival at "Yankee Town" with concern.

As Thayer's men were building their cabins, about two hundred Missourians, who were encamped just north of the village, approached the emigrants to inform them that one of their tents was on land claimed by a pro-slaver and demanded its removal. The abolitionists stood their ground and began organizing themselves for defense. The next day the Missourians returned with reinforcements and gave Lawrence until 2 PM to take down the tent and leave the Territory. When Lawrence and his men refused to depart, the Missourians began wrangling among themselves whether to remove the tent. By sundown they were still quarreling and decided to return to Missouri.[†] Before departing they warned the abolitionists they would return in a week and "wipe them out."[29]

That fall more free-soilers arrived from Massachusetts, Illinois, Maine, and Ohio, traveling the well-worn paths of California gold rushers a few years earlier. Some settled in Lawrence,

---

[*] In August, Thayer returned to Boston on a series of lecture tours to recruit more emigrants. In all, he would give over seven hundred lectures and travel over six thousand miles.

[†] The great irony was that most Missourians and Northerners were more interested in obtaining or speculating in cheap land in Kansas than in exporting slavery. Many Northerners hadn't even heard of the Emigrant Aid Society.

while others founded new towns such as Topeka, Manhattan, and Grasshopper Falls. In late October, a band of twenty-five settlers arrived under the auspices of the New York–Kansas League founded two months earlier on the model of Thayer's society. Among the twenty-five abolitionists and pioneers in the party was Orville Brown.

By then the battle lines in Kansas had already been drawn.

Chapter Three
THE BOGUS ELECTIONS

"Free ferry, a dollar a day, and liquor gentlemen."
—Blue Lodge promise to Missourians

THE OCTOBER AIR WAS CRISP AND THE SUN SHINING clear and bright when Orville bid farewell to his wife and boarded the train for Chicago. As the train stopped along the way, more men boarded, alone or with families, all bound for a new life in Kansas. Some were abolitionists going to ensure Kansas became a free state; still more with no dog in the fight were simply headed for cheap land. From Chicago, Orville took the Illinois Central to Alton. When the train stopped to disgorge passengers in the southern river town, Orville and other abolitionists took a moment to pay homage to Elijah Parish Lovejoy, a Presbyterian minister and abolitionist who had been murdered there by a pro-slavery mob in 1837. The next day Orville boarded the steamer *Sam Cloon* to Kansas City. On board he made the acquaintance of three kindred spirits who would become major players in the free-state movement: Gaius Jenkins, Martin F. Conway, and Kersey Coates. Large numbers of Southerners were also on board. Although the two groups eyed each other with suspicion, little outright hostility was shown. Later, cholera, that haunting scourge of nineteenth-century pioneers, struck passengers on the lower deck. Orville attempted to minister to one afflicted Kentucky man, but he died within hours. In the evening, his body was laid unceremoniously upon the riverbanks as his bereft family looked on.

On his way up the Missouri River, Orville got his first glimpse of the horrors of slavery. The river being low, slaves were brought aboard to ease the boat over the sandbars. As they pushed and prodded with long poles, their master periodically lashed them with a long switch to spur them to greater effort. Further on, when the *Sam Cloon* ran aground, Orville wandered ashore where he stumbled upon a Missouri tobacco plantation. Noticing some low kennels four or five feet high with low entrances, he inquired as to their purpose. He was stunned to learn they were slave quarters.

After five days on the river, the *Sam Cloon* pulled into Kansas City, the main entrepôt for Kansas-bound emigrants and goods. Failing to find a Kansas League agent who was supposed to welcome them, he overnighted at the Gilles House Hotel. There he chanced to meet a Baptist missionary, Dr. David Lykins. Lykins, who had been in Kansas since 1844 ministering to the confederated tribes of the Wea, Piankeshaw, Peoria and Kaskaskia, briefed him on the region and the best locations to settle.[*]

After provisioning, the party of twenty-six League members broke up into two groups to prospect for homesites, with Orville heading one of them. Since Lawrence and its environs had already been staked out, he led his party to the Miami Indian village on the Osage River, bearing a letter of introduction from Dr. Lykins to the Indian agent in the region, Eli Moore. In anticipation of the rush of settlers, the US government had recently purchased all but seventy-two thousand acres of the five hundred thousand acres

---

[*] Lykins later became a pro-slave member of the territorial legislature.

that had been originally allotted to the Miami and other Midwest tribes under the Indian Resettlement Act of 1830.

As they surveyed the countryside, Orville found Kansas a singularly beautiful land that was anything but the barren desert depicted in explorers' descriptions. Burnished prairie tallgrass shimmered in the autumn winds and thick stands of walnut, hickory, oak, hackberry, buttonwood, cottonwood, linwood, and sugar maples traced the course of pellucid streams teeming with fish. On the rolling prairie uplands, game bristled in abundance: buffalo, antelope, sage grouse, deer, turkey, rabbits, mountain cock, and waterfowl of every variety. And the black prairie soil surpassed in richness anything back home. Along the way they cooked fish they caught on pin hooks and camped on beds of leaves, serenaded by prairie wolves howling in the distance.

With the information furnished by Lykins, Orville led his party to the former Potawatomi Indian Reserve, a seven-square-mile wedge-shaped piece of land at the confluence of the Osage and Potawatomi Rivers.* At first sight, Orville thought it the most picturesque and promising piece of land he had seen. North of the Osage a level prairie extended for several miles to the eastern terminus of a high divide that ran to the Bull Creek Valley. The Potawatomi, which drained the tributaries of the high prairie, offered abundant power for a planned mill. South of the Potawatomi Creek, the prairie lifted gradually to high tablelands skirted by timber for building. Nearby was limestone, clay for brick, and artesian water for crops and cattle. Coal was twenty-five to thirty miles distant. To the west lived the Sac and Fox tribes, to the south the Chippewa, Kaskaskia, and Peoria, and to the east the Wea and Miami.

---

* The tribe's name Potawatomi, meaning "keepers of the fire," grew out of the tribe's practice of burning the prairie each year.

Orville was on horseback leading two ox-drawn wagons when he was suddenly ordered to halt by a bearded man standing by the roadside. It was Eli Moore, the Indian agent assigned to the Five Tribes area. Of late, Moore had been busy helping the Indians protect their land from encroachment by emigrants. Orville immediately brought up his mare and dismounted. Moore gruffly informed him they were trespassing on Indian land and should leave at once. "If I am on Indian land," Orville said, "I have been misled by a number of persons who assured me that all land north of the Osage was public land."[1] Taking a map from his pocket, Moore showed him that the spot he was on was marked as belonging to Baptiste Peoria, chief of the Peoria and the French-Indian interpreter of the Five Tribes. Noticing a storm rapidly approaching and some of the party looking "badly worn," Moore invited them back to the agency mission to rest, leaving two Indians to look after the oxen and wagons.

That night Moore had a long discussion with Orville, whom he found courteous and congenial in every way. In the morning Moore sent his son to summon Baptiste to the mission for a powwow. After a long discussion with Orville, Baptiste agreed that a city, not a squatter's claim, could be established on the south bank of the Osage on the condition that a name for the town be adopted early.

On the date agreed upon, a large crowd of licensed traders and Indians showed up for the christening, including a Peoria chief, Ed Black. At first Orville proposed the names of Brooklyn and Brownville, which Baptiste rejected. Baptiste then proposed Peoria or City of Kansas, which Orville opposed. Finally, Moore stepped in and settled the deadlock by proposing Osawatomie, blended from the names of the two rivers so close at hand. From that day forward, Chief Black would refer good-naturedly to Orville as

Osawatomie Brown.[2] Little did the chief know that so harmless a nickname would one day hang like a millstone around the necks of Orville and Spencer.

This account of the founding of Osawatomie related years after by Eli Moore's son is far less colorful than Orville's more prosaic version. According to Orville, it was Baptiste who had informed him of an old government reserve between the Osage and Potawatomi Rivers. On October 25, 1854, he and several emigrants rode to the site where they found several Quakers residing in tents. Orville proposed they join together and start a town. Not yet ready to settle permanently, and seeing that Orville and his party were also abolitionists, the Quakers relinquished their claim and moved on. Early the next morning, Orville and his companions mounted their Indian ponies and followed a trail across Bull Creek that led past Pilot Knob to a beautiful piece of prairie stretching four miles to the Osage and crowned by a mantle of dark pines in the tableland beyond. The emigrants who had accompanied Orville left to look at another site eight miles away. Just then a young couple appeared in a wagon, the Wilkinsons, who professed to be abolitionists from the South and showed an interest in settling there. Taking an ax he had carried all day, Orville cut four poles and, laying them out four-square, marked his claim for a town. In the waning light, he then carved the date of the town's founding on a nearby tree: "October 26, 1854." That night he and the Wilkinsons crossed the Osage and camped in a grove of tall oaks. In the morning they rode along the Potawatomi River to survey their new claim. While Orville was crossing the Wea portion of the old reserve, an idea for the name of the town suddenly struck him. Halting in a driving rain, he pulled out a piece of paper and penned the two words—*Osage* and *Potawatomie*. Compounding the two names he came up with Osawatomie.

In the evening they made camp, the Wilkinsons in a tent and Orville in a wagon. Upon waking, Orville consulted his watch and, mistaking the time for morning, fetched his pony in the river bottoms. Wishing to survey the land around his claim, he crossed the Osage to the high prairie, where he was overtaken by a sudden prairie storm. In the waning light, the low dark clouds had obscured Pilot Knob, the landmark by which he was navigating, and he was suddenly lost. Unable to move until daylight, he sat in his saddle all night blasted by wind, rain, and hail. At daybreak he was awakened by the crowing cocks at Baptiste Peoria's home. After a breakfast of cornbread and coffee at the chief's cabin, he returned to camp where some of the first emigrants, having found nothing better, had returned and set up tents on the site. Suddenly, the Wilkinsons decided to relinquish their claim and left for Dutch Henry's Crossing, located seven miles north. As it turned out, the Wilkinsons were ardently pro-slave and cringed at the thought of having to live among the many Eastern abolitionists who were settling there. It would not be the last Orville would hear of Mr. Wilkinson.

To manage Osawatomie, Orville established a town company with William Ward, Sam Geer, William Chestnut, and Samuel C. Pomeroy, a manager for the New England Emigrant Aid Company. Each held equal interest. Orville became president. They purchased over $12,000 in machinery for the town, including a sawmill, which they would build on the south bank of the Potawatomi. On a hill overlooking the Osage, Orville staked off his own homestead of 160 acres and began work on his cabin.

As the agent for the promotion of the town, Orville set about issuing circulars advertising the site in Kansas to new immigrants. He also attempted to interest investors back East. One flyer boasted the richness of the soil, the various types of produce that grew there, the composition of the forests, the easy availability of stone and other building materials, and other benefits of living in Osawatomie. Homesteads of 160 acres went for $200. Letters from prospective immigrants all over the country began pouring in, inquiring about Osawatomie or making arrangements to purchase tracts of land. Within a few months he commissioned A. D. Searl to survey the town and mark it on a territorial map he was about to publish. With the assistance of Thayer's New England Emigrant Aid Company, the steam sawmill was erected on the Potawatomi to provide lumber for settlers.

Each day brought fresh loads of emigrants to Kansas. Braving typhoid and malaria, they staked claims on every open tract of land in and around Osawatomie, built cabins, dug wells, and cleared fields. They sewed sacks of unbleached cotton and filled them with prairie grass for mattresses. Within a year Osawatomie would boast a hotel, a blacksmith, several homes, and the first four-horse mail service to Kansas City in the Kansas Territory. It would soon become the third free-soil town in Kansas after Topeka. Still, because the town was far from emigrant routes, most settlers were New Yorkers, and so the area would remain an enclave of free-soilers in a largely pro-slave region. Orville delighted in the climate. That fall brought no rain and the air was clear and mild, so mild that many evenings he wrote letters in the open air by the light of the moon.

One day, John Robert Everett and his wife, Sarah, appeared in Osawatomie. The Congregationalist couple had arrived a few weeks earlier with their two small sons from Oneida County, New York, having abandoned a plan to migrate to Minnesota in order to lend a hand in making Kansas a free state. Having met Orville in St. Louis on their migration west, the couple decided to seek him out for assistance in locating a suitable tract of land. In mid-November the couple set out from Kansas City for Osawatomie with a small party of other interested settlers. Upon arrival, John was dismayed to find the land around Osawatomie poor for farming and the streambeds bone dry. Though ambivalent about the place, he nonetheless filed a claim for a parcel of land and commissioned John Serpell, a New York abolitionist who had come with Orville, to build a cabin on it.

When the Everetts later returned with all their belongings to move into their new home, they were stunned to find the lot empty. John demanded an explanation from Serpell, who told him that a claim jumper had seized the lot and threatened him should he attempt to build Everett's house on it.[3] * After speaking to the neighbors, Everett found this to be a complete fabrication. When the Everetts learned Orville was holding, quite illegally, four or five claims for speculative purposes, suspicion immediately fell on him. Whether out of guilt or sympathy, Orville offered the bereft couple his half-built house to stay in until his family arrived from New York. With mixed feelings they accepted.

In February three young men from Ohio rode into Osawatomie bearing letters for Orville. The young men were Frederick, Owen, and Salmon Brown (no relation to Orville). Orville thought them hale, fine looking men, "far superior to the eastern emigrants." [4] The Brown boys quickly settled on a tract of land eight miles north of Osawatomie on the Osage. There they cleared the woods and made improvements to the land with a view to permanent occupation. In May their brothers John Jr. and Jason arrived with fruit saplings and cattle for breeding. As Osawatomie was the nearest trading and mail point for forty miles, Orville frequently saw them in town hauling wood or livestock to sell. They told Orville they

---

* The following year Serpel would accidentally drown while bathing in the Osage.

expected their father to arrive in several months—the arch abolitionist John Brown.

All that fall Orville worked to finish his log cabin, cutting and
splitting post oaks and puncheons for the floor. For several months
it had no roof or door, and he continued to live in a tent, sleeping
on buffalo robes and blankets. He also was using the house to store
goods and supplies until a store could be built in town. Eventually
he put up roof shakes, held down with heavy logs.

On top of his duties as town president, there was the business
of ensuring Kansas became a free state. Soon after his arrival he
began traveling fifty miles to Lawrence, which, because of the New
England Emigrant Aid Company colony, had already become the
heart of free-soil activity in Kansas. There, in a sod hotel with a
floor of straw, crowds gathered nightly to discuss the latest news
in the Kansas Territory. And the topic of keenest interest was
the election for a delegate for the remaining four months of the
thirty-third Congress. The new territorial governor, forty-seven-
year-old Andrew H. Reeder, had arrived from Pennsylvania in
October. Stout, florid-faced with bulging eyes and bushy mutton-
chop sideburns, Reeder wasted no time in setting an election date
of November 29.

Three candidates stood for the congressional seat: a free-soiler,
a pro-slave, and a Democrat. Although little was at stake, David
Atchison, the US senator from Missouri, was meanwhile not
taking any chances. Having served in the Missouri militia that
drove Joseph Smith and his Mormons from the state, he knew
how to deal with people he considered to be his enemies. On Election Day the bellicose senator led a large number of Blue Lodge
men across the border to vote, a tactic Orville sardonically dubbed
"Missouri methods." Other Missourians were enticed to cross over
with offers of money, food, and whiskey, and a free ferry across

the Missouri. In total, almost two thousand Missourians crossed over to cast fraudulent votes in almost every district. When the polls closed, Missourians triumphantly mounted their horses and wagons crying out, "All aboard for Westport and Kansas City!"[5] In one isolated settlement called 110, of the 604 votes polled, only 20 were legal. Not surprisingly, the pro-slavery candidate and former Indian agent, J. W. Whitfield, was elected.* Yet Whitfield's victory only spurred free-soilers to redouble their recruitment efforts in the North in preparation for the more important territorial elections.

Inexplicably turning a blind eye to the voting irregularities, Reeder proceeded to order a census for legislative elections. On the last day of February, the census was completed and made public. It revealed 8,601 inhabitants in the Territory, among whom 2,905 were eligible to vote. Among those eligible, 1,670 were from Southern states and 1,018 from the North (217 were from other countries). With 62 percent of eligible voters from the South, pro-slavery men were assured a legal victory.

Even so, Missourians were not about to take any chances. In March a Missouri delegation met with Reeder to urge him to move up the election date to preempt expected Northerner emigrants from voting. When Reeder asked the delegation's leader, F. Gwinner, his place of residence, Gwinner replied that he had a claim on Salt Creek, though not a house. "I believe I have your claim in my pocket," Reeder said coyly. He then produced a playing card marked "Gwinner's Claim—October 21, 1854." Gwinner had posted it to a tree to mark his claim, which was later found by Reeder's secretary while hunting. As the card was

---

* When Whitfield arrived in Washington, the House refused to seat him on the suspicion that he had enlisted his Indian friends to vote for him.

a three of diamonds, Reeder quipped, "Why your card was rather low—some fellows might have come along with the four of diamonds and jumped your claim!"[6] Everyone had a good laugh, but when Reeder set the election date for March 30, 1855, Missourians accused him of delaying elections so more Northerner emigrants could reach Kansas. Even though the charge was baseless, fears of an influx of Northerners spurred Atchison to redouble efforts to flood the polls with Missourians on voting day.

According to Reeder's election proclamation, only "residents" could vote, residents being rather loosely defined as those residing or having the intention of permanently residing in Kansas. With voters having only to swear an oath to that effect, both sides rushed to bring in as many "residents" as they could muster. Thayer might have brought in an additional nine hundred emigrants in time for the election, or at least that was Atchison's suspicion. In the rush to settle Kansas, free-soilers saw themselves as honest residents; Missourians and migrants from Southern states saw them as interlopers, which gave them the right to do the same.

Five days before the election Atchison went to work. To ensure a favorable outcome, he marched into Kansas with eighty men and twenty-four wagons of supplies. In St. Joseph, John Stringfellow was exhorting Missourians to "mark every scoundrel among you that is the least tainted with free-soilism, or abolitionism, and exterminate him. . . . Enter every election district in Kansas . . . and vote at the point of Bowie knife or revolver."[7] Once again, Missourians who crossed over received free food, liquor, and transportation. The day before the election, Atchison sent over a thousand more Blue Lodge men, guns in hand and Bowie knives stuffed in their boots, whom he told "not to follow the law." Ferries operating on the Missouri could not handle the crowds.

On Election Day nearly a thousand more heavily armed Mis-

sourians under the command of Colonel Samuel Young and Claiborne Fox Jackson, a former chemist and state senator, rode into
Lawrence to vote. With fifes and fiddles playing and flags flying,
they led young and old, educated and illiterate, drunk and sober,
on horseback and mules and in wagons loaded with tents and
rifles. One caravan pulled two cannons loaded with musket balls.[8]
Meanwhile, Atchison was in Nemaha voting with a large group
exclaiming, "There are ten hundred men coming over from Platte
County, and if that isn't enough we will send five thousand more.
We've come to vote, and will vote, or kill every God damned abolitionist in the Territory!"[9]

On his way to the precinct at Dutch Henry's Crossing, Orville
was astonished to encounter 150 armed Missourians who had just
voted there that morning and were on their way to Paola twenty
miles west to vote that afternoon. While voting in Orville's district, they had stayed at the home of Allen Wilkinson, the emigrant who had first surveyed Osawatomie with Orville and who
would very soon be elected as a pro-slave legislator.

At some polls, judges who refused to allow men to vote who
would not take an oath of residency were threatened or replaced
with more compliant judges. Other judges, fearing for their lives,
simply failed to turn up at polling sites. Seeing they were outnumbered, many eligible free-soilers became disheartened and refused
to vote. Polls stayed open until late in the evening. When the vote
was tallied, Missourians had once again swept the boards. Missouri's newspapers were jubilant. The *Leavenworth Herald* cel-
ebrated the election results as the definitive end of the Kansas
question: "All Hail! Pro-slavery Party Victorious! We have met the
enemy and they are ours. *Veni, Vidi, Vici.* Free White State Party
used up."[10]

Atchison had won, but it was a Pyrrhic victory. On election day over 6,000 ballots were cast, of which 5,427 were pro-slavery. Since legal pro-slavery voters greatly outnumbered free-soilers, Missouri settlers would have prevailed easily in a free and fair election. Now, however, free-soilers declared the election a fraud and refused to recognize it.

The day after the election Orville and other free-state men in Osawatomie signed a petition declaring the election in his district fraudulent. He took it to Governor Reeder at his home in Shawnee Mission. It was the first of several election protests to be submitted to the governor. Even though he was outraged by the proceedings, Reeder said meekly that he thought protests would be "unavailing" but promised to give Orville's "due consideration." Orville found the governor strangely quiet, "bewildered and confounded," concluding he had already gotten wind of threats to his life if he tried to withhold legislative certificates.[11] Just then, several free-staters rushed into his office to provide protection for the governor, placing several pistols on his desk covered with papers for good measure. Even though Reeder had the right to order new elections, he was mulling a course of action that would not antagonize the overwhelming number of Missourians in the Territory. He therefore allowed only four days for filing protests, leaving too little time to canvass voters as to irregularities in their districts. Even though Missourians had invaded all but four of the eighteen election districts, he then called for a reelection in only the six districts that submitted protests.[12]

From Reeder's home, Orville rode to Kansas City to meet with Charles Robinson, who had just formed the Free-Soil Party in Lawrence. Having taken note of the heavily armed Blue Lodge men around the governor's mansion and in Lawrence on Election Day, Robinson said he had begun to feel completely at the mercy of pro-slave power. The day after meeting with Orville, Robinson sent an urgent letter to Thayer requesting two hundred Sharps rifles and two cannons. "Give us the weapons," he wrote, "and every man from the North will be a soldier and die in his tracks if necessary, to protect and defend our rights."[13] A breech-loading rifle, the Sharps was the latest invention in weaponry, coveted both for its ability to fire rapid rounds (about eight to ten shots per minute) as well as its long-range accuracy. Armed with the superior Sharps, free-soilers could easily overpower Missourians' heavier buffalo guns and clumsy army muskets. To ensure his request got through, he sent an identical letter to Edward Everett Hale. Fearing both letters would miscarry or be intercepted by Missourians, he dispatched one of his clerks, George W. Deitzler, to hand deliver the letter to Thayer. Within hours of Deitzler's arrival in Boston, the company board approved a hundred Sharps rifles for shipment to Kansas. The boxes were marked BOOKS in the event they were intercepted in Missouri.

Despite the deteriorating situation, Orville sent for his family in April. He was waiting on the levee when Mary and the four children, Spencer, Rocky, Fanny, and Freddy, landed at Kansas City. A few weeks later Orville and Rocky returned to Osawatomie to finish work on the house while the rest of the family stayed in town for a week at the home of Morgan Cronkite, an emigrant from New York. When Orville and Rocky arrived at the cabin, the Everetts, who were still living in the cabin, refused to vacate. With the assistance of neighbors, Orville took their belongings and set them out in the prairie. Sarah Everett, however, refused to budge from her rocking chair. Picking up the chair with Sarah clinging resolutely to the arms, Orville took it outside and added it to the household goods. In June the couple bought a half claim three miles from Osawatomie, harboring bitter feelings toward Orville to their dying days.

As April gave way to May, the atmosphere in and around Osawatomie was relatively calm—apart from the shooting of a free-soiler by a pro-slavery man in Leavenworth in a claims dispute. Orville and the boys planted corn and onions, and they fenced the land while the women set up house. In the bright sun, the crops burst forth as the prairie beyond blossomed with wild strawberries and flowers of every hue and color. Mary and Orville found the drier climate agreeable and were excited to be part of the founding of the new state, even if it was not yet the harmonious frontier they had envisioned when they set out. Still, in those early days, they were on amicable terms with the Missouri border men on whom they depended for trade. They also traded with the Indians, with whom they enjoyed cordial relations. Indeed, when a Sac chief became smitten with one of Orville's daughters, the chief offered $300 in gold for her.

As more settlers arrived in Osawatomie, tents were replaced with log cabins and grass-thatched mud huts. On mail day, men from forty miles around would arrive while the postmaster Sam Geer tossed envelopes over the heads of hundreds of excited shouting men. Osawatomie was becoming a real town.

Yet there was still no school in Lykins County. Unable to get the education he longed for, Spencer worked the family farm, breaking ground and planting seed. It was a life the frail boy felt unsuited for, physically and temperamentally. When not working the farm, he spent his leisure time reading history and literature and fishing with his brothers for jack salmon, perch, or blue catfish in the many streams. In the fall they hunted wild turkeys and prairie chickens with Orville.

On May 22 new elections were held in the disputed districts. Free-staters won in all but Leavenworth, where Atchison had once again been up to his old tricks. Reeder subsequently departed for Washington to solicit President Pierce's backing for the holding of new elections, this time with military force to ensure they were free and fair. Instead, Pierce attempted to pressure Reeder to resign, but the governor refused to abandon his post, even though pro-slavery men had threatened to lynch him if he returned to the Territory.

Upon his return in June, Reeder announced that the legislature—which free-staters were now calling the Bogus Legislature—would convene in an unfinished building on the first Monday in July at the new capital in Pawnee. Since Pawnee was in the middle of nowhere and over a hundred miles from Missouri, Reeder's choice of a capital city proved unpopular with the largely Missourian legislature. He had already come under criticism for illegally purchasing Indian lands in Pawnee to profit from the anticipated growth of the new capital.

The legislature's first act was to call for the ten remaining free-state members to resign. The eleventh, Martin Conway, whom Orville had befriended on his journey up the Missouri in October, had already stepped down as part of a strategy conceived by Robinson to demonstrate that the legislature as it was constituted was illegitimate. Conway had written a letter to this effect, which the legislature promptly tossed aside before proceeding to unseat, one by one, the remaining free-staters on grounds that they had been irregularly elected. On the fourth day the legislators passed a resolution over Reeder's veto to move the capital to Shawnee Mission, located two miles from the border from Westport. It was the briefest time a city had ever been a state capital.

All that summer and fall the legislature was busy passing the most draconian pro-slave laws in the country. Residents of the Territory could be jailed for reading free-state newspapers or sentenced to two years hard labor for circulating anti-slavery material. Stealing or abetting in the theft of slaves was punishable by imprisonment or death. Aiding a slave to escape was also punishable by death. Even though implementation of these laws was somewhat lax, Southern papers heralded the new codes. But when the legislation landed on

Reeder's desk, he promptly vetoed it on the grounds that by meeting in Shawnee Mission, the legislature was not in legal session. His action further antagonized the legislature, which petitioned Washington for his removal. On August 15 he was sacked for unethical land speculation and replaced with Wilson Shannon of Ohio.

Reeder wasn't alone in rejecting the legislature. From June to August, seven free-state conventions were held in Lawrence, all but one favoring the repudiation of the Bogus Legislature. The most enthusiastic rally occurred at an Independence Day celebration in a grove outside Lawrence. As two companies armed with Sharps rifles paraded in uniform before a crowd of between one to two thousand people, Charles Robinson urged rejection of the new laws in language that hinted at the violence that was to come:

> Let us repudiate all laws enacted by foreign legislative bodies, or dictated by Judge Lynch over the way. Tyrants are tyrants and tyranny is tyranny, whether under the garb of law or in opposition to it. . . . I seem to hear the millions of free men and the millions of bondmen in our land, the millions of oppressed in other lands, the patriots and philanthropists in all countries, the spirits of the Revolutionary heroes and the voice of God, all saying to the people of Kansas, "Do your duty!"[14]

In mid-August free-soilers met in Lawrence and recommended sending delegates to a convention to draft a free-state constitution and apply for admission to statehood. While the proposal met with general approval, some felt Robinson's Fourth of July speech had gone too far and recommended moving the convention site from Lawrence—perceived as a hotbed of Northern abolitionism—fifteen miles west to Big Springs, a tiny trading post of four or five log cabins on the California emigrant road. Because Big Springs was inhabited by so called Western abolitionists, those who had come from west of the Appalachians who opposed slavery on economic as opposed to moral grounds, the venue was deemed more politically moderate.

On September 5, one hundred free-soil delegates from nearly every district in the Territory converged on Big Springs. Because of the lack of accommodations, delegates camped in tents. Orville was a delegate, as were Fred and John Brown Jr., from the area known as Pottawatomie Creek. So heavily armed were the attendees that the landlady refused to fetch one man's coat, saying, "Go in and get it. I would not touch that armory for all the property in the room."[15] What portended to be the most significant free-soil event thus far in the battle for Kansas would take a bizarre and unexpected twist: the acceptance of the Black Law proposed by James H. Lane.

Tall and lanky, forty-one-year-old Lane was part lawyer, part politician, and all actor. He had arrived in Kansas that spring a recently defeated Indiana Democrat saying he would "just as soon buy a nigger as a mule."[16] He was convinced Kansas would become a slave state and wanted to be on the right side when it did. But when he failed to secure support for the territorial government under the banner of the Democratic Party, he promptly changed sides. By the time of the Big Springs convention, he was hoping to replace Robinson, who was not in attendance, for leadership of the free-state movement but on a decidedly different platform. Chewing tobacco and dressed in frontier garb of buckskin breeches, the oratorical genius mounted the podium and proceeded to give a spellbinding speech. Objecting to Robinson's lukewarm condemnation of slavery, the persuasive Lane called instead for a prohibition of black emigration—free or slave—into the Territory altogether. When he finished speaking, ninety-nine out of the one hundred delegates accepted his resolution. Orville had been so transfixed by the power of Lane's speech that he voted with the majority, as did John Brown's family.[17]* The bizarre outcome prompted one Kansan to observe, the delegates' "hatred of slavery was not as strong as their hatred to Negroes."[18] Later, however, a committee recommended the resolution be killed as "untimely and inexpedient."[19] As a concession to Lane, they adopted a law that forbade anyone from enticing a slave to run away from his master on penalty of death.

Next to speak was Andrew Reeder, who, after his untimely removal from office, had thrown himself wholeheartedly into the free-soil cause. Reeder denounced the territorial government as a "monstrous consummation of an act of violence, usurpation, and fraud . . . trampling down as with the hooves of a buffalo, the Kansas-Nebraska bill, libeling the Declaration of Independence, and staining the country with indelible disgrace."[20] Reeder proposed the party form its own government and send him as the Free State delegate to Congress, both of which the convention accepted. Delegates also vowed to boycott the October 1 election and meet again in Topeka on September 15 to prepare its own free-state constitution.

When it was over, the convention had succeeded in giving form to free-soil resistance by formally transforming it into a Free State Party.[21]

In early October the Shawnee legislature elected its pro-slave candidate, J. W. Whitfield, by a near unanimous margin as representative to Congress. When both Reeder and Whitfield showed up to take their seats in Congress, a bewildered House refused to seat either of them and called for investigation into the Kansas troubles.

On October 22, a constitutional convention was held at

---

* The lone holdout was a missionary, James H. Byrd.

Topeka to draft the Free-State Constitution, prohibiting slavery. In attendance were Democrats, Republicans, Whigs, free-soilers, and "nothingarians" from every part of the Territory. Men of every occupation were represented, including doctors, lawyers, preachers, farmers, and teachers. Of the fifty-two members elected to the convention, forty, including Orville, took part in the lively deliberations. There were caucuses, committee meetings, electioneering, buttonhole fingering, and speech making. Newspaper reporters were admitted to a seat within the bar and dispatched reports of the proceedings of the convention to all parts of the country. After sixteen days, a constitution was produced. Lane, who dominated the convention, was elected president, but was once again unable to get his Black Law written into the document despite the fact that a majority of delegates were in favor of it.[22]

Even though the convention had distanced itself from "radical" abolitionism, Orville was nonetheless pleased with the outcome. "We are becoming a force to be reckoned with," he said, "and with God on our side we will prevail."[23] With two governments now in Kansas, one North and the other South, one free, the other slave, one official, the other provisional, each side was coalescing. Now the long fuse of discontent needed only a spark to ignite the hostilities simmering just beneath.

Chapter Four

WHISPERS OF WAR

"Sharps Rifles are the religious tracts of the new free-soil system."
—Democratic Review

IN LATE FALL OF 1855, A GRIZZLY LOOKING MAN claiming to be a federal surveyor arrived in Osawatomie leading a team of oxen and a wagon filled with tents and rifles. If questioned en route by Missourians, his surly reply was that he was going to Kansas to survey the lands for "them and the abolitionists to quarrel over."[1] This surveyor was the man who would in a single stroke escalate the Kansas conflict from simmering hostility to outright war—John Brown.

Tall and gaunt with a heavy beard, Brown had the grim look of an Old Testament prophet. When Orville first met the fifty-five-year-old abolitionist he took to him instantly, calling him a "wonderful man." His description of Brown is in sharp contrast to the popular image of a dangerous man who was mostly a failure in life:

His personal appearance was that of a gentleman of the old school. Tall, erect, not portly, nor slim, broad shouldered, well-proportioned [with] a heavy head of iron-grey hair, silvering to white, stiff and bristling back from the forehead [with] graceful well-formed ears, [with] grey eyes and clear-cut vision but very

mild and gentle in expression, canopied by heavy dark brows
and full-flowing long, clean white beard, embellishing as fine
a head as ever crowned the shoulders of man. He was a true
gentleman, listening to you patiently and replying in a pleas-
ant and brief but decided manner. He never minced matters in
giving expression to unpopular truths.[2]

The two Northern abolitionists had much more in common
than a surname. Growing up on the Ohio frontier in the early
1800s, John experienced a life of extreme privation. At sixteen, he
enrolled in preparatory school, but lack of money and an eye ail-
ment forced him to drop out. Both Browns were deeply religious
Congregationalists, though John had withdrawn from affiliation
with a particular church. And like Orville, John had also had an
epiphany in which he resolved to consecrate his life to the cause
of abolition—his provoked at a much older age by the murder of
Elijah P. Lovejoy in 1837. After moving to Springfield, Massachusetts, in 1846, John worked on the Underground Railroad. He
later worked for Gerrit Smith assisting indigent blacks to obtain
land grants in New York. Orville respected him as much for "his
trust in God and man" as for his courage and self-reliance.[3] He saw
John Brown frequently, at his house, in town on business, and at
public meetings on free-soil issues, and he and his family became
good friends.

Despite their affinity, the two did diverge on one important
point. Whereas Orville felt the path to a free Kansas lay in pop-
ulating the Territory with abolitionists, John believed that only
with "the remission of blood" would Kansas become a free state.
During the Convention of Radical Political Abolitionists held in
Syracuse in June of 1855, John had declared that no one should
go to Kansas without weapons, and that if the attendees were the

ultra-abolitionists they claimed to be then they should be willing to provide his three sons in Ohio the wherewithal to travel to Kansas and with arms. The following day in open session, Smith presented John Brown with three revolvers, seven muskets with bayonets, and a purse of gold, instructing Brown to send a report of his actions in the Territory in defense of human freedom.[4]

Once in Kansas, the old man stayed at the home of his half-sister Florella Adair and her husband the Reverend Samuel Adair until he could build his own cabin. The Adairs were a missionary couple using their house as an Underground Railroad station for slaves fleeing Missouri. Not surprisingly, the hawkish Brown chafed at Charles Robinson's lily-livered policy of nonviolent resistance. Yet, as a newcomer he agreed to abide by the free-soil leader's policy—albeit with great reluctance.

In October, Orville and Eli Thayer traveled to St. Louis to purchase a boiler for the mill before going on to New York to seek financing for more improvements to Osawatomie. Rumors of an invasion of Kansas by Missourians were already afloat when they boarded the outbound boat in Kansas City. The water being low, the boat was put ashore on the east bank at Hill's Landing for a time. In the streets Orville observed Missourians armed and mounted, drilling for an attack on Lawrence. Recruits were being sought and additional ones were being drawn from the prisons. Orville was alarmed by the freedom with which they confided to him, a total stranger, their plans to attack Kansas. When the boat stopped in Boonville, he encountered the same hostility and bitterness toward Kansas free-soilers.

In New York he met with the Kansas League in Manhattan's luxurious Astor House where the New England Emigrant Aid Company had also set up its headquarters. (Unbeknownst to him, six years later Abraham Lincoln would stay there on his way to the presidential inauguration.) While in New York, Orville succeeded in getting a Kansas Fund started for the construction of a number of undertakings in Osawatomie, including a church and a school house.* Whether out of guilt or conviction, New York and Boston abolitionists who were unable or unwilling to move to Kansas contributed handsomely to the cause. They were "wide awake and doing nobly for the friends of all our enterprises," Orville enthused. "Everyone seems ready to help the good work."[5]

Later he and Thayer went to Brooklyn to attend a Kansas free-state lecture at the home of Henry Ward Beecher, clergyman, abolitionist, and brother of Harriet Beecher Stowe, author of *Uncle Tom's Cabin.* Of late, the South had been calling on free-staters to respect law and order, and to use their Bibles to voice their opinions. A Bible had even been presented to one of the pro-slave leaders in Kansas, a gesture Southern newspapers unanimously applauded. But in his address to a public audience that day, Beecher had something more persuasive than the Holy Book in mind to convert advocates of slavery: Sharps rifles, often referred to as Beecher's Bibles.[6] According to the *New-York Tribune:*

> He [Beecher] believed that the Sharps Rifle was a truly moral agency, and that there was more moral power in one of those instruments, so far as the slaveholders of Kansas were concerned, than in a hundred Bibles. You might just as well . . . read the Bible to Buffaloes as to those fellows who follow Atchison and Stringfellow, but they have a supreme respect for the logic that is embodied in Sharp's rifle.[7]

---

* When he returned in late winter, Orville opened the first school in Osawatomie in a one-room log cabin on his property. His daughter Kitty was the school's first teacher, and his wife, Mary, would teach there as well.

Beecher believed the superior weapon had true moral agency and was the only thing that could tame the wild beasts of the South. In his fiery sermons, Beecher called on his congregation to donate money for the purchase of rifles. He donated to the cause himself. Thanks to Beecher, money came in from all parts of the North: Bangor, Maine; Randolph, Vermont; Albany, New York; and elsewhere. New Haven, Connecticut, alone contributed $4,000.[8] But as Orville would soon learn on his return trip in March, the real question wasn't any longer whether to use weapons but how to get them into Kansas.

While Orville was rallying support in the East for the free-soil cause, Missourians he had seen mustering for an attack on Lawrence had finally gotten their pretext for war. On November 21, 1855, at the village of Hickory Point outside Lawrence, a free-soil settler named Charles Dow swung a two-foot piece of iron at a pro-slave squatter named Franklin Coleman in a dispute over the boundary between their claims. In return Coleman gave Dow a load of buckshot to the chest, killing him instantly. Because of his pro-slave sympathies, Sheriff Samuel J. Jones, who was also the postmaster of Westport, made no attempt to arrest Coleman even though he had fled to Missouri.[9]

A few days after Dow's funeral, free-state men formed a vigilance committee to bring Coleman to justice. When the vigilantes learned that Coleman's neighbors planned to testify that he had shot Dow in self-defense, Dow's roommate, Jacob Branson, and several others set the homes of Coleman and his two neighbors ablaze. Terrified by the lawlessness, the few pro-slave families living in Hickory Point fled to Missouri, giving rise to rumors that free-state men were arming with Sharps rifles and had begun to expel all pro-slave settlers from the Territory.[10]

When informed of the house burnings, Jones formed a posse

of twenty men and set out to arrest Branson. Arriving at Branson's cabin late at night, Jones burst through the door and with pistols cocked, thundered, "Don't you move or I'll blow you through!"[11] As Jones was escorting his prisoner to jail in Lecompton, a band of fifteen free-state men led by Samuel N. Wood intercepted them at Wakarusa River and demanded to see the arrest warrant. When Jones refused—or was simply unable to produce it—the free-state men rescued Branson and escorted him to Charles Robinson's house in Lawrence.

Jones, who had been itching for a pretext to attack free-state men, immediately sent a dispatch to Governor Wilson Shannon requesting three thousand men to put down an "open rebellion" and assist him in "enforcing the law."[12] Since Branson's rescue came just two months after the Big Springs convention, Shannon construed Jones's message as part of a larger free-state plan to defy territorial law. The same day he instructed the commander of the Kansas militia, Major General William P. Richardson, to collect "as large a force as you can" and place his force under the command of Jones in Lecompton.[13] A similar order was sent to the commander of the Southern militia, Brigadier General Samuel Strickler. The following day Shannon sent a message to President Pierce, informing him of the gravity of the situation in Lawrence: "It is vain to conceal the fact," he wrote, "we are standing on a volcano."[14]

Even though Shannon was concerned civil war could break out along the border, the next day he added fuel to the fire when he issued a proclamation urging citizens of the Territory to rise up and resist "this confederate band of lawless men."[15] In response, Colonel Albert G. Boone, a Westport merchant and grandson of the legendary frontiersman, immediately issued an inflammatory appeal claiming that homes of Missourians were being burned down and atrocities of all sorts were being committed against them. Over a thousand pro-slavery and Blue Lodge men from all over Missouri mustered for an armed invasion. One volunteer, a seventy-year-old Irishman toting his father's Revolutionary War flintlock musket, set out with his sixteen-year-old grandson. Those who could not go were asked to contribute money to defray volunteers' expenses for the causus belli.

For his part, Robinson was none-too-pleased to have the Hickory Point's troubles laid at his door, for it had given Missourians the pretext they had long been looking for to attack the city. To avoid being compromised, he ordered Branson and the three Lawrence men involved in the rescue to leave town immediately.

Upon hearing of the advance of the pro-slave forces, Robinson called up residents to defend the city. Additional men from outlying areas were summoned to come to the aid of Lawrence. Among the four hundred to six hundred men who heeded the call were John Brown and his four sons, all armed to the teeth. Timber and cylindrical barricades made of earth five feet high were thrown up, and other preparations were made for a vigorous resistance. By day Jim Lane drilled the troops while the women frantically made cartridges and took target practice with pistols.

On December 1, Jones's forces amassed along the Wakarusa River just south of Lawrence. For three days each side warily watched the other, waiting for the slightest provocation as a pretext to strike. Despite the tension, free-state men allowed Missourians to freely enter the town to reconnoiter. During one such reconnaissance Jones ran into lawyer Sam Wood, one of the Lawrence residents who had participated in the Branson rescue. During the bizarre encounter, Wood invited Jones to dinner but Jones declined. While on another reconnaissance Jones was asked in the presence of Robinson what he intended to do; the hotheaded sheriff replied, "I'll show you when I get ready."[16]

As the siege dragged on, Robinson braced for the worst and ordered more ammunition brought in. Since men were needed to defend against an attack expected any moment, two women, Lois Walker and Sam Wood's wife, Margaret, were sent to fetch ammunition buried at Mud Springs on the Santa Fe Trail. The day being cold, the women had put on extra layers of clothing. It turned out to be fortuitous for they were able to use the extra clothing to conceal the matériel. They tied the gunpowder around their waists, and the cartridges in cloth around their ankles. Bullet molds and gun wipers were stuffed in the sleeves, pockets, and waists of their billowing petticoats. Bars of lead were secreted in their stockings. So burdened were they that the women needed assistance getting into and out of the wagon.[17] "When I saw those two wimmin," a free-soil man told a reporter, "I just allowed that bustles had come into fashion again, for they were swelled out awful."[18] A twelve-pound howitzer was also smuggled in from Kansas City in a box marked "store goods." Along the way the wagon got mired in the mud and was aided by two of Jones's men who had no idea they were extricating the enemy's artillery.

Meanwhile, reports had reached Shannon that a howitzer and fifteen hundred Sharps-bearing fighters were in Lawrence. Having thought he could easily put down the free-staters with his unruly mix of citizens and militia, he now feared a bloodbath. On December 4, he called up the 1st Calvary at Fort Leavenworth under Colonel Edwin V. Sumner, a cousin of the Massachusetts senator. In an abrupt change of strategy, Shannon wrote, "It is peace, not war that we want, and you have the power to secure peace."[19] Sumner, however, wisely refused to act without authorization from Washington.

Upon hearing the governor had attempted to call up federal dragoons, Jones became concerned that he would lose control of the plot he was hatching. He began to press the governor for authorization to attack, insisting reports of the strength of free-state men were exaggerated. If the governor did not, he said, "more than two-thirds of the men now here will go away very much dissatisfied."[20]

Just how keen Jones was for war was revealed in a conversation he had with *New-York Tribune* correspondent William Phillips, whom he stopped on the Lawrence–Wakarusa road. Suspicious that Phillips was spying for the free-staters, Jones stopped and interrogated him for several minutes before allowing him to pass.

"Well, sir, let me tell you," Jones said, "You're well out of Lawrence. That place will be wiped out one of these days. By God, sir, they are all traitors, there, and damned abolitionists. We've got to wipe them out. There will be no peace in the Territory till it's done; and we'd better do it before they get any stronger." When Phillips pointed out that such an action would lead to a war, Jones thundered, "Well, damn it, that's what we want. . . . Damn the Union! We have gone in for peace long enough. We have got to fight some time or other, and may as well do it now. We have got the law and the authorities on our side, and we will take that town. It's no use talking; we have got to fight!"[21]

Shannon was still at Shawnee Mission when he received a message from Robinson complaining that Missourians were "committing depredations upon our citizens, stopping wagons, opening and appropriating their loads, arresting, detaining, and threatening travelers."[22] Robinson threatened to go above the governor if he did not act immediately to contain the situation. The men who had delivered the letter explained to the governor that Lawrence had nothing to with the Charles Dow affair. Nor were sixteen houses burned down, but only three whose occupants were not at home but in Lawrence at the time of the attack. The forces amassing at

Wakarusa were thus preparing to destroy Lawrence for something in which they had no involvement.

The news came as a shock to Shannon. He now feared the irregulars he had instigated would become uncontrollable. On December 5 he crossed over to Weston and asked Colonel Boone to accompany him to Wakarusa and use his influence to calm the men. Reaching the encampment at three in the morning, Shannon discovered that pro-slave forces had been separated into two groups to prevent the wanted men from escaping Lawrence. Jones was on the Wakarusa, and the militias, which had not placed themselves under his authority, were twenty miles to the northwest at Lecompton. To make matters worse, Atchison had shown up on the north side of the Kansas River with two hundred Blue Lodge men from Platte County.

Arriving in the Wakarusa camp Shannon was struck by the "strong disposition, which appeared to be almost universal, to attack Lawrence."[23] To diffuse the tension, he requested an escort to take him to Lawrence to consult with Lane and Robinson. The two free-soil leaders assured him they had every intention of respecting territorial laws and would respect Jones's arrest warrant—if he had one. Although Shannon felt their statements clearly contradicted the resolutions made at the constitutional convention in Topeka, under the circumstances, for once, the bumbling governor thought better than to argue the point. Shannon was also surprised to learn Robinson wasn't harboring Branson's rescuers or even Branson. All of them had left town days earlier (one showed up at Orville's house, much to Mary's vexation). Shannon admitted he had grossly overestimated the free-state threat and that an assault on the town would now be totally unjustified. Yet without some concession from free-staters, he would be unable to disband the militia. Estimating there were now some twelve hundred Sharps rifles brought in to arm free-state men, Shannon suggested they turn over the weapons to Major General Richardson until such time that "in the opinion of the chief executive" the arms could be restored to them. Robinson flatly declined, saying the rifles were brought in to defend freedom at the ballot boxes.

Shannon returned to Wakarusa with nothing to show for his attempt to negotiate a way out of the impasse he had largely created. He was still clinging to the hope that Sumner would arrive any moment and bail him out. When Sumner did not appear he called together three dozen men from the two camps and asked them to explain what kind of settlement they wanted. Only one expressed a desire for a peaceful ending to the standoff. Most were clamoring for nothing less than the total destruction of Lawrence. Once again, Shannon called on Sumner to come to his rescue. Still having received no orders from Washington, the colonel regrettably declined.

Just after midnight, Richardson informed Shannon that a plan was afoot to hoist "the black flag" as a signal to attack Lawrence. Richard believed if that occurred, nine out of ten men would disobey orders, including the forces at Lecompton who were aware of the plot. Fearing a collision between soldiers and volunteers was imminent, Shannon ordered Generals Richardson and Strickler to put down any unauthorized attack on Lawrence.

In the morning, Shannon was distressed to see the orders had little effect in stifling the volunteers' urge to fight. Jones's posse was still threatening blood and murder. One of the volunteers told Shannon that unless the citizens of Lawrence surrendered their arms, Missourians would attack the city and that the governor himself should now take care for his own safety. Desperate for a solution, Shannon turned helplessly to his aides for advice. One of them suggested he form a committee to negotiate with Robinson in Lawrence. With the situation deteriorating and Sumner refusing to budge, Shannon immediately approved the idea.

On December 7, Shannon set out for Lawrence with Colonels Boone and Kearney and General Strickler. A few hours later the party arrived at the Free State Hotel to meet with Robinson and Lane. Unbeknownst to the governor, on the previous day the first casualty of the war had occurred. Thomas Barber, his brother Robert, and their brother-in-law were on their way home from Lawrence when they were stopped by Potawatomi Indian Agent Major George W. Clarke and a Missouri merchant. After a testy exchange, the merchant ordered the Barbers to accompany them to Wakarusa. The Barbers refused. Precisely what happened next is unclear, though it appears that Clarke drew his pistol and fired first. A quick exchange of gunfire followed before each side rode off. The Barbers had not gone far when Thomas groaned and announced with a wan smile that "a fellow had hit him." Thomas then slumped, slid from his saddle, and died.

Robert brought his brother's body back to Lawrence where the sobbing of his wife caught the attention of free-state men who resolved to wreak havoc on their enemies. When Robinson got wind of their plans he immediately checked in. Now, as Shannon was ascending the hotel stairs, he glanced in an adjoining room and was shocked to see Barber's body laid out on a bench with his lifeless eyes staring out at the stairway. Ever the clever strategist, Robinson may well have staged the tragic scene to win the governor's sympathy going into negotiations. In any event, the feckless Shannon was about to be played even better by free-staters, just as he had been played by Missourians.

The first meeting lasted an hour, after which Robinson invited the governor to his house for dinner. Negotiations resumed the following day, Saturday, and concluded in the evening with the signing of a "treaty." The document, signed by Robinson, Lane, and Shannon, exonerated Lawrence from any complicity in the Jacob Branson affair in return for which free-state men agreed to assist in arresting any Lawrence men involved in the rescue. For his part, Shannon agreed to remunerate citizens of Lawrence for any damage caused by Jones's men and to never again call residents from another state to execute the territorial laws. Cleverly inserted into the end of the document was the free-state declaration: "We wish it understood that we do not herein express any opinion as to the validity of the enactments of the Territorial Legislature."[24]

When word of the treaty terms reached Lecompton, Missourians felt betrayed. "Shannon has played us false!" John Stringfellow exclaimed. "The Governor of Kansas has disgraced us and the whole proslavery party."[25] Others cursed the "cunning abolitionists" instead. Some believed that pro-slavery forces would have attacked Lawrence that very evening had a vicious sleet storm not come up.[26]

But free-staters were not quite finished with Shannon. That evening, Robinson and Lane invited him to a dinner party at the Cincinnati House. During the party, Lane anxiously approached Shannon with a report that a large irregular force had assembled on the outskirts of town and asked for written permission to repel the assault. Having already drafted the document, Lane handed it to Shannon who, warmed by abundant liquor and the conviviality of the event, signed it with hardly a glance. It read:

> *You are hereby authorized and directed to take such measures and use the enrolled forces under your command in such manner, for the preservation of the peace and protection of the per-*

sons and property of the people of Lawrence and its vicinity, as in your judgement shall best secure that end.[27]

Not only had the tipsy governor cosigned a settlement document acknowledging free-staters' refusal to recognize territorial laws, he had now authorized them to form a militia. Only later did he learn that the threat Lane referred to had been a ruse to obtain sanction for any aggression on the part of free-staters. Later, Shannon said he signed it because he had been genuinely concerned that Missourians posed a threat to Lawrence and insisted that his authorization was simply to repel the one attack.[28]

The following day, Shannon issued orders to Richardson, Jones, and Strickler to disband. Lingering doubts about the volunteers' intentions caused him to remain at the camp until the forces had retired. The Wakarusa War, as it was called, had been averted at last.

On December 10, the ladies of Lawrence sponsored a ball at the Free State Hotel to celebrate the lifting of the siege and the departure of Missourians. To smooth ruffled feathers, Robinson invited Jones and the governor. Surprisingly, Jones attended; the governor, having pressing business back in Shawnee Mission, did not attend. Despite the festive atmosphere, not everyone was as willing to extend the olive branch as Robinson was. Lane could be heard in different rooms describing the killing of poor Barber, still fresh in the minds of attendees, in an unsuccessful attempt to incite an attack on Jones. One free-soiler in particular—John Brown—refused to recognize the terms of the treaty. To protest its signing, the old man mounted a dry goods box in the corner of the hotel and called for the shedding of Missouri blood to atone for Barber's murder and the outrageous siege of Lawrence.[29]

Whether he knew it or not, Shannon had settled nothing.

Chapter Five

AN ARMY OF LOCUSTS

"Let your young men come on in squads as fast as they can be raised, well armed. We want none but true men."
—David R. Atchison

THE BITTER COLD THAT HAD HASTENED THE DISPERSAL of Missourians at Wakarusa retreated for a time, only to be followed by several weeks of brutal subzero temperatures, high winds, and heavy snow not seen in living memory. Even the Indians and traders, longtime residents of the area, had never seen such a winter. Log cabins, hastily thrown up and riddled with chinks and fissures in the roof and walls, afforded little protection against the punishing cold. Orville's family burned a cord of black walnut a week to stay warm. Writing his dispatches from the Robinson home, correspondent William Phillips had to keep his inkpot on the stove to keep it from freezing. Worse off was old John Brown, who huddled in a three-sided lean-to with a fire at the open end to shield temperatures as low as minus thirty degrees Fahrenheit. Looking out over the landscape, one settler was prompted to remark, "Siberia itself could not look more frigidly repulsive than these frozen, snow-drifted wastes of Eastern Kansas."[1] A few welcomed the bitter temperatures, believing it was the weather alone that had kept Missourians from invading Lawrence again.

While Mother Nature was imposing a truce in hostilities, free-state men adopted the Topeka Constitution in mid-December 1855. Among the forty representatives to ratify the document was Orville Brown. A month later, the election of free-state officers was held—in homes, as the mayor of Leavenworth, fearing violence, had prohibited polling. Charles Robinson was elected governor by an overwhelming margin, signaling widespread approval of his policy of nonviolent resistance. Surprisingly, the only major incident occurred at a home where pro-slavery men attempted to seize the ballot box. This led to a scuffle in which Reese Brown, member-elect of the free-state legislature, was killed by a hatchet blow to the head.

Senator Atchison viewed the elections with alarm and set about with renewed resolve to crush the free-state juggernaut once and for all. On February 4, 1856 he called fellow Missourians to action in a speech in Platte City:

> *They have held an election on the 15th of last month, and they intend to put the machinery of a State in motion on the 4th of March. Now, you are entitled to my advice, and you shall have it. I say prepare yourselves. Go over there. Send your young men and if they attempt to drive you out, then, damn them, drive them out. Fifty of you, with your shot guns, are worth two hundred and fifty of them with their Sharp's rifles. Get ready—arm yourselves, for if they abolitionize Kansas you lose $100,000,000 of your property. I am satisfied I can justify every act of yours before God and a jury.* [2]

The Blue Lodges in Missouri began selling shares in land companies that planned to send men when the weather improved. Atchison also called on men in Southern states to come to Missouri and Kansas "well-armed with money and a determination to see this thing out. . . . I do not see how we are to avoid civil war," he said, "come it will."[3] General Benjamin Stringfellow traveled through the South urging support in the form of men and money. In response, "Kansas aid societies" sprang up from as far away as Mississippi, Kentucky, South Carolina, and Georgia.[4] One Georgia county sent a hundred men. The Alabama legislature contributed $25,000 to the emigrant cause. Mississippi pledged to send seven hundred men, and its former governor, General John Quitman, donated $2,500 to the Southern Kansas Emigration Aid Society.[5] In April, Alabaman major Jefferson Buford, who had served in the Creek Indian wars, sold forty of his slaves to finance an emigration of four hundred men, mostly from Alabama, Georgia, and South Carolina. Senator Andrew P. Butler of South Carolina boasted, "Even in my own state, I perceive parties are being formed to go to Kansas, adventurous young men who will fight anybody."[6] Smaller companies set out in spring from Kentucky, Tennessee, Virginia, and Florida. On the whole, however, the Southern response was too little too late, as one historian noted, as most legislatures were unwilling to finance emigrant societies.[7] Perhaps, too, the South was simply lacking the righteous ardor of burned-over abolitionists.

Anticipating another invasion when the weather broke, Robinson began laying in provisions, weapons, and a half ton of lead. "We are purchasing ammunition and stores of all kinds for a siege," he wrote Amos Lawrence.[8] More men were mustered into service and drilled. Fortifications were strengthened, the largest being five feet high and one hundred feet in diameter on which patrols marched daily. Robinson still feared being outnumbered by Missourians willing to fight, and he sent a letter to President Pierce requesting federal troops to protect Lawrence citizens. Never sympathetic to the abolitionist cause, Pierce instead issued a proclamation in which he denounced the free-state movement as "revolutionary" and reaffirmed the territorial legislature's authority to enact laws. Equally concerned by reports of Missourians amassing along the border in response to Atchison's call, Pierce ordered them to disperse and for all states, North and South, to abstain from meddling in the Territory's affairs. To preempt the free-state movement, President Pierce subsequently recommended to Congress that it draft a bill authorizing the people of Kansas to frame a constitution with a view to admission to the Union. Two weeks later he placed federal troops at Forts Leavenworth and Riley, and put them at Governor Shannon's disposal "for the suppression of insurrectionary combinations, or armed resistance to the execution of the laws."[9]

But in his attempt to short-circuit the free-state movement, Pierce had overlooked the resolve of Northern abolitionists not only in Kansas but in the North as well. Newspapers in New England were urging more people to emigrate to take up the fight. As soon as the river ice thawed, emigrant societies in New England and New York sent more settlers. So, too, did the Kansas Emigrant Aid Society of Oberlin, Ohio, and a German society in Cincinnati. In Albany, New York, Gerrit Smith called on free-staters to resist the territorial legislature, Congress, and even President Pierce himself.

With Northern emigration came superiority in money and weapons. The new director of the New England Emigrant Aid Company, Dr. Samuel Cabot, secured $12,000 in donations with which to arm Kansas-bound migrants. A colony, consisting mostly of Yale graduates, was given Sharps rifles, half of which were funded by Henry Ward Beecher, who threw in a Bible upon departure for good measure. "We go with the Bible to indicate the peaceful nature of our mission . . ." declared their leader, Deacon C. B. Lines, "and a weapon to teach those who may be disposed to molest us."[10]

In New York the abolitionist Frederick Law Olmsted attempted to raise money for the purchase of another hundred Sharps rifles. After securing only $400, on the advice of an army officer he used the money to purchase a howitzer and ammunition instead. Eli Thayer managed to raise money for twenty-three Sharps rifles, ten of which the miserly abolitionist purchased himself.

But the largest shipment of weapons sent that spring had fallen into the hands of Missourians a few months earlier. Nearly one hundred Sharps had been stowed away on the steamer *Arabia,* which was bearing Orville up the Missouri on his return. As it was March and early in the season, only thirty passengers were aboard, mainly Missourians returning from Washington where they had attempted to bring in fighters and obtain political support for their cause among Southern Congressmen. Among the several Northern passengers was a thirty-four-year-old abolitionist disguised as a soldier from a Southern state, David Starr Hoyt of Massachusetts. Just when and how the thirty-four-year-old Hoyt had taken up the cause is unclear. Having served as an officer in the Mexican War, he was now leading a small group to fight in Kansas.

While boarding in St. Louis, Hoyt had confided to Orville that he was smuggling two boxes of weapons, each containing fifty Beecher's Bibles, into the Territory for the New England Emigrant Aid Company—"with more courage than wisdom," Orville noted. In his stateroom, Hoyt carelessly left a letter he was writing to his mother intimating the true purpose of his trip. The letter fell into the hands of the ship's captain.[11] Wishing to expose Hoyt, the captain read the letter aloud to a crowd of passengers in the saloon. Irate Missourians turned to confront Hoyt and throw him in the river, but the abolitionist stood his ground. With his back to the wall, Hoyt slowly drew back his waistcoat displaying heavy pistols and a large bowie knife prominently at his sides.

While Hoyt was squaring off against the Missourians, the captain referred the question of the boat's liability to a pro-slavery lawyer among the passengers. The lawyer was returning from his former hometown of Baltimore, where he had just printed the new territorial laws. In the spirit of justice, the good lawyer opined that the boat could be detained at any landing for the full value of the rifles ($4,000 on a letter drawn up by Samuel C. Pomeroy). The opinion did not sit well with pro-slavery men who were anxious to see Hoyt punished. They now turned on the lawyer, demanding to know who he was. Protesting that he had been unfairly assailed for giving an honest legal opinion, the lawyer indignantly defended himself as the son of a slave holder who had come to Kansas "as a Democrat true to the interests of the South."[12] Moreover, he was a Kansas legislator who had helped draft the Territory's legal code and had just spent the winter getting them printed in Baltimore. "Hoyt had raised a one-sided storm," Orville quipped, "the lawyer a two-sided tornado." To the most vocal of his attackers, a Dr. Porter from Independence, the lawyer thrust a finger in his face, paraphrasing a line from Shakespeare: "On what meat has this, our Caesar, fed that he hath grown so great?"

"Did you mean me sir?" Porter asked.

"If the coat fits, you can put it on."[13]

The two then lunged at each other, the doctor tall and agile and the lawyer short and stout. The lawyer was getting the better when Porter shouted for his weapons, which had fallen from his belt. Just then the captain entered and pulled the lawyer off of Porter. With the boat soon to land in Missouri and the captain facing possible liability for the contraband, a merchant from Westport, Charles Kearney, son of Major General Stephen Watts Kearny, pulled Hoyt aside and pointed out the gravity of the situation to him. Nodding sheepishly, Hoyt finally relented and turned over his weapons. Kearny, who commanded a great deal of respect from Missourians, then mounted a chair and proceeded to give reasons why, "as law and order men," everyone on board should refrain from further violence and post bonds in order to indemnify the boat's captain for the rifles. All aboard unanimously agreed and handshaking was followed by a short feast.[14]

As the boat approached the landing at Lexington, Missouri, about a thousand pro-slave men, notified in advance by telegraph, were waiting to confiscate the rifles. Pulling Kearny aside on the deck, Orville asked, "How are you to get Hoyt by that landing?"

"When the boat is nearing the dock and the passengers are rushing to that side of the boat," Kearny said, "the Captain will slip Hoyt out of his stateroom to the other side and run him up to his personal quarters on the upper deck."[15]

When the boat landed, Missourians rushed aboard to seize Hoyt. They scoured every nook and cranny but failed to find him, secreted as he was in the captain's quarters, which they dared not enter. In the end, Hoyt managed to slip away, though the rifles were confiscated and he had nothing to show Pomeroy for his money when they met a few hours later in Kansas City. As it turned out, the guns were useless because the breach slides and ammunition had been sent overland via Iowa. Hoyt later sued the *Arabia* and recovered the full amount of his loss, though Governor Shannon, after much deliberation, refused to return the rifles. The Hoyt incident had confirmed Missourians' worst suspicions: free-staters were smuggling large numbers of weapons—superior ones at that. To intercept contraband, river patrols and cargo inspections were stepped up.

One day a large suspicious-looking box arrived in Kansas City on the boat *Genoa* addressed to Orville Brown. As a large crowd gathered, the Law and Order Committee of Lexington was called, and they proceeded to tear open the box. To their embarrassment, it revealed not Sharps rifles as they were expecting, but a piano for Orville's daughter Kitty. Seeing the disappointment on the faces of the Missourians, a bystander mocked, "Music hath charms to sooth the savage breast."[16] This prompted the crowd to laugh in derision at the pro-slavers who skulked off in shame. Because of its amusing history, John Brown later told Orville that if the piano belonged to him, "one thousand dollars should not buy it."[17]

On March 4, 1856, the free-state legislature convened at Topeka. As legislators took their oaths of office, Sheriff Jones looked on silently, recording names of those he intended to arrest later. During its two-week session, the legislature proceeded to codify its laws and elect James Lane and Andrew Reeder as US senators for Kansas in preparation for when the free state would be admitted to the Union. "The last of March, and still all quiet," Charles Robinson's wife Sara wrote. "The grass is growing everywhere, and the tiny flower-bells sway gently in every breeze. In many places they spring up without leaves, and in the dusty roads."[18]

On April 16 officials came to Osawatomie to collect taxes. Free-state residents in the area called an urgent public meeting chaired by John Brown. According to Orville, the old man was "the Gabriel of the occasion," as he delivered an impassioned speech in which he indignantly compared taxation by the Bogus Legislature to the oppressive British tea tax during colonial times.[19] At the conclusion of the meeting, a resolution was passed to resist payment of any tax to the territorial government on the grounds that it was illegitimate. "This is the first gentle breeze put in motion in central Kansas towards subjecting us to the yoke," Orville wrote, "May the earthquake swallow us after the tornado hath blasted us if we submit to this fiendish enactment."[20] A few weeks later a grand jury in Lykens County District Court in Paola found that Orville,

John Brown, John Jr., Charles Crane, and several others "being persons of evil minds and dispositions . . . did unlawfully and wickedly conspire, combine, and confederate and agree together mutually to aid and support one another in a forcible resistance to the enactments of the laws passed by the legislature of said territory of Kansas . . ."[21] Later, Orville was staying in a Lawrence hotel on business when several men burst in and arrested him. When asked by what authority they were acting, one of the leaders bellowed, "God Almighty and Governor Shannon!" Orville insisted on seeing an arrest warrant but was told he would see it "when they reached the prairie." He was then forced into a two-horse carriage. As the carriage was making its way up the street, several free-staters spotted him and came to his rescue. If anything, the attempted abduction had only hardened Orville's resolve:

> Our cause daily brightens. Let them curse! God reigns, and right will rule. Let the Border Ruffians rage and the Missourians imagine a vain thing! The "Yankees" are not the pusillanimous creatures they had supposed from seeing the poor white men of the slave States. Let us have more men (settlers and their families), and money to aid in paying expenses of our Free-State movements, and mills to cut lumber for houses, and in two years we will defy Missouri and F. Pierce in the bargain![22]

On April 19, Sheriff Jones arrested Sam Wood, one of the old Jacob Branson rescuers who had just returned from Ohio with one hundred fighters. A crowd of free-staters soon gathered around the two, taunting and mocking Jones. While Jones's attention was diverted, his pistol was slipped from his belt, allowing Wood to escape. Exasperated, the next day Jones returned to Lawrence with a small posse from Lecompton. It being Sunday, he was unable to find Wood at home or any of the other Branson rescuers about. As he was hitching his horse in front of the Free State Hotel, he suddenly spotted one of Branson's rescuers, Sam Tappan, strolling down the street.* As Jones rushed over and grabbed him, Tappen wheeled and punched him in the face. Jones actually appeared pleased, for it had now given him the pretext he needed to lead the long-awaited assault on Lawrence. The next day he went to the governor to request a military force to assist him in executing what by now had grown to twenty arrest warrants. On April 23, Jones reappeared with a small number of US dragoons under the command of Lieutenant McIntosh. A band of Lecompton men was stationed by the river to prevent any of the wanted men from escaping. Six men were taken prisoner and placed in a small building in town.

None of the six, however, were Branson's rescuers, for they had already fled town and were now moving from house to house and hiding in ravines. Late in the day it began to rain and Jones, still not having found the main culprits, encamped along the river out of town. Around ten o'clock that night, while sitting in his tent, an assailant fired into the tent striking Jones in the back. The identity of the assailant was never learned and some even speculated that it was a Southerner attempting to incite an attack on free-staters.[23] The next day, the Committee of Safety in Lawrence issued a statement repudiating the "atrocious" attack on Jones and offered $500 for the apprehension of the shooter.

In early May a Lecompton grand jury indicted Reeder, Robinson, and Lane for treason. Judge Samuel D. LeCompte ordered US Marshal I. B. Donelson to arrest the free-state leaders and

---

* Cousin of the New York abolitionist Lewis Tappan.

shut down the newspapers and the Free State Hotel as public nuisances. Lane had already fled to Iowa; Reeder, Robinson, and his wife now prepared to flee eastward. Disguised as a wood chopper in a battered straw hat, a clay pipe in mouth, and an ax in hand, Reeder sauntered out of the Free State Hotel undetected. Robinson and Sara got as far as Lexington, where he was caught and detained by authorities.

Unaware the free-state leaders had absconded, Donelson issued a proclamation that was circulated in eastern Kansas and border towns of Missouri calling on "law-abiding citizens" to rally at Lecompton for his assistance. An enormous eight-hundred-man posse of Missourians and Southern chivalry responded. After rewarding them liberally with whiskey, Donelson began scouring the Kansas prairie. In Lawrence, rumors were swirling that Donelson intended to destroy the now leaderless town. Even if he had no intention of doing so, residents feared he would be unable to control his inebriated men once they entered. In the absence of Robinson in mid-May, a committee of free-staters appealed to Governor Shannon for protection but to no avail. As free-staters floundered, Sam Pomeroy returned from the East and was made interim head of the Committee of Safety. Pomeroy immediately appealed to Colonel Sumner to station troops in the vicinity as a deterrent. Once again, Sumner replied that while he wished to do something, he had no authority to act. The next day Pomeroy sent a desperate letter directly to Donelson, pledging free-staters would henceforth respect the law. That the territorial government had grown weary of free-state promises is evidenced by the marshal's cynical reply:

> *Your declaration that you "will truthfully and earnestly offer now, or at any future time, no opposition to the execution of any legal process," etc., is indeed difficult to understand. May*

I ask gentlemen, what has produced this wonderful change in the minds of the people of Lawrence? Have their eyes been suddenly opened, so that they are now able to see that there are laws in force in Kansas Territory, which should be obeyed? Or is it that, just now, those for whom I have writs have sought refuge elsewhere? Or it may possibly be that you now, as heretofore, expect to screen yourselves behind the word "legal," so significantly used by you. How am I to rely on your pledges, when I am well aware that the whole population of Lawrence is armed and drilled, and the town fortified—when, too, I recollect the meetings and resolutions adopted in Lawrence, and elsewhere in the Territory, openly defying the laws and the officers thereof, and threatening to resist the same to a bloody issue, and recently verified in the attempted assassination of Sheriff Jones, while in the discharge of his official duties in Lawrence? Are you strangers to all these things? Surely you must be strangers at Lawrence.[24]

While Donelson was advancing on Lawrence, attempts to resolve the Kansas question in the US Congress was also reaching the tipping point. In March, in response to President Pierce's request, Senator Stephen A. Douglas introduced a bill for Kansas's admission as a slave state. Senator William H. Seward countered by announcing he would introduce a bill to admit Kansas as a free state. On May 19, free-state supporter Charles Sumner of Massachusetts rose to the floor of the US Senate and began an emotional two-day speech, "The Crime Against Kansas," in which he personally attacked Douglas and South Carolina senator Andrew P. Butler. Sumner's worst vitriol, however, was directed at Butler, whom he charged with taking "a mistress ... who, though ugly to others, is always lovely to him; though polluted in the sight of the world, is chaste in his sight—I mean the harlot, Slavery."[25] As Butler was known to colleagues as a courteous and congenial man, even Butler's opponents felt Sumner had gone too far. Three days later, while Sumner was seated at his desk on the Senate floor, Preston Brooks, a cousin of Butler, savagely beat him over the head with his gutta-percha cane, breaking it in the process. All that summer a bitterly divided Congress would struggle in vain to find a way to admit Kansas as a state, prompting pro-slavery Texas senator Louis T. Wigfall to remark, "Let Kansas bleed if she has a fancy for it."[26]

Bleed it would. At dawn on May 21 an advance party of Donelson's men, armed with muskets, gathered on Mount Oread, overlooking Lawrence. On the brow of the hill nearest the town was Robinson's house, which had been taken over as headquarters. Just before noon US marshal Donelson sent US deputy marshal W. P. Fain into town. Fain proceeded to arrest a few lesser free-state men without incident. Donelson then turned over his posse to a fully resuscitated Sheriff Jones to execute his warrants, declaring, "He is a law and order man and acts under the same authority as the Marshall."[27] The men gave Jones a resounding ovation. Armed at last with federal authority and a formidable force of men at his command, Jones advanced on Lawrence. At that moment Atchison and Benjamin Stringfellow had come up with two brass six-pound howitzers and the Platte County Rifles that Atchison had organized. Major Buford was leading a large force of Southerners, and Colonel Boone was leading a company from Westport. Orville was in Kansas City buying supplies when he received word that pro-slavers were marching to Lawrence to destroy the town. Being on the Committee of Safety he hastened to Osawatomie to bring up as many fighters as he could to protect the beleaguered town. "Captain" O. V. Dayton, founder of Osawatomie's weekly newspaper, the *Kansas Herald,* promptly assembled the Osawatomie Company, and John Brown came up with his sons and the hundred-man Pottawatomi Rifles.

Around three o'clock in the afternoon, Jones descended into Lawrence with banners unfurled. Emblazoned on one was, "Let Yankees tremble, abolitionists fall; our motto is, 'Give Southern rights to all.'" Backed by a small force, Jones went to the hotel and demanded Pomeroy turn over all free-state weapons. After consulting with the Committee of Safety, Pomeroy offered to give up the artillery, but the Sharps rifles, he insisted, were private property. Jones then ordered the men to destroy the *Kansas Free State* press, which was smashed and thrown into the Kansas River. Books and papers were scattered in the street. A company of South Carolinians proceeded to demolish the other press, *Herald of Freedom.* In a curious act of foreboding, the South Carolinians had hoisted their state flag over the *Herald* building before moving it to the Free State Hotel. Next, Jones brought up one of the cannons and trained it on the hotel, the bastion of free-state activities. Somewhat comically, the first balls overshot the hotel and landed in a ravine. After adjusting the cannon's trajectory, a few dozen balls struck the hotel but did little damage. Jones then ordered the men to torch it, though not before the wines and liquors had been salvaged for immediate consumption. When the walls of the hotel had finally fallen, Jones exclaimed triumphantly, "I have done it by God, I have done it!" He then turned to his men and said, "You are dismissed, the writs have been executed."[28] The men, many of whom by now were soused, went on a rampage looting and destroying the town. Homes and stores were broken into and robbed of anything of value: money, books, clothing, guns, and provisions. Seen at one store was Benjamin Stringfellow, contentedly helping himself to two boxes of cigars. By evening the town was in ruins.

The mob drifted off with their plunder. Miraculously, no one was killed except a Southerner who had been hit by a falling piece of mortar from the hotel wall.

Orville and his men had gotten as far as the Wakarusa when they realized they were too late to save Lawrence, and so they returned to Osawatomie. But with the sack of Lawrence, John Brown's patience with inaction had finally reached the breaking point. The truculent Brown had always thought Robinson's free-state strategy of nonviolence weak and pusillanimous. Looking for some action, he and the Pottawatomi Rifles moved on to Bull Creek while deciding what to do. At noon the next day, a man named Hank Williams rode up to their camp and announced old man Morse, who had refused to sell ammunition to Southerners, was being threatened at his store at Dutch Henry's Crossing. Now the old man said, no less an authority than God Almighty decreed him to "make an example" of the pro-slavery men living on the Pottawatomie Creek. James Townsley, who was against slaughtering pro-slaver settlers, asked Brown, "If God is such a powerful man as you say, why doesn't He attend to this business himself?"[29] After sharpening their cutlasses on a grindstone, John sent Jason and John Jr. home to be with their families. A few of the men then bowed out, unwilling to kill men in cold blood, whatever their beliefs. This left only Theodore Weiner, his son-in-law, Henry Thompson, John's sons Salmon, Watson, Fred, Owen, and Oliver, and a reluctant James Townsley. Brown refused to let Townsley drop out, fearing he might reveal their plans. To appease him, the death list was shortened.

Just before midnight on May 24, Brown led some of his men to the house of James Doyle, a pro-slave man who owned no slaves. They were greeted by some of Doyle's savage dogs that Townsley and Fred immediately "laid out" with their swords. When Mrs.

Doyle answered, John announced he was from the Army of the North and ordered James and his sons, William and Drury, outside. Another son, John, was not ordered outside because Mrs. Doyle had pleaded with them to spare his life. As the sons were being led from the house, Mrs. Doyle rebuked her husband, "I told you, you would get into trouble for all your devilment."[30] So as not to alarm pro-slave neighbors, Owen Brown and another of Brown's men took Doyle and his two sons away from the Doyle house and hacked them to death with their broadswords. As he was leaving, the old man shot Drury in the head for good measure. At daybreak Mrs. Doyle and her son went in search of them.

> *I found my father and one brother, William, lying dead in the road, about two hundred yards from the house. I saw my other brother lying dead on the ground, about one hundred and fifty yards from the house, in the grass, near a ravine; his fingers were cut off and his arms were cut off; there was a hole in his breast. William's head was cut open and a hole was in his jaw as though it was made by a knife; and a hole was also in his side. My father was shot in the forehead and stabbed in the breast.[31]*

When one of the men in the party protested the killings, John countered it was better that a score of pro-slave men should die rather than one free-state man be driven from the Territory.[32]

Four nights later, Brown led the men to the homes of Morton Bourn and J. M. Bernard. Although the men admitted to owning slaves they swore they never participated in any activities against the free-state movement. Brown warned them to leave the Territory immediately or they would be killed. The next night Brown went to the home of territorial legislator Allen Wilkerson, who had first surveyed the Osawatomie site with Orville. Wilkerson, half-dressed, was ordered outside and marched some distance from the house, where two of Brown's men cut him to pieces.

Crossing Pottawatomie Creek, they arrived at the cabin of James Harris just after midnight where they found Harris and a few overnight guests, including Dutch Henry's brother, William Sherman. After questioning each of the men, Brown decided none but William Sherman had been involved in the attack on Lawrence and spared them. They then took William to the edge of the creek where one of John's sons hacked him to death. His body was later found with the left hand cut off and his skull split open in two places, his brains washed partially into the water.[33]

When news of the massacre reached Lecompton, Henry Clay Pate, a captain in the territorial militia, set out with the pro-slavery militia called Shannon's Sharp Shooters to find the Browns. Unbeknownst to Pate, Brown was hiding in a thicket near Ottawa Jones's house, guarded by a dozen men. Jason Brown, who had spoken to his father at Jones's house before he went into hiding, asked him if he had killed the men on the Pottawatomi. The old man said he had. Jason said, "Then you have committed a very wicked act," to which John Brown replied, "God is my judge."[34] Jason then went to Osawatomie to give himself up but was arrested on the way. Orville, who thought it no crime to have murdered Missouri state men, rode out to the Joneses with a message of warning that Pate was searching for Brown with a large force.* To elude Pate the old man began moving from place to place. Eventually, Pate abandoned the search though not before torching the cabins of John Jr.

---

* Later, however, at a public meeting in Osawatomie, free-staters would denounce the slayings.

and his father and the shop of Theodore Weiner whom they suspected of being complicit in the killings.

On his way back to town Orville intercepted John Jr. who was riding back to Osawatomie with the Pottawatomie riflemen. Orville warned them they would be shot on sight if they tried to enter town. Immediately, the men disbanded and fled into the thickets along the Osage River. For several days and nights John Jr. wandered in the prairie, hungry, sleepless, and crazed. Some days he would stop at the house of his uncle Sam Adair to get a few hours rest and some food. Fearing sooner or later he would be captured and killed by vigilantes, Orville suggested he turn himself in to federal forces under one Colonel Coffee in Paola. As it was arranged, the US troops were to remain on the north side of the river while Coffee was to receive Brown in town in his private covered carriage and turn him over to federal troops who would lead him to Paola. John Jr. agreed to the plan. When he emerged from the bush he was gaunt and his clothes were in tatters from days of hiding in the brambles. Orville found him a new suit and he was able to enjoy a night's rest, free from fear at his uncle's house. In the morning John Jr. showed up at the colonel's carriage, and he was charged along with his brother Jason with murder, although they were the only two sons not to have been involved in the massacre. With their arms tied tightly behind their backs the Brown boys were forced to march eight miles in the hot sun, holding one end of a rope, the other end of which was held by a mounted soldier. John Jr. had to maintain a brisk pace to keep from being trampled by the horses. When they reached Tecumseh, their ropes were replaced with chains and ankle manacles, and the men were marched to Lecompton. The grueling march was said to have driven young John Jr. insane.[35]

Upon hearing of the arrest of his sons, John Brown took off

in pursuit of Pate. He knew Pate was somewhere in the area of Hickory Point, for there were reports men had been plundering and harassing free-staters in the area. While scouring the prairie for Pate, Brown came upon the twenty-five-man Prairie City Company and united with them, thus enlarging his force. As his combined force was still half the size of Pate's, he sent for reinforcements camped on the Wakarusa while he continued his search. At daylight on June 2, he found Pate camped in a grove of blackjacks, eating breakfast. Moments later the two sides began firing. Fighting went on for nearly three hours, until Pate's ammunition began to run low. Just then Fred Brown mounted his horse and appeared on a land rise, shouting in mock excitement as if their reinforcements had arrived. Even though Fred's antics had been a ruse, it fooled Pate into surrendering. By then half of his men had deserted.

Meanwhile, Colonel John W. Whitfield, the pro-slave delegate to Congress, was leading a new invasion of three hundred Missourians to avenge John Brown's murders. When Whitfield heard of fighting in the grove, he had hastened to the scene only to arrive just after Pate's surrender. The next day Whitfield moved on to Bull Creek, twelve miles east of Palmyra, when Brown and the other free-state companies gathered nearby to oppose him. At that moment Colonel Sumner arrived on the scene with 160 dragoons and drew up between the two armies. Sumner announced he was acting on behalf of the governor and ordered the free-state men to disperse.

Although Sumner's purpose for being there was to arrest John Brown, no one in Sumner's party could find the warrant. After a good deal of parlaying, John Brown agreed to turn over Pate and his other prisoners to Sumner who offered to release them on the condition that they depart immediately. Sumner then went over to Whitfield camp and ordered his men to disperse, and he also agreed to comply. Assuming both men would honor their word, Sumner returned to Fort Leavenworth, leaving only a small detachment behind. But the next morning, as Whitfield marched back to Missouri, a detachment of half his men under Captain John W. Reid, a Missouri attorney and legislator who had been decorated in the Mexican War, broke off and turned south for Osawatomie.

On June 4, Reid set up camp eight miles outside Osawatomie. Between Reid's men and the town was a company of federal dragoons that Orville had requested for the town's protection. To reconnoiter the town, Reid dispatched a spy who pretended to be sick. Among the intelligence he gathered was that, for no apparent reason, the dragoons protecting Osawatomie had moved off in the direction of Ottawa Creek several miles away.[36] Some of the dragoons may well have harbored pro-slave sympathies. Whatever the reason, it left Osawatomie protected by only twenty armed men. Still, most residents believed Reid would not attack the town but had encamped on the fringes to cut off travelers and supplies on the roads leading to it.[37]

With the dragoons gone, Reid now advanced. As he entered town, it was so quiet he suspected an ambush, even though his scouts had reported only a few men about who were engaged in building defenses. Approaching by the Westport road from the west and not from the east, as John Brown had expected, they took residents completely by surprise. So unprepared were they that no attempt was made to resist as Reid's men began robbing and ransacking shops and houses. The spy who had been aided by local residents the previous day led the men from place to place, showing them where the best booty in the form of arms, jewelry, and money could be obtained. Many of the men pinched petticoats as trophies.

Orville was sick in bed when Spencer rushed in with news

that the town was under attack. Fortunately, armed neighbors rushed to protect Orville's house and family, though his three horses and a dozen others were stolen while he and the other owners looked on helplessly.

The Missourians then began looking for the *Kansas Herald* press, which had just printed its first edition. When they failed to find it or the editor, Dayton, who was out of town, they began threatening residents to talk. They threatened to hang a woman who they felt sure knew of its location, but she pleaded ignorance. When they finally found the press, they smashed it to bits.

As destructive as the sacking of the town was, a still worse fate awaited Osawatomie in retaliation for John Brown's murders.

Chapter Six

OSAWATOMIE REDUX

"Take more care to end life well than to live long."
—John Brown

JOHN BROWN HAS BEEN DESCRIBED AS A BIT PLAYER in the Kansas conflict, yet the old broadswordsman was anything but. His massacre of innocent men on the Pottawatomie marked the moment when what had thus far been largely a political conflict turned violent. With Charles Robinson in jail, free-state firebrands like James Lane were now emboldened to go on the offensive. Determined to drive pro-slave settlers from the Territory once and for all, Lane organized a large, well-equipped army that roamed the countryside terrorizing pro-slave settlers. Missourians rushed to the aid of friends and family under attack. Amid the escalating violence, local militias proliferated. By the summer of 1856, a full blown guerilla war had broken out all across the Kansas prairie, as both sides indulged in an orgy of killing, looting, stealing, and destruction of crops in the name of liberty and the right to determine the future of Kansas.

In Missouri, efforts were stepped up to curb the influx of abolitionists into the Territory. Emigrants caught passing through the state with weapons (and they usually were) were disarmed and turned around. Kansas-bound cargo was inspected at points of entry to ensure no weapons were being smuggled in from Northern abolitionists. Northerners began using alternative routes through Iowa and Nebraska to send matériel and thousands of dollars in hard cash to free-state settlers perceived as beleaguered.

Writing to Mary in early June, Orville described Osawatomie as living in a state of siege. Small parties of Missourians, some in army uniform, roamed the area day and night, terrorizing rural settlers and plundering wagons and homes. To prevent theft and to be at the ready in case of a surprise attack, settlers had their horses saddled and brought into the house or hitched to windows or doors. At bedtime, weapons were laid within easy reach. The few pro-slave men living in and around Osawatomie had now turned spies for Missourians who raided the homes of suspected free-state fighters and dragged them off to Lecompton. At night the barking of dogs signaled to nervous residents that raiders had struck at yet another home and arrested its occupants. Fearing a similar fate, some took shelter in the woods, coming home during the day to eat before returning to their hiding places. Others lived together in groups protected by guards. A few weeks later Orville took his boys to stay at the Shawnee Friends Mission, a Quaker settlement located three miles south of town, before returning to stand guard over Osawatomie. Stationed at Pilot Knob five miles north of town, he was to fire a signal shot if Missourians were seen crossing Bull Creek. For many days and nights he and other volunteers kept lonely vigils in the hills around the town. With Kansas in turmoil, the stream of new free-state emigrants to Osawatomie—indeed to all of Kansas—slowed to a trickle that summer.

Caught in the middle of the fighting were Sumner and his troops. Less than five hundred federal dragoons had been assigned to the entire Territory, far too few to establish even a modicum of law and order over the vast Kansas prairie. Complicating the situation was Sumner's concern for respecting individual rights on both sides of the conflict. When the free-state legislature attempted to convene in Topeka, Sumner was ordered by both President Pierce and acting Territorial governor, Daniel Woodson, to disperse the legislators. He arrived at noon on July 4 with two hundred dragoons and two brass cannons, which he trained on the assembly building. Sam Tappan, the clerk, had just called the legislature to order when Sumner appeared at the door and announced:

Gentlemen, I am called upon this day to perform the most painful duty of my whole life. Under the authority of the President's proclamation, I am here to disperse this Legislature, and therefore inform you that you cannot meet. I therefore order you to disperse. God knows that I have no party feeling in this matter, and will hold none so long as I occupy my present position in Kansas. I have just returned from the border, where I have been sending home companies of Missourians, and now I am ordered here to disperse you. Such are my orders, and you must disperse, I now command you to disperse. I repeat that this is the most painful duty of my whole life.[1]

Despite his apologetic tone, loyal soldier that he was, Sumner threatened to use the entire force at his command to enforce his orders. The legislature complied, though not before some civilities between the two sides were exchanged. Sumner's respect for free-state rights elicited three cheers for himself, Governor Robinson, the national flag, and the free-state legislature . . . and three groans for Pierce.[2] A few days after the incident, the US House attempted to attach a proviso to the army appropriations bill to prohibit use of federal troops against free-state activities. It failed, though narrowly. Secretary of War Jefferson Davis later censured Sumner for using military force to disperse a political meeting, even though he was merely following orders.

By August, violence across the Territory had reached a fever pitch. On August 12, Lane's army attacked Fort Franklin, Sheriff Jones's new stronghold in the Territory. Having failed to dislodge the occupants after three hours of fighting, Lane brought up a wagonload of hay against the fort and torched it. Everyone inside fled, allowing him to recoup Old Sacramento, the cannon used in the Mexican War that had an almost mystical value in the conflict.* That there had been no casualties was something of an embarrassment to Lane who was looking to show them he meant business. The attack had not been entirely in vain, however, for three days later John Brown used Old Sacramento to attack a hamlet in Douglas County.

Meanwhile, two of the most active militias had finally squared off after months of near clashes. Back in June, Major Henry Titus of the pro-slave Law and Order militia had put a $300 bounty on the head of the free-state militia leader Sam Walker. Getting no takers, Titus decided to torch Walker's cabin, which was located at the junction of the California and Lecompton roads. When Walker got wind of the plan, he invited some thirty men to his house to give the militia commander a proper welcome. Knocking out some of the chinking in the walls of the cabin, they waited for Titus and his men to arrive. They had almost given up waiting when Titus's militia appeared around midnight. They were greeted with a hail of gunfire. Titus turned and fled. Amazingly, no one was killed,

---

* On the night of June 4, 1856, two companies of free-state irregulars had seized the cannon in an attack on a blockhouse in Franklin. Old Sacramento had been stolen by Missourians from the US arsenal in Liberty, Missouri, and used by Sheriff Jones in the attack on Lawrence.

though two of Titus's men were taken prisoner to Lawrence. With the courts sympathetic to the pro-slave side, Titus later got a writ for Walker's arrest, forcing him to flee into the prairie.

In mid-August, Walker resurfaced upon hearing several free-state prisoners were to be hanged in Lecompton. Setting out with his militia, he encountered Titus and his men eight miles from town conducting one of their nightly raids of free-state homes. This time, however, darkness prevented a final resolution of their feud.

In the morning, a coach driver tipped off Walker that Titus was holed up at his house, a stout log cabin dubbed Fort Titus. Walker quickly sent a runner to Lawrence to retrieve Old Sacramento from Lane. A few days earlier, a federal dragoon had confided to Walker if he wished to nab Titus and could make short work if it, the dragoons might look the other way. As he waited for the cannon to come up, Walker and his men approached Fort Titus and opened fire with their Sharps rifles. Titus quickly returned fire, killing one free-stater. During the firefight, Old Sacramento was brought up. Using balls made from the type from the *Herald of Freedom* press, salvaged from the Kansas River, Walker blasted a hole through the blockhouse wall. Raising a white flag, Titus surrendered. Emerging from his blockhouse, injured and bloodied, Titus was taken to Lawrence with several other prisoners.[3]

On August 17, Governor Shannon rode to Lawrence to arrange a peace deal between the two militias. As part of the deal, both sides agreed to release their prisoners, including Titus. It would be Shannon's last official act, because the following day he resigned in frustration. Years later he would bemoan his troubled tenure, "Govern Kansas in 1855 and '56! You might as well attempt to govern the devil in hell."[4]

Shannon's departure left State Secretary Daniel Woodson as acting governor. Ardently pro-slave, Woodson wasted no time in declaring Kansas in a state of rebellion and calling for Missouri citizens to rise up, much as Shannon had done on two previous occasions. In response to Woodson's call, Colonel Boone raised several hundred volunteers, as did Missourians in other counties. Cooper County raised $5,000 for the relief of pro-slavery families in Kansas. Atchison, who felt too much blood had been shed to abandon the cause, assembled his men at New Santa Fe and placed them under the command of Colonel John Reid. Reid's objective: to capture "Osawatomie Brown."

By this time the town of Osawatomie was in a virtual state of siege, with sixteen armed companies of Missourians encamped around the town.[5] There was a large company of Major Buford's Alabama boys on Bull Creek, and two miles east one hundred Georgians were staying on the farm of Charles W. Ballard under the pretense of making homes. For weeks both companies had been intercepting supply wagons, and by late August the town had exhausted its stock of flour.

On August 28, Orville received intelligence that pro-slave men were preparing for another attack on the town. With only two dozen armed men to protect it, he once again requested federal troops, who set up camp on his property. He then rode to Lawrence to request that the Committee of Safety dispatch a thousand men to Osawatomie. Before departing, he sent Spencer, Rocky, his sister, and her husband, Charles Crane, to stay at John Carr's heavily guarded house. To those fleeing the countryside, he opened his home as a shelter.

Upon reaching Lawrence, Orville sent Fred Brown to Osawatomie to bring up his family from Carr's house. That very day, federal troops who were protecting Osawatomie had once again inexplicably decamped some twenty miles west. At sunrise on August 30, Fred Brown set out with a team of horses and a wagon for Osawatomie. Arriving at Orville's house, he fed the horses before going to Carr's house to arrange with the family an immediate start after breakfast. Fred then set out for his uncle Adair's house. Little did he know that a detachment of about three hundred of Atchison's men was advancing on Osawatomie under Reid's command. This time Reid planned to destroy Osawatomie entirely. On his way, Reid encountered the Reverend Martin White, a pro-slavery Baptist minister who was headed to Osawatomie to reclaim horses he believed had been stolen from him by residents of Osawatomie. As he neared the town, Reid spotted free-state men guarding the southern crossing to town from the Osage, so they circled around and approached from the northwest. There they came upon Fred Brown on his way to the Carr house to collect Orville's children. Reverend White shot him through the heart, killing him instantly. White later claimed the shooting was in self-defense as Brown refused to halt when he was ordered to.[*] Hearing the shot, Mr. Garrison came out from the Carrs' house and set out in the direction of the noise when Reid's men shot him as well.

John Brown was in camp making breakfast when word reached him that his son had been killed on the Lawrence road. Immediately he ordered his men to intercept Reid's men before they reached Osawatomie. But Reid had already reached the high ground overlooking the town. Even though he was greatly outnumbered, John Brown sent ten of his men to hold a blockhouse on the edge of town, while he and the rest of his men took up a position in the woods along the Osage River. The river ran nearly parallel to the road down which Reid's men were now advancing. Brown, with

---

[*] Late in life Orville said he felt indirectly responsible for the death of Fred Brown.

seventeen men, was on the right; Dr. W. W. Updegraff, with ten men, was in the center; and Captain Cline was on the left with fourteen men. There was also an independent command still farther to the left, in the mill consisting of "Pap" Austin, an ex-soldier whose large rifle carrying a one-ounce ball he had named Kill Devil. As the Missourians descended the hill below Orville's house in crescent formation, John Brown and his men, strategically placed behind rocks and trees, raised their Sharps rifles and fired. Mounted and exposed as they were, Reid's men were thrown into confusion. With his son Jason at his side, Brown walked the line of his men, encouraging and urging them to shoot carefully. At one point John stopped to ask one of his men if there was blood on his back. When he said there wasn't, John grumbled, "Well, something hit me a terrible rap on the back. I don't intend to be shot in the back if I can help it!"[6]

Meanwhile, Reid had regrouped. Bringing up a cannon, Reid fired into the woods. The cannon hit high into the treetops, bringing down some branches but failing to hit any of Brown's men. Reid's men then dismounted and rushed the woods, forcing Brown and his tiny force to retreat along the bank using the trees as cover. When they reached the sawmill, they jumped into the river and began to swim to the other side while others jumped into skiffs. Caught under Reid's heavy fire, two of Brown's men were wounded and one was killed. Three others, including Charley Keiser, were taken prisoner.

Even though the attack occurred in broad daylight, the town had been taken completely by surprise. At the moment of attack, Spencer and Rocky Brown, as well as Brennan (a cousin), were preparing breakfast. Spencer was setting the table, Rocky was cutting beefsteak, and Brennan was tending to the fire and coffee when they heard a shot ring out—the shot that killed Fred Brown. Looking out the window, Brennan spotted some of Reid's men. "Spencer, the Missourians are coming!" he cried out. Running to the door, Spencer saw a large number of armed mounted men moving slowly down the hill. "They were in full view and pretty close," he later wrote.[7] He told Brennan and Rocky to buckle on their guns as he grabbed his hat and started to town to warn others.

Spencer was not yet fourteen years old at the time, but he already exhibited some of the same heroic qualities that marked his final days. As unarmed neighbors were fleeing their homes, he ran a half mile into town at breakneck speed to warn the townsfolk. The first house he came to was that of the Lakes, who were eating breakfast. When Mrs. Lake heard the news, she began to cry inconsolably. He then went to the home of women whose men were in the fields and helped them hide their valuables in the woods. On his way to town he stopped at the homes of several more free-staters to warn them that four hundred Missourians were gathering on the hill for an attack. Once in town he went to the hotel's barn and dug up several muskets buried in the hay. Next he checked on his father's office. Finding it locked, he slipped through a window and found the safe was still intact. There was one rifle in the office belonging to his cousin. He took it and hid it in a nearby cornfield. Just then the Missourians attacked, and Spencer mounted a pile of logs to observe the battle. It was as if he had suddenly become an actor in a great theater of war, much like the heroes of epic battles he had read about in the works of Sir Walter Scott. After a few minutes he ran to the blockhouse where John Brown's men were and asked if they wanted some rifles. They told him to bring them along, but by the time he got back, the men, having seen two columns of men approaching with a cannon, had abandoned the blockhouse and fled into the woods to join John Brown.[8] Spencer started after them into the brush but paused at the Sears house to check on Mrs. Sears, as her husband was in the field fighting. Seeing a horse tied near the house, he helped Mrs. Sears into the saddle and led her over the river out of danger. He then returned to the house and hid her trunks and valuables in the bushes.

After a ninety-minute gun battle, the settlers were driven back over a hill. Now they watched helplessly as Reid's men descended on the town like an army of locusts, plundering food stocks, looting shops, destroying crops, and stealing horses. With the men fighting in the fields, the Missourians burst into homes, demanding rings from women's fingers, pulling jewelry from ears, and stealing anything of value before setting the houses ablaze. Some families fled to nearby woods while others huddled together in houses with young men to protect them. Others were taken prisoner. In the rampage, the mill was spared only because the miller had put up such a spirited defense.

Sometime during the melee Spencer had slipped over to the Missouri side. Just what impelled him to do something so daring and reckless is unclear. Whatever his motive, Spencer was chatting amiably with the men when a man named Taggert suddenly recognized him. Rushing over, Taggert grabbed the boy by the arm and said, "Follow me."[9] At the sound of the man's voice, Spencer's blood ran cold. Saying nothing, Spencer followed him to a house where fourteen other prisoners—some boys like himself—were being held. Four other prisoners arrived including "Dutch Charlie"—Charley Keiser. Placing Spencer in a chair, the Missourians began to question him as to how many free-state men there were and if he was old John Brown's son. Spencer said he wasn't sure but thought there were at most fifty men and that he was most certainly not John Brown's son but the son of Orville Brown. At this the men scoffed, convinced he was lying on both counts. It was then that Spencer heard the order to burn down the town.

As the Missourians prepared to destroy Osawatomie, they began loading their booty onto the wagons. One of the men ordered Spencer to lend a hand loading some chairs in a wagon. When he refused, the man rushed at him with his bayonet, threatening to stick him if he did not obey. After Spencer complied, he was ordered into a wagon with several wounded men, one of whom had been shot in the mouth and another through the lungs.

Retreating up the hill west of town, they stopped at Spencer's house that thus far had been untouched. All this time Spencer had been without shoes or stockings, so his captors allowed him to retrieve some clothing from the house. When he entered, "a very hot fire" was already raging in one of the rooms. He spotted a man about to make off with his precious violin, which he was able to retrieve, though "not without some trouble."[10] He then hastily collected some underwear, two or three suits of clothes, and a pair of flimsy moccasins. In a momentary act of kindness, one man handed Spencer his fish hook and line, and another, his saddle which was too bulky to take. After they finished plundering the house, they set it ablaze. At the last minute, two men attempted to take Kitty's grand piano, but the rapidly spreading flames forced them to drop it in the doorway where all but two legs and the iron frame would perish. As Spencer walked back to the wagon he turned to see his house, barely one year completed, now engulfed in the conflagration.

In town, virtually every free-state house and store—some twenty to thirty including the church and Kitty's little school—had been burned to the ground. Only the mill and the house of Samuel Adair had been spared, because it was full of sick people, mostly women and children, whom Florella, John Brown's half-sister, was ministering to. Orville's office had been broken into and his safe emptied of all his papers and valuables. Two free-state men had been killed in the battle, as had two dozen Missourians. Reid thought he had killed John Brown, but in fact the old man was on a hill overlooking the river watching in tears as Osawatomie was being destroyed.

In the evening when the fighting subsided, a few settlers ventured out of their hiding places and buried Fred Brown's body by the side of the road where he had been shot. Behind Carr's house they found a man named Powers wounded and bleeding from fourteen buckshot wounds to the groin. He had been spared thanks to the kindness of a Missourian who, after Reid's army had departed, told the Carrs that Powers was lying badly wounded in a thicket.

As Missourians retreated, free-staters continued to fire upon them at the Osage Crossing. For his protection, Spencer was placed in the charge of a Missourian named John Hancock from Howard County. After riding a short distance, Spencer voluntarily gave up his place in the wagon to a sick man. He then rode one of his family's horses the Missourians had stolen. When they stopped late in the afternoon to eat, it was the first meal he had eaten all day. Resuming their march, they left the main road and bivouacked across the prairie. Along the way, Reverend Martin White and his brother came up to boast how the reverend had shot Fred Brown on the Lawrence road. "Poor Fred!" Spencer cried when they later passed his bloody body lying on the side of the road. Next to the body was a plain board on which was inscribed: "Wm. Garrison, Fred Brown, and Wm. Powers, murdered by Rev. Martin White and Gen. Reid's men, August 30, 1856."

When the Missourians were within five miles of Bull Creek camp, a man came to move them along saying James Lane was in pursuit. As soon as news of the attack on Osawatomie had reached Lawrence, Lane had assembled his army of three hundred men. Wishing to avoid an encounter with Lane's fearsome army, the Missourians rode east at full gallop. After several miles of hard riding, one of the men asked Spencer if he wanted to rest but Spencer, who was nearly out of breath, said he preferred to continue. In the evening they arrived at Bull Creek on the Santa Fe Trail, where General L. A. MacLean was encamped with some twelve hundred men and six cannon, preparing to confront Lane's forces. But when Lane reached Bull Creek, he decided to halt until the infantry came up, allowing Reid and MacLean to slip away into Missouri. Upon hearing from his scouts that Reid had decamped, Lane returned to Lawrence.

Any hope the boy had of being rescued was now gone. In the evening he was given a piece of tough bread and placed in a tent with a dozen other prisoners. All night he tossed and turned, tormented by the day's trauma.

In the morning, Spencer was formally placed under arrest. As he was being returned to his tent, one of the men warned the guards, "Look out for him, he's sharp as a thorn."[11] Crowded as it was with Osawatomie prisoners, there was barely enough room to sit. Spencer squeezed onto the ground, his feet soaking wet from the porous moccasins. Next to him was Charley Keiser, also known as Dutch Charley. Charley began to openly worry that Franklin Coleman, the murderer of Charles Dow who was in Reid's army, intended to kill him.

When the sun came up, the prisoners were marched in single file to camp headquarters. Seeing Spencer, one of the officers from Texas, Colonel John Anderson, approached him. "My you're awfully young to be in such a place," he said. "What's your name?" After the boy replied, Anderson admonished, "Now Spencer, if you will be a good boy and obey your father and mother, and obey the laws, I will let you go home."[12] But Spencer only stared at him saying nothing. Anderson repeated his offer but still the little captive refused to respond. Anderson then led him to the officers' tent and asked General MacLean to make him out a "passport" in order that the boy might return to Kansas. While MacLean was preparing it, someone came up and whispered to the colonel who then spoke to MacLean. Returning to Spencer, Anderson said there were men who were adamantly opposed to freeing the son of John Brown. Indeed, some were actually planning to shoot him as soon as he left camp. For his safety Anderson decided to take Spencer to Westport after breakfast, after which he could go home by another, safer, route. Upon hearing he would be released, Spencer turned to the prisoners and asked if they had any word they wished to send home. But before anyone could answer he was whisked away to the officers' mess tent. "Those were the last words I was able to speak to them," he wrote, "and I was obliged to leave the disappointment as best I could."[13]

While eating in the officer's tent, Spencer noticed Joseph Anderson, the colonel's son and a member of the Bogus Legislature, holding his mother's knife basket with twelve silver forks and a music book belonging to his aunt, Mary Crane. Although it was Sunday, one of the officers pressed Spencer to play his violin but he refused, as much from shyness as from a stubborn refusal to gratify his captors.

Fearing Lane was still in pursuit, in the afternoon the Missourians hurriedly broke camp. Spencer was placed in a wagon with a wounded man named Klein, whose shin had been shattered by a Sharps rifle ball and whose disfigured leg he was told to support. For fifteen miles the boy held on to the gruesome bloody stump. "I should not like to do it again," he said.[14]

Early the next morning, before breaking camp, Coleman took Dutch Charley out and executed him, a cold-blooded act that MacLean defended.* Spencer was in the surgeon's tent where he had been ordered to tend to the wounded when he heard the disquieting shot. The other Osawatomie men who had been taken prisoner with Dutch Charley were taken on to Kansas City, put aboard a boat, and sent downriver with the warning that if caught again in the Territory they would be hanged.

Spencer gave little inkling of the kind of questions the Missourians posed, but whatever his responses he clearly impressed his questioners with his intelligence. While he was assisting one of the surgeons, Dr. James Keith, Keith asked him if he would be interested in staying on his farm for a year to study law or medicine. At first Spencer said nothing, thinking under the circumstances the offer was made in jest. When Keith repeated his offer, the other surgeons encouraged him to accept, saying the doctor was rich and had some pretty daughters. Long wanting an education, and fearing, as a Brown, he might well end up like Dutch Charley, Spencer accepted on the condition that he be allowed to return home if his father summoned him. Later that day General MacLean told Spencer he was sending a letter to Lawrence, and he allowed Spencer to write home on the condition that he say nothing about the strength of his army. Spencer agreed. He then penned the following:

DEAR FATHER:

I write this to ease your mind of any apprehension you might have on my account. I was taken in town. As I passed by our

---

* Dutch Charley's body was never found.

house I saw it burned, and the piano in it. I was allowed to take what I wanted in the shape of clothing. I am as well treated as I should be under your own care. There is nothing to fear on my account. Brennan, Whit*, and Rock are safe. So is Uncle Charley [Crane] and family. No more until I write again. September 2, 1856.

Your affectionate son,
SPENCER[15]

In the morning the Missourians broke camp for Indian Creek, thirteen miles away. Dr. Keith had business in Little Santa Fe. Before departing, Keith put Spencer in one of Reid's wagons with all his worldly possessions: his violin and clothing, his mother's knife basket, and his aunt's sheet music that he had managed to recoup. "That [wagon master] Poole totally disgusted me with tobacco and bad whiskey before I arrived at Westport," he groused.[16] As they marched, companies of a hundred or more fighters now began to peel off and head home with their plunder.

General MacLean arrived in Westport to find the town bracing for an attack by Lane. Ironically, it was through Orville that Lane had sent his threatening message: "Brown," he said, "you know Colonel Boone. Write him that Jim Lane will be in Westport tomorrow with three thousand abolitionists to breakfast with them."[17] Little did Orville know at the time that his son was among them. In the streets, Atchison was giving a speech about John Brown having taken "McKinney's train," a local allusion to his presumed death. Upon seeing the prisoners in the wagon, Mis-

---

* A cousin of Spencer's.

souri boys began hooting "Damned Yankee" and other epithets. Poole had a horse that needed shoeing and ordered Spencer to follow him to the blacksmith shop. Inside, Poole handed the boy a file and told him to begin filing the animal's hoofs as he did the same. When they finished, Poole sent Spencer back to wait in the wagon. At some point Spencer had jettisoned his wet moccasins. As his feet were now bare, he gave a passing man some money to buy several pairs of stockings. Saying nothing the man went off and returned with two pair of socks and returned Spencer's money. Later he learned the kind man was Lieutenant Beedroe of Lexington, Missouri.

After some time, Poole started for Missouri. He continued to drink whiskey and chew tobacco along the way until "he became positively disgusting."[18] From time to time he would give Spencer the reins and ask him to sing, which Spencer refused to do. Two miles down the road, Dr. Keith came up. Noticing his dislike of Poole, Keith offered Spencer his old grey mare, Puss, to ride. They rode until dark when they stopped at the house of a friend of Keith's to spend the night. In the morning they resumed their journey, conversing all the while. When the subject of the Fugitive Slave Law came up, Spencer, ever his father's son, said it was "contrary to the Bible."[19] Keith politely said he was mistaken. Just then they stopped at a field filled with ripe melons, and there they gorged themselves. At Chapel Hill, Keith stopped to buy Spencer an expensive pair of shoes. Despite their differing views on slavery, the boy had warmed to Keith, thinking him an intelligent and kind man with a lively sense of humor. When they arrived at the farm, Mrs. Keith came running out of the house to greet the doctor, shedding tears of joy at his safe return. Spencer was baffled by her crying, showing, for all his precocity, just how emotionally young he really was. Also at the door was Keith's pretty daughter

Molly who, upon seeing Spencer said, "Do, Ma, send Perry [her brother] out to ask him to come in. He looks so sad."[20]

Spencer's sadness would soon evaporate, for Keith's residence, known as Hazel Glen, was an opulent antebellum mansion set on a two-thousand-acre plantation. The house, a large, two-story brick affair, was surrounded by a carpet of lush blue grass "so thick and soft as to feel like feathers under your feet," Spencer marveled.[21] Hickory, honey locust, and thorn trees, pruned to perfection, adorned a plantation worked by twenty slaves. The boy with the odious name of Brown could very well have been dead by now, but thanks to the kindness and chivalry of a few Missourians, he instead found himself ensconced in a life of luxury not found on the harsh Kansas prairie. "It seemed like an ideal dreaming home which I have so often wished for," he said.[22] After days of loneliness and anxiety in being carried so far from a home now in ruins, his happiness was all the greater.

Dr. Keith and Spencer sat down to supper alone as the rest of the family had already eaten. Two of Keith's twenty slaves served them, Harry and Oliver, whom Spencer thought "little imps." The cook, Avina, he described as "very black and fat, and her flesh fairly quivered all over her when she laughed which happened neither few times nor far between."[23]

A few days later, Spencer was taken to Lexington, where he was permitted to write a letter to his father. Colonel Boone forwarded it along with a reassuring message of his own.

MR. O. C. BROWN SIR:

I inclose the letter from your son. I saw and conversed with him in camp. He is very well, and is now at Lexington with Colonel Oliver Anderson who will take good care of him. I asked the staff to let me have him, but they thought he would be safer from insult there than here. I saw an Indian, to-day, from Paola, who said your other son, perhaps the younger one, was much distressed about you and his brother. I sent him word that his brother was safe and well, and for the citizens to send him to me and I would take good care of him and send him to his mother, or keep him until I had orders from you. As a number of persons, I understand, will leave there next week for the East, it is possible they may bring him in. If so, I will write you immediately, as I am sure you will be uneasy about him. Should he come, I will do all I can to make him happy, and so will my father. Your son saved the likeness of his grandfather, which General McLean found in the things of one of the soldiers.

Be pleased to hear from you,
Respectfully,
A. G. BOONE[24]

Given that the two men were on opposite sides of a war, Boone's expression of concern for Spencer—and the solicitous courtesy he showed toward Orville—was remarkable. It was a testament to the fact that, for all their coarseness and espousal of the abhorrent institution of slavery, Missourians did not conform to easy abolitionist stereotypes of Border Ruffians and Pukes, as they were called. Indeed, some were refined men who adhered to a code of Southern chivalry even in their dealings with the enemy.

Others, however, were none too pleased about the solicitude shown toward Spencer. One day a Missourian stopped by to tell Keith that if he continued to harbor the son of an abolitionist, a fuss would be made not only by the boy's father (Orville) but by "the rest of the anti-slave world in general," concerns Keith evidently dismissed.[25]

Knowing he could (or would) not attempt to escape, Keith treated Spencer more like an esteemed house guest than a prisoner. He placed a fine horse at his disposal and allowed him to come and go as he pleased. Spencer availed himself of Keith's large library and read many books he had never had the opportunity to read, such as *Rienzi, The Last of the Romans* and *The Last Days of Pompeii* by Edward Bulwer-Lytton. In the gardens he played his violin and was even allowed to take target practice with Keith's shotguns and rifles.

"As I said I have no desire to leave now," he wrote his mother. "I sit at the table two out of three meals to the exclusion of the Doctor's children. I have no lack of employment as there are plenty of books in the house which I always wanted to but never had the opportunity to read, besides when these fail there is either a shotgun or a rifle and plenty of ammunition, besides my violin and plenty of nuts and apples and a young lady to court."[26]

The young lady was Keith's eldest daughter, Molly. On long walks together, he and Molly would talk, gather walnuts, and playfully flirt. In the evening the two played checkers, mostly, he admits, so he could gaze upon her comely face. One night he had gotten a wishbone and broken it with her. Having gotten the longer piece, when Molly left the room Spencer placed it above the door evidently so that he might get his secret wish of a kiss when she passed beneath. One of the servants, Dinah, who was in the room, was privy to the little joke and when Molly returned they both began to tease her, though nothing came of it. Coming from a boy on the cusp of manhood, the adolescent nature of their flirtation showed just how little experience Spencer had with the opposite sex on the Kansas frontier.

Although relieved to hear from her son and his happy circumstances, Mary nonetheless urged him to tell Dr. Keith to put him on the next train to Chicago to stay with his Uncle Horton at his home on LaSalle Street. Yet Spencer was just beginning to enjoy the good life at Hazel Glen and said nothing to Keith. In October, Spencer received a letter from his father through Colonel Boone asking him to return to Utica, New York. Boone concurred, asking that Spencer stop at his home on his way through Lexington. As the county fair was being held in Lexington, Dr. Keith decided to take the children and Spencer to the fair for a few days before his departure. On a raw cold morning they set out, Spencer and Perry on horseback and Molly and her sister Belle in the buggy with Dr. Keith. At the gate, Mrs. Keith kissed Spencer goodbye, causing him to fairly blush at the act of a woman he had come to regard as a second mother. Reaching the fairgrounds in the afternoon, Dr. Keith gave Spencer and Perry some money for dinner and they went off with Molly to enjoy the fair. Because the hotels were full, Perry and Spencer spent the night at Colonel Anderson's while Keith stayed at Walton's Hotel.

The next day, they all returned to the fair. In the evening on his way back to Colonel Anderson's, Spencer stopped by the hotel to see Molly. He came away from the encounter "deeper in love than ever." At Colonel Anderson's, his daughter Katie played the piano, which, Spencer said, so reminded him of home "as to sadden my heart."[27] Just then it was announced a Baptist Tea Party was about to take place across town and they all repaired to the party. On the way, Spencer stopped at Walton's Hotel where, just as he had hoped, Mrs. Keith asked him to accompany Molly to the party, giving him six shillings for expenses.

At the fair the next day he bought some gifts for Molly: a penknife and pocket book in which he inscribed with adolescent infatuation, "I love you." When Keith announced the family would be

returning to Hazel Glen in the morning, Spencer took the opportunity to present his gifts to Molly, whose expression of thanks he
could read in her eyes.

On the morning of October 5, Spencer's enchanting interlude
drew to a close as he prepared to return to Utica. For the journey he
bought an overcoat, two handkerchiefs, and some clothing for ten
dollars. Mrs. Anderson hemmed and inscribed the handkerchiefs
SKB for him. As he said goodbye to Molly, Spencer kissed her on
the hand. Just before they parted, he whispered to Mary, a friend of
Molly's, to keep him apprised of her activities.

Just after midnight Spencer boarded the steamer *William
Campbell* bound for Alton, Ilinois. As he was boarding, Colonel
Anderson handed Spencer some money for the journey, asking
that he tell his father to pay him back when he could. He immedi-
ately went to sleep, though not before kissing the ring Molly had
given him. In the morning he boarded the Illinois Central Railroad for Chicago where he stayed briefly with his uncle, Charles
Crane, who had fled Kansas after the attack on Osawatomie.
Crane had been in the countryside lecturing on the situation in
Kansas to large numbers of abolitionists. The following day his
uncle took him to a rally for the Democratic presidential candidate
James Buchanan who, despite being a northerner, was running in
support of popular sovereignty in Kansas. His opponent was the
abolitionists' choice, General John C. Frémont, who was running
on a Republican platform of a slave-free Kansas. While at the rally,
Spencer met several individuals who knew his father and expressed
admiration for the work he was doing in Kansas. After listening
to a lecture on slavery by Frederick Douglass, Spencer started for
Utica by the Lake Shore rail line.[28]

Once home in New York, abolitionists were quick to exploit
Spencer as a promotional tool. At a public meeting he was placed

upon a stand and displayed as an innocent boy whom the Missourians had cruelly held prisoner for nearly six weeks. At the village of New Graffenberg, he was asked to make an extemporaneous speech on behalf of a free Kansas but stumbled miserably. He also attended several abolitionists' lectures including one by William Lloyd Garrison, the founder of the anti-slavery newspaper *The Liberator*.

In the two years since he had been gone from Utica, fourteen-year-old Spencer had already lived a lifetime.

Chapter Seven

GOVERNING
THE DEVIL IN HELL

*"That Constitution [Lecompton] cannot be forced upon us
without the shedding of blood..."*
—Charles Robinson

FOR SEVERAL DAYS AFTER THE ATTACK ON OSAWATOMIE, Orville remained in Lawrence fighting in Lane's army. When he returned home, he was aghast to find the town he had built from scratch as well as his home had been burnt to ashes. His shop had been ransacked and the safe emptied of its contents, including $125 in cash. All that he had worked two years to build had been wiped out in a flash. When he learned his eldest son had been captured and whisked off to Missouri, he was devastated. At least the rest of the children were safe, having taken refuge at the house of their uncle, Charlies Crane. Writing to Mary, he bemoaned his loss while affirming his determination to fight on:

> *No other alternative is left us. It is fight or starve, for adhesion to the bogus laws never will be given.... Many of our people are prisoners, and some we have reason to believe have been murdered.... Leavenworth is shut out from us and the mails have stopped.... I am utterly stripped of everything but the clothes on my back, and not the first dollar... all is burnt and stolen but my claim.[1]*

Not knowing that Spencer was already in Utica, Orville refrained from mentioning Spencer's abduction to spare Mary further grief, especially as he had no idea precisely where his son was. Mary responded by suggesting he approach Samuel Pomeroy in Atchison and apply for aid from the Kansas Relief Committee. This group had been taking up a collection in all the New York churches to aid Osawatomie victims.

Yet aid would take weeks to arrive. With no means to support himself, Orville collected the children and brought them to temporarily stay with friends in Lawrence. A few weeks later, he set out for Utica with the children. In his care were the widow of Fred Brown and the wife of John Brown Jr. Their homes had also been destroyed by Pate. John Brown Jr., meanwhile, was awaiting trial in a Lecompton jail.

Looking around at the other free-staters on board returning east, Orville was struck by the look of weary defeat displayed on their faces: "The boat bore a sad company," he wrote. "Many were leaving all their earthly possessions behind, including relatives who had fallen in battle."[2] As the steamer descended the Missouri, free-staters huddled in their rooms like church mice, afraid of encountering the pro-slave men on board.

After all the suffering Orville had endured, one might have expected him to abandon the Kansas cause for the stability and security of life in New York, if not for his own sake then at least for his family's. Yet he remained as committed as ever to a free Kansas. Indeed, more was at stake now than ever, for it was an election year. The Democratic Party was wagering heavily on the merits of the Kansas-Nebraska Act, though it had snubbed its author, Senator Stephen A. Douglas. The Democrats were expecting the nomination of James Buchanan. Although decidedly pro-slave, Buchanan was running on a platform of unionism. Having just returned from

England where he served as ambassador, he was safely removed from the divisive Kansas debacle. By contrast, the Republican Party was waging all on a platform of a free-state Kansas under the candidacy of the immensely popular and charismatic soldier-explorer John C. Frémont.

In the fall, Orville embarked on a speaking tour about Kansas while campaigning for Frémont at venues all over New York State. He delivered lectures in Jefferson, Oswego, Oneida, Herkimer, Otsego, Delaware, and several other counties to audiences eager to hear about the Kansas conflict firsthand. In Utica's Mechanics Hall he spoke before a crowd of sixteen hundred with Henry Jarvis Raymond, politician and cofounder of the *New York Times*. He appealed to listeners to emigrate, while making no attempt to sugarcoat what they faced. Anyone going to Kansas, he said, should expect continued conflict. "Be prepared to buckle on the armor," he warned.[3]

In November, Buchanan won by a landslide, taking all but one slave state and even some free ones. Free-staters in Kansas now faced an uphill battle and more emigrants were needed. Under the auspices of the New England Emigrant Aid Company, Orville set up headquarters in the swank Astor House in New York City. He then placed an advertisement in the *New-York Tribune,* inviting those interested in immigrating to Kansas to call upon him to obtain information. The response was overwhelming. Hundreds of men descended on the hotel and pressed upstairs to his room. "Men of all nationalities, of all occupations, professional men, tradesmen, hair-brained adventurers, gentlemen and beggars, men clean and dirty men, strong men and invalids," came in a surging tide.[4] So many came that eventually he was forced to lock his door and ask the hotel clerk to control the flow of visitors.

That winter John Brown also returned east with sons Jason and

Owen but with a different purpose in mind: to raise money for more weapons. The old man was convinced that the only way to make Kansas free was through the shedding of blood. In speaking tours in New York and Massachusetts, Brown managed to raise $30,000 for the free-state cause. Despite concerns that he was wantonly violent, the Massachusetts State Kansas Committee voted to give Brown two hundred Sharps rifles, four thousand cartridge balls, and thirty-one thousand percussion caps—then in a reverend's cellar—and $500 for expenses. During his tour, he met Henry David Thoreau who, in his effusive praise of the old man, appeared to have been ignorant of his slaughter of pro-slave men at Pottawatomie Creek.[5]

By contrast, Orville saw more to be gained by increasing the number of free-staters in Kansas than in conducting guerilla warfare. He saw greater power at the polls than at the end of a gun barrel. By spring he had managed to entice some fifteen hundred Northerners to emigrate, many of whom were interested in a large tract of unclaimed land in southern Kansas. These were not impoverished "driftwood populations," he felt, but successful people whom had received Orville in their homes during his speaking tour.

In March 1857, Orville uprooted his family once again and returned to Osawatomie. Accompanying him was a large group of emigrants who planned to assist him in rebuilding the town. Ironically, Missouri steamship operators were happy to see them, grateful for their business. Most Missourians, however, were alarmed by the avalanche of Northerners.

Upon arrival, they were stunned to find Osawatomie completely rebuilt. Churches were open, and the settlement looked just as it did before Reid's attack. Yet there was still no public school for Spencer, and so the boy resumed working on the family farm and cutting and hauling logs to rebuild the family house. It was backbreaking and exhausting labor for which he was physically and temperamentally unsuited. When not working in the fields, he assisted his father in reorganizing the town records. Come spring he would help his father plant an orchard of forty trees and large flower gardens around the house. Every free moment was spent reading works of history, literature, and poetry. On a regular basis he made entries in his diary, which he had been keeping for some time, written in a cypher of his own invention, which by now was several hundred pages in length.

He also wrote regularly to his newfound friends in Missouri. The time he had spent "incarcerated" on Dr. Keith's plantation turned out to be one of the happiest of his young life. In Hazel Glen he had been in the company of soul mates, educated and sensitive people his own age who liked to discuss literature and play music. There were pretty girls to boot. Dr. Keith's idyll stood in stark contrast to the harsh life on the Kansas prairie with its backbreaking labor and endless conflict. Too shy to write Molly directly, he wrote to Mary, whose father was the principal of a school where she sometimes taught. "Ah, my soul yearns for music," he pined.[6] "If I ever marry, may I marry a girl who can sing and play!" he wrote in his diary. "If I am tired, music rests me; if I am angry, it tames me in a minute. The 'Marseillaise Hymn' makes me uncontrollable at times. The sweeter the music, the sadder I am."[7] He often confided his innermost feelings to Mary who became something of a sister confessor. He admitted to having obtained a picture of the sculpture *Indian Girl* by the Albany-based neoclassical sculptor Erastus Dow Palmer, which he likened to Molly. In private moments, the moonstruck boy would gaze at it for hours, stirring a longing to see her again. But in July, disappointment came when Molly's friend Mary wrote that she expected Molly to be "set up as a young lady" in about a year. Still, he refused to give up on Molly. "How can I?" he asked, "She is my main hope."[8] He also wrote Mrs. Keith, who responded with an invitation to Hazel Glen to attend the many winter parties with her children.

To satisfy his son's yearning for music, Orville returned from Lawrence with a chess set and a flute, fife, and flutina, a type of accordion. Despite his father's attempts to bring some culture to Osawatomie, Spencer saw little future for himself on the prairie. In the spring of 1858, he began making efforts to enter West Point to get a good education inexpensively. Evidently unaware the school was an army academy, he planned to get into the navy with his degree. To prepare financially, he sold his shares of town stock to his brother Rocky for eighty-five dollars. His friend Mary counseled him against the move, suggesting he study in Missouri, "if you are not too strong free-soil to patronize them."[9]

It was a decidedly pacified Kansas that Orville returned to that spring, thanks to the forceful strategy implemented by the new governor, John W. Geary. Pennsylvanian by birth, Geary had been the first mayor of San Francisco and former infantryman in the Mexican War where he sustained several wounds. On his trip up the Missouri in early September, Geary got a quick—if disturbing—schooling on the governability of Kansas even before he set foot in the Territory. When his steamer *Keystone* docked at Glasgow, Missouri, he and his secretary John H. Gihon were astonished to see on the hill above the dock throngs of men, women, and children who had turned out to bid farewell to Claiborne Jackson and his company of volunteers who were heading off to Kansas to "hunt and kill abolitionists." All were armed with an odd assortment of weapons, some new, some old, still others, according to Gihon, "unfit to shoot robins or tomtits."[10] While Geary and his secretary were observing the parting ceremonies, the steamboat carrying ex-governor Shannon chanced to come up. When the ex-governor heard his successor was on the *Keystone,* a visibly agitated Shannon came aboard to give Geary an earful on the situation in Kansas. Having fled in haste, Shannon drew a picture of a Territory in total anarchy with roads everywhere strewn with the bodies of slaughtered men. It was not an entirely inaccurate depiction, and Geary may well have begun to wonder just what he had gotten himself into. As the *Keystone* continued upriver, Geary observed town after town frantically girding for war. When the boat paused at Kansas City, self-described ruffians came aboard to ensure no abolitionists were on the boat. At Leavenworth, Geary and his aide disembarked to the sound of a crier riding through town alerting free-staters to leave or be driven out. On their way out of town, they encountered a barricade of wagons clumsily thrown up by citizens expecting any moment an attack from Lane's dreaded army of fifteen hundred strong. It was a fitting introduction to a situation he now had to bring under control.

Although a loyal Democrat, Geary was nonetheless committed to stabilizing the Territory and promoting the image of popular sovereignty the Democrats endorsed. He judiciously took no sides in the conflict, feeling both were to blame. He urged pro-slavery men to keep Missourians from interfering in the Territory and free-staters to respect its laws.

Rather than waiting for bloodshed to begin, Geary sought to prevent violence from erupting by using the army to accomplish his goals. His first test came within days of his arrival. Three thousand pro-slave forces, many of them Missourians, were encamped near Franklin, mustering for an attack on Lawrence. From the capital, Geary hastened to the encampment with three hundred dragoons and some light artillery. Pulling into the camp at dusk, Geary found the usual suspects: Commander John Reid and his subordinates Atchison, Whitfield, Ben Stringfellow, Sheriff Jones, Deputy

Marshal Fain, and General L. A. MacLean. Addressing Atchison, Geary said the last time he saw him, Atchison was acting vice president of the United States and president of the US Senate. Geary was thus distressed to see the once-respectable politician now preparing to lead a ragtag militia to slaughter the citizens of Lawrence. Geary then ordered them to disband immediately or face his dragoons. Taken aback by the governor's aggressive posture, the Missourians reluctantly disbanded. Geary then set out to break up Lane's men who fled to Nebraska, though not before attacking pro-slave settlers in route.

In a letter to the Secretary of State William Marcy, Geary described the situation as he found it in his first week in office:

The whole country was evidently infested with armed bands of marauders, who set all law at defiance, and travelled from place to place, assailing villages, sacking and burning houses, destroying crops, maltreating women and children, driving off and stealing cattle and horses, and murdering harmless men in their own dwellings and public highways.[11]

With the departure of Lane and the dispersal of the Missourians, however, the situation gradually improved and by early November peace had settled over the prairie. Geary then set out to clean up the judiciary. Meeting with Chief Justice LeCompte and Judge Cato, he urged them to dispose of the many prisoners awaiting trial. He also ordered the release of free-state men who had been arrested on political or trumped-up charges and were being held in tents in Lecompton under federal guard. For the most part LeCompte stonewalled, though John Brown Jr., who had not been indicted, was released on bail. (Brown sent the chains that had so unnerved him to Henry Ward Beecher as a souvenir of bleeding Kansas.) Geary also asked Missouri Governor Sterling Price to order the boy's release, unaware he was already home. Thanks to Geary's efforts, by the end of the bloody year of 1856, Kansas's bleeding had stopped—at least temporarily.

The greater challenge for Geary, of course, was to find a lasting solution to the political conflict. In spite of his accomplishments and attempts at neutrality, he was mistrusted and unappreciated by both sides. Pro-slave men felt that in failing to distinguish the lawfully constituted party from the rebel free-state one, Geary had in effect sided with the latter. Free-staters were no less wary of the governor's intentions, believing his moderation toward them was merely a political ruse for Buchanan to carry key states in the election.[12] On March 20, 1857, frustrated by the lack of support from the Pierce administration and tired of the privations of life on the prairie, Geary resigned, having served just six months. In an eerily prophetic farewell address in Lecompton, he assessed what was at stake in the Kansas conflict. "You are intrusted, not only with the guardianship of this Territory, but the peace of the Union, which depends upon you in a greater degree than you may at present suppose."[13]

Geary's departure marked a trying period for free-staters and for Orville personally. Until a new governor was appointed, free-state men were once again at the mercy of Woodson loyalists in the Territorial administration who resumed using federal troops as a posse, dragging free-staters from their homes and sending them before partisan judges. Often the charges were trumped up, such as simply attending a free-state meeting. Easterners who had only recently arrived flush with hope and the romance of life on the prairie were soon discouraged by the difficulties and pulled up stakes and returned home. "It required solid staying qualities to combat the many opposing elements in Kansas life during these years," Orville noted.[14]

To make matters worse, no sooner had Orville rebuilt his house when disaster struck once again. One afternoon in early June he spotted a ferocious storm on the horizon and sent Spencer to secure the town's ferryboat on the Osage. As the boy was returning home, a dark funnel cloud suddenly came churning through the woods, tearing up trees by their roots. He began to race for the house to avoid being struck by a falling tree or flying debris. Just as he arrived the tornado struck, demolishing the entire house. The family, who was supposed to move in the very next day, was staying in town at the Greer Hotel where the roof was sheared clean off. Orville's own "staying qualities" were being severely tested.

In late May, Geary's replacement arrived. Kansas's forth governor in three years was fifty-six-year old Robert J. Walker. A wee man five feet in height and weighing barely a hundred pounds, Walker possessed a towering political reputation. A graduate of the University of Pennsylvania, Walker had served as a Democratic senator from Mississippi and secretary of the treasury. Somewhat unrealistically, it was believed his North-South credentials would appeal to both sides. Friends warned him about going to the netherworld of Kansas, but Walker confidently asserted that he possessed the solution to the Kansas conflict, and it was enshrined in theKansas-Nebraska Act. His plan was to give expression to the will of the majority.

Upon arriving in Kansas on May 27, 1857, Walker traveled the Territory giving speeches and pledging justice, fair elections, and honest administration of peoples' rights. After listening to one of Walker's speeches, Orville came away shaking his head in disbelief. "Our experience had taught us to doubt his ability to fulfill his pledges. He was attempting to give us justice under the Bogus Laws and Missouri rule. He needed a better understanding of the situation, oil and water could not mix."[15] Everyone wondered just how long Walker would last.

To make good on his promises, Walker proceeded to call the Lecompton constitutional convention proposed by the legislature during Geary's tenure as a preliminary step for admitting Kansas to the Union. Although Geary had attempted to veto it, Walker supported the convention, not least because it had been authorized by the legislature. The move angered free-staters. Pro-slavers were equally angered by Walker's recognition of free-staters' right to vote for whatever constitution that emerged from the convention. Like Geary, Walker would soon find himself the proverbial man in the middle—if he hadn't already.

A few days before Walker's arrival, territorial Secretary Frederick P. Stanton had decided to base the apportionment of convention delegates on a recent census that free-staters had rejected as defective. Among its many flaws was that voters had registered in only twenty out of thirty-four counties. Even in registered counties, proportional representation was wildly imbalanced. Over tea with Stanton, Charles Robinson urged him to jettison the elections formula and start over. But Stanton refused, noting free-staters were contributing to the problem by refusing to participate in the election. "The trouble," he groused, "is that you Free-State men are not willing to take any steps to the correction of the evils you complain of." When the election was held on June 15, it was thus simply a matter of deciding which pro-slave delegates would be going to the convention.[16] This time Missourians did not flood the polls, and only twenty-two hundred pro-slave men bothered to vote. At Charles Robinson's direction, free-staters stayed at home, prompting Representative James Hughes of Indiana to caustically remark, "Men who could expend thousands, and travel many a weary mile to fill Kansas with rifles could not walk across the street to vote."[17]

Robinson, however, had other plans in mind. As pro-slave forces were gearing up for the convention, free-staters met in August at Grasshopper Falls to carve out a strategy for legislative elections in October. Orville was among the forty-three delegates in attendance. The move signaled renewed confidence that the free-state movement could prevail at the polls if elections were fair. Even pro-slave men expected free-staters to win and, for this reason, decided to put the Lecompton referendum on hold pending the outcome.

On October 5, Kansans went to the polls to elect legislators. At precincts where Missourians were expected to vote, Walker placed federal troops. The pro-slave party won, but there was a glitch: In two counties, McGee and Oxford, where few whites lived and where Walker had not stationed troops, the number of votes had mysteriously been a thousandfold greater than in the constitutional convention voting in June. Walker now faced a dilemma. If he accepted the election results, then the pro-slave party would continue but under decidedly fraudulent circumstances and contrary to the principles of popular sovereignty he had so publicly espoused. If he threw out the election results, the Territorial legislature would come under free-state control, which could spark a renewed outbreak of violence. After visiting Oxford precinct and determining hardly anyone lived there, he concluded the votes in the two counties had been forged and threw out the returns. What remained were twenty free-state and fifteen pro-slave representatives. For the first time in its history, the Kansas legislature now consisted of a free-state majority.* After

---

* One of the elected candidates tossed out with the Oxford and McGee ballots was Sheriff Jones, who marched into Secretary Stanton's office and demanded a certificate of election be made out on the spot to which Stanton bluntly refused.

four years of sporadic violence and unremitting political maneuvering, each side was now on separate and quite antagonistic legal
paths to determine the fate of Kansas—free-state men were in
control of the Territory's law-making body while pro-slavery men
controlled the convention that would write the Territory's constitution. The two sides were like two trains hurtling on parallel tracks—one via the constitutional process, the other via the
legislative—toward the same destination.

With free-state forces in control of the legislature, Southerners
saw the Lecompton Constitution as their last best hope of making
Kansas a slave state. Since legislative elections had demonstrated
free-state dominance at the polls, the Lecompton Constitution
framers realized they would be doomed if they presented the referendum in binary terms of "for" or "against" slavery. So when they
reconvened in November to finalize the document they devised a
diabolical solution. The people of Kansas would be given a choice
between two propositions: one *with* slavery and one *without*. But
the one without slavery contained a catch. For if Kansans voted
for a free state, slaveholders would be prohibited from importing
new slaves into the territory but still be entitled to retaining existing slaves as long as they existed and reproduced. This alternative,
free-staters complained, "was like submitting to the ancient test
of witchcraft, where, if the accused, upon being thrown into deep
water, floated he was adjudged guilty, taken out, and hanged; but if
he sunk and was drowned he was adjudged not guilty—the choice
between the verdicts being quite immaterial."[18]

On November 7, convention delegates approved the constitution. Although ratification by Kansans was set for December 21,
delegates sent the document to Congress for ratification in the
hope of preempting free-state rejection. Infuriated, Governor

Walker hastened to Washington in late November to make his case directly with Buchanan for a revision of the constitution. Even some Southerners like John Stringfellow refused to accept the outcome on the grounds that it was against the will of the majority. So, too, did Stephen Douglas, who urged Kansas to start the constitutional process over from the beginning. Nevertheless, most Southerners continued to cling to the Lecompton Constitution as their best hope for a slave Kansas, and they lobbied Buchanan hard for its passage. Some states even threatened to secede if Kanas was not admitted to the Union as a slave state.[19]*

With Walker absent, free-staters now pressured the acting governor, Fredrick Stanton, to call the new legislature into session, issuing veiled threats to unleash Lane's army if he didn't. Reluctantly Stanton called the body into session on December 7, 1857. When the legislature convened, it cleverly moved to schedule a second ratification vote on the Lecompton Constitution on January 4, 1858, the same day the Lecompton convention had set for election of state officers under its own constitution.

This time, voters would have the added choice of rejecting the constitution outright—precisely what legislators expected Kansas voters would do if given the chance. To back its actions, the legislature also authorized the belligerent James Lane to serve as head of the free-state militia, a job normally reserved for the governor.

When news of Stanton's actions reached Washington, Stan-

---

* Four months later, Walker would be shocked to read President Buchanan's opening address to the opening session to the thirty-fifth Congress, wherein the president wholeheartedly endorsed the rigged constitution and urged representatives to do the same. Appalled at the president's backing of a fraudulent election process, Walker left the territory on business and never returned.

ton was promptly sacked for reopening the Lecompton issue. He was immediately replaced by Commissioner of Indian Affairs James Denver, who happened to be visiting the tribes in Kansas at the time.

On December 21, Kansans went to the polls to ratify the Lecompton Constitution. Faced with spurious options, free-staters declared the constitutional convention process fraudulent and boycotted the polls. Not surprisingly, the constitution carried "with slavery" by a margin of ten to one.

Southern celebration over the outcome would be short-lived, however. Two weeks later, Kansans again went to the polls to ratify the constitution a second time and to vote for state officers under the Lecompton Constitution. This time free-state voters turned out in large numbers, overwhelmingly rejecting Lecompton. Election of officers, however, was marred by massive vote tampering. One of the most egregious frauds had occurred at the Delaware Crossing precinct where the ballot box had mysteriously disappeared. Pollster John Henderson claimed to have given it to territorial official L. A. Maclean, who swore he had passed it on to the surveyor-general, John Calhoun. But Calhoun denied ever having received it. A few weeks later an unidentified Lecompton man tipped off investigators that Maclean and another man had buried the missing ballots in a candle box under a woodpile near Calhoun's office in Lecompton. After the ballots were recovered from the woodpile, they were found to be a fraction of what pro-slave men had claimed was the talley. The result: free-state advocates had not only overturned the constitution but won the election of officers under Lecompton as well.

Southerners still had an ace up their sleeve—the Dred Scott decision of the United States Supreme Court handed down the previous year. Dred Scott was a slave whose owner had sold him

Capture of Fort Henry by US gun boats under the
command of Flag Officer Foote, February 6, 1862.
*Courtesy of Library of Congress, Prints and
Photographs Division.*

Castle Thunder prison, Richmond, Virginia.

Courtesy of Library of Congress, Prints and Photographs Division.

Charles Grandison Finney,
fiery Presbyterian preacher in
the Second Great Awakening.
*Courtesy of New York Public
Library.*

Commodore William D.
Porter, gallant commander of
the USS *Essex*.
*Courtesy of Library of Congress,
Prints and Photographs Division.*

The abolitionist John Brown.
Courtesy of Library of Congress, Prints and Photographs Division.

Underground Railroad routes through New York.
*Created by Alexander C. Flick (1866–1961) and
Wilbur Henry Siebert (1869–1942).*

Orville Chester Brown, abolitionist and founder of Osawatomie, Kansas.
Courtesy of Kansas State Historical Society.

Illinois Senator Stephen A. Douglas.
Courtesy of Library of Congress, Prints and Photographs Division.

Spencer Kellogg Brown, Union spy.
Courtesy of Kansas State Historical Society.

in Missouri to an army surgeon named Dr. John Emerson. After purchasing Scott, Emerson took him to free-state Illinois and later to Wisconsin Territory where, under the Northwest Ordinance of 1787, slavery was also prohibited. Over the years, Emerson was reassigned several times, sometimes taking Scott with him, other times leasing him out for profit. In 1843 Emerson died, leaving his brother John Sanford as executor of his estate. Three years later Scott was living in Missouri when he sued to win freedom for himself and his family on the grounds that the years spent living in free soil had made them free. After several trials in several Missouri courts, the case eventually went to the US Supreme Court. On March 6, 1857, just two days after Buchanan was inaugurated, in a seven-to-two decision the Court ruled against Scott on the grounds that he was not a citizen but property. The Dred Scott decision essentially strengthened the hand of pro-slavers for it reaffirmed the right to own slaves in the Territories. In light of the decision, the convention had only to get their constitution past Kansas voters and a Democratic Congress, and the White House would be sure to approve it.

Determined to push the Lecompton Constitution through Congress, Buchanan now drew on all the resources at his disposal. A House select committee to consider the constitution was packed with sympathetic members while cabinet members lobbied fence-sitters and liberally doled out patronage. Some Southern congressmen even threatened to secede if the constitution was not passed. Supporters argued Lecompton was a perfectly legal document, and if free-staters chose to sit out the vote that was their prerogative. Opponents countered that free-staters had boycotted the constitutional election because Lecompton had been a rigged document from the very start. Arguments for and against did not follow strict party lines, and when the vote was taken, the

Senate accepted Lecompton while the House did not. After weeks of wrangling, Indiana Congressman William English finally brokered a compromise, called the English Bill, whereby Kansas would receive a reduced land grant in exchange for acceptance of Lecompton. If they accepted the bill, they would automatically accept Lecompton; if they rejected it, they would have to wait until the territory reached a population of 94,000 before they could vote on another constitution. On August 2, 1858, Kansans resolutely rejected the English Bill by a vote of 11,812 to 1,926.

Thus did the year 1858 close with no resolution of the conflict in sight.

Chapter Eight
JAYHAWKING

"In the old country, we have a bird called the Jayhawk,
which kind of worries its prey. It seems to me, as I ride home,
that that's what I've been doing."
—Pat Delvin, Irish free-soil guerilla

BY 1858, WITH THE FREE-STATE MOVEMENT IN CONTROL of the legislature and the Lecompton Constitution dead, pro-slavery forces had lost any hope of making Kansas a slave state. As a result, eastern towns that had seen so much violence and destruction—Lawrence, Osawatomie, Leavenworth—now enjoyed relative peace for the first time in years. But south of the Kansas River, fighting erupted with a vengeance, touching off a vicious cycle of violence and anarchy not seen since the terrible summer of 1856. This time, however, the conflict was not about whether Kansas should be free or slave but was simply a matter of settling old scores. Orville Brown would eventually broker an agreement between the territorial government and guerillas to end the last major fighting in the territory, an achievement he would come to regard as his finest contribution to the making of the free-state of Kansas.

These old scores went back to the fall of 1856, when Indian agent Major George Clarke had begun raiding isolated northern settlements in Linn and Miami counties, seizing horses and cattle, robbing and burning homes and crops, and turning families out. Said one of the victims, they "took everything they wanted, and I think they took what they did not want to keep their hands in—had ribbons on their hat, side combs in their hair, and other things they did not need."[1] Of Clarke's brutality one soldier said, "I was in the Black Hawk War, and have fought in the wars of the United States, and have received two land-warrants from Washington City for my services, but I never saw anything so bad and mean in my life as I saw under General Clarke."[2]

Most of the violence centered around Fort Scott, a military post from 1842 to 1854 and the main town in the southeast region embracing Linn, Bourbon, and Miami counties. Because the region was not on the northern emigration lines, most of those who had settled there were pro-slave sympathizers from the South. These men had long been keen to participate in the fight against free-soilers but were frustratingly far from the center of action. Their first chance had come in 1856 when Captain Reid issued a call for men to attack the hometown of John Brown in Osawatomie. About 150 men, eager to retaliate for the Pottawatomie Creek massacre and share in the spoils, had gathered at Fort Scott, and marched northward to join Reid. When they reached Liberty Township, located several miles outside Osawatomie, they halted to make camp. They were about to partake of supper when a band of free-state guerrillas suddenly materialized out of the prairie. So taken by surprise were they that in their flight back to Fort Scott, they abandoned "baggage, horses, boots, coats, vests, hats, a dinner ready cooked, and a black flag on which was emblazoned 'Victory or Death.'"[3] Apparently, they were not quite prepared for either.

Free-staters had responded in kind, giving better than they got with an adroitness that earned them the nickname Jayhawkers, possibly after the fictional bird of prey. Whatever the etymology, the term came to mean rapacious free-booting and destruction, and stealing horses, guns, money, farm implements, and anything else that was not nailed down. The most fearsome Jawhawker on a par with James Lane was James Montgomery. Born in Ohio, Montgomery was a fervent abolitionist who had come to Linn County in August 1854. A year after being driven out by Clarke, Montgomery organized his own guerrilla band called the Self-Protective Company. He then set out to compile a list of Clarke's accomplices by going to Missouri and posing as a teacher in search of a job. He had actually begun teaching for a few weeks when, his list of Clarke's raiders completed, he closed his school and returned to Kansas. Montgomery captured twenty of Clarke's raiders and stole their money, horses, and other valuables. Seeking retribution for wrongs committed against other free-soilers, Montgomery began circulating southeastern Kansas, raiding homes and driving out pro-slave settlers. When farmers began returning from Missouri to reclaim land they had been driven from, Montgomery dealt with these "claim jumpers" by capturing them and trying them in a kangaroo court in his camp on the Little Osage. By spring of 1857 he was conducting more ambitious attacks on pro-slavery men in Missouri, many of whom he had ejected from southeastern Kansas.

This tit-for-tat raiding went on intermittently for many months. What displaced farmers needed to strike back was a leader, and by spring of 1858 they found him in one Charles A. Hamilton, a wealthy Georgian who had moved to Kansas to win the territory for pro-slave forces. Only weeks before, Montgomery had ejected Hamilton from his log cabin near Fort Scott. Meeting with other ejected farmers in western Missouri, Hamilton compiled a list of Montgomery's men he intended to arrest and execute in retaliation. On May 19, 1858, Hamilton crossed into Kansas with a company of men and began seizing anyone he regarded as a political or criminal enemy. Near Chouteau's Trading Post in Linn County, Hamilton encountered an old foe, a blacksmith named Eli Snyder.

"Where are you going?" Hamilton demanded. "You are going to Trading Post."

"If you know better than I do, why do you ask?" Snyder retorted.

"If you don't look out, I'll blow you through," warned the Georgian.

Snyder then raised his shotgun, warning, "If you don't leave I'll tumble you from your horse."[4]

A week later Hamilton was rounding up men near Trading Post when he found Snyder at his shop. After a brief tussle, Snyder was shot. Though seriously wounded, he succeeded in reaching his cabin where his son covered his retreat with a double-barreled shotgun, killing one of Hamilton's men. Enraged, Hamilton gathered his prisoners and marched them into a defile near the Osage River. When he ordered his men to fire, one of the Missourians refused saying, "I'll have nothing to do with such a piece of business as this!"[5] Hamilton then withdrew his pistol and fired, provoking a hail of gunfire from his men. In what was called the Osage Massacre, five were killed and five seriously wounded. One man was unharmed by pretending to be shot.

The massacre ignited an all-out war between Montgomery and Hamilton along the border region. Both sides rampaged the countryside killing, looting, and destroying property. Civil authorities were all but powerless to enforce law and order. In trying to raise a posse to arrest some of Montgomery's men, the sheriff of Linn County was overcome and disarmed by the very men he wished to arrest. To stabilize the border Governor Denver issued a warrant to Deputy US Marshal Samuel Walker for Montgomery's arrest. When Walker reached Raysville, ten miles outside Fort Scott, he found a large gathering of men.

"What are you after?" one of them asked.

"I've come down to take Montgomery."

"You can't do it. That thing's out of the question," the man replied.

Tucking the warrant in his pocket, Walker said diffidently, "I don't know Montgomery, and I don't wish to have him pointed out. If he is, I shall have to make an effort to take him."[6]

Walker rode on to Fort Scott where many of the perpetrators of the Osage Massacre were holding out. Believing free-state men were justified in retaliating for the massacre, Walker then joined with Montgomery in arresting three men, including Clarke.[7] Yet before Walker could bring them back to Lecompton, they escaped.

On the night of June 6, 1858, Montgomery returned to Fort Scott where he torched several buildings before taking cover in a ravine. When residents rushed out of their homes to extinguish the flames, Montgomery's men opened fire. Surprisingly no one was hurt, nor were the buildings damaged.

A week later Governor Denver and Charles Robinson conducted a tour of the territory's southeast and found that small guerrilla bands had been organizing out of mistrust of local authorities. In an effort to defuse the violence, Denver spoke to a large crowd at Fort Scott. "I shall treat actual settlers," he promised, "without regard to former differences. I do not propose to dig up or review the past. Both parties, I believe, have done wrong and are worthy of censure, but I shall let all that go. My mission is to secure peace for the future."[8] He quickly dispatched federal forces to patrol the border, hoping it would encourage guerilla leaders to disband. On the Missouri side, Governor Robert M. Stewart had ordered militia to Bates and Cass Counties for the same purpose. The measures helped quell the disorder, and it seemed there would be no further trouble. Feeling peace was finally restored, on September 1, Denver resigned from a post he never wanted in the first place and returned to his job as commissioner of Indian affairs.

If Denver thought that he had been able to resign on his own terms, he couldn't have been more mistaken. A few months earlier the old man himself John Brown reappeared, flush from his fundraising tour in the East. On his way to the southeast, Brown stopped in Lawrence to see Charles Robinson. Once and for all, Brown wanted to lay out the fundamental differences between them. "You have succeeded," Brown said, "in what you undertook. You aimed to make of Kansas a free state, and your plans were skillfully laid for that purpose. But I had another object in view. I meant to strike a blow at slavery."[9] Strike he would. A few months later, he and Montgomery built a fort on Little Sugar Creek and resumed raiding and driving off pro-slavery men from the southeast of the territory. In some cases bands of fifteen or twenty of their men would ride up to a dwelling and, after displaying their weapons, feed their horses from the farmer's crib while demanding food for themselves. After satisfying themselves they would take whatever they wanted and order the residents to leave the area under penalty of death. In mid-December Montgomery attacked Fort Scott, arresting most of the officers of the court and looting its stores of over $5,000 in goods. When the son of US Deputy Marshal John Little attempted to defend his store from attack, Montgomery's men shot him in the head.

Meanwhile, having recovered, Eli Snyder had gone into Bates County, Missouri, and attacked the home of Jeremiah Jackson, a wealthy farmer. Jackson and his son-in-law put up a fierce resistance. To force them out, Snyder torched his house, forcing Jackson and his family to flee. He then entered the burning home and stole $6,000 in valuables before burning the remaining buildings.[10]

While Montgomery and Snyder were busy jayhawking, John Brown slipped into Vernon County, Missouri, where he destroyed property and stole eleven slaves, intending to transport them via the Underground Railroad to Canada. But when they attempted to take a female slave at the home of an old German immigrant, David Cruise, things went horribly wrong. Attempting to fend off the intruders, Cruise's gun misfired and he was shot and killed. Before fleeing, Brown and his men helped themselves to virtually all the dead man's property.

Into this unremitting chaos the new governor of Kansas, Samuel Medary, arrived in late December 1858. He was the fifth Kansas governor in as many years. That few expected Medary to last was comically illustrated when he was asked to pay his barber's bill on a monthly basis. The black barber, known as Ethiopian Sam, is said to have replied, "If you please, master, I prefer to have you pay by the shave; these new governors goes away so mighty sudden!"[11]

Lacking sufficient funds and forces at his disposal to quell the disturbances in the southeast, now buried in early snow, the new governor sent Samuel Walker to gather information and discuss with Montgomery terms for surrender. On January 3, 1859, in a report to the governor, Walker described the region in a state of anarchy, with individuals fleeing homes in panic and Montgomery and John Brown robbing, killing, committing arson, and driving men out at will. Walker warned the governor that the Jayhawkers were too fortified at Little Sugar Creek to remove by force. Montgomery vowed to resist any attempt by state or federal authorities to be arrested, claiming he was well-armed and could muster a thousand men. The only terms by which Montgomery would consent to disband would involve a full pardon for him and his men for all offenses committed; he (Montgomery) would also have to be allowed to select the sheriffs of the counties of Bourbon, Linn, and Lykins, and the deputy marshal for the southern district. If not, he would lay waste to the entire region and give Medary "more trouble than the Seminole Indians."

The governor's reply to Montgomery's offer was equally reso-
lute. "I have no compromise to make with crime," he gnarred.[12] Yet
he had no funds with which to pay volunteers or raise a militia. He
was even paying his messengers from his own pocket. Determined to
crush Montgomery and bring him to justice, the hamstrung governor
turned to the federal arsenal at Jefferson Barracks in St. Louis. His
intention was to form a posse comitatus by arming local residents with
arsenal weapons. He then ordered four companies of dragoons from
Fort Riley to Linn and Bourbon Counties. Many, including Orville,
saw the territory inching toward another destructive civil war.

On January 4, six hundred muskets and five thousand rounds
of ammunition arrived in Lawrence from St. Louis. Four days
later Walker and Deputy Marshal Fain set out with a posse from
Fort Riley to arrest Montgomery and his men. Fearing a bloody
collision was imminent, James Lane, now the head of the Territorial militia, offered to act as mediator between Medary and
Montgomery and John Brown. In a rare reversal of his role in
bleeding Kansas, Lane announced, "I am moved only by a sincere
desire to restore peace and quiet to that portion of Kansas."[13] But
Medary was more interested in crushing the rebellion and punishing Montgomery. When Fain and Walker arrived in the area
with the cavalry, they were ordered to return immediately to their
forts. Secretary of War Jefferson Davis had refused to allow federal
troops to be used against the Jayhawkers. By then, the situation was
so bad that residents of the territory's southeast were demanding
the governor declare martial law in Linn, Bourbon, Anderson, and
Lykins Counties. Fearing civil war was imminent, Orville rode to
Lawrence and requested an audience with Medary to inform him
of the true state of affairs. The two met in Medary's chambers with
James Lane. The governor inquired about Eli Snyder, Montgomery, and the other "desperadoes." Orville responded by explain-

ing the legitimate free-state grievances for atrocities committed in 1856. Montgomery, he argued, was not the desperate criminal that Medary thought him to be, but was merely settling grievances for wrongs done to him by pro-slavery men. While they would not be taken alive, Orville said, they would come to Lawrence at the governor's behest. When Medary expressed disbelief, Orville assured him that if the governor promised safe escort for them, he (Orville) had only to send a message and he could have the presumed "desperadoes" in his chambers in a day.

The very next day the Jayhawkers appeared at the governor's office in good form. Outside, an angry crowd of dispossessed Southerners had gathered demanding protection against Montgomery's men. When Medary appeared on the veranda, some of the crowd instantly drew their weapons. Seeing Orville appear at his side, the men lowered them. Medary then made a conciliatory speech followed by James Lane who, in the words of Orville, "could always move the masses as the tree tops are moved by the wind."[14] A bill was subsequently enacted by the legislature and signed by Medary that exempted from prosecution all those committing crimes for a political offense. Orville later considered his intercession "the most important act of my territorial life" for it led to the passage of an Amnesty Act by the legislature which, once and for all, ended the strife throughout the countryside.[15]

Within weeks the situation calmed. In a letter to the governor, Orville reported on the peace prevailing in Osawatomie. The news elicited this reply in late February from Medary:

My Dear Sir:

Your letter of the 22nd is just received. I am very much gratified to learn that all things are working for good in your formally distracted region. If your people all go peaceably and industriously to work, [you] will soon know the difference between a state of riot and disturbance and that peace industry.

Everything seems to wear a more hopeful and quiet appearance all over the territory, and within a year of prosperous emigration and full crops of the present settlers, Kansas by the opening of next spring will scarcely be known from its appearance to its old acquaintance. Excuse me for thus troubling you. Your letter gives me great delight and I feel content.

Very respectfully,
S. L. Medary[16]*

As for John Brown, Missouri's Governor Robert Stewart had put a price of $3,000 on his head, but by then Brown had quit Kansas for good. He was now in Detroit assisting his bondsmen into Canada before heading to what would be his last and final destination—Harpers Ferry, Virginia.

Early in 1859 Orville's health took a turn for the worse and his spirits began to "sink with his mortal frame."[17] To seek better care, he briefly returned to New York. As he was preparing to depart for the east, Orville finally received a $1,000 award from the territorial treasury in Lecompton for damages incurred during the attack on Osawatomie in 1856.

---

* As a footnote to the incident, shortly after pacification of the region, the arms Medary had requested finally arrived, having been delayed by muddy roads. When Captain Weaver attempted to unload some of the rifles from a wagon, he accidentally shot himself and was killed.

Meanwhile, the Kansas legislature got down to the business of abolishing slavery. After heated wrangling over three versions of a draft, a bill was finally sent to Governor Medary repealing slavery. Medary, who thought the body had no power to legislate the issue, waited until the legislative session ended before reviewing it, essentially issuing a pocket veto. To appease legislators angered by his perceived "treachery," he approved a measure calling for a constitutional convention, which voters subsequently approved.

In July 1859, convention delegates met at Wyandotte. Three months later the constitution passed by a margin of two to one. When the constitution went before Congress, it passed the House handily. But when it reached the Senate, Missourian James Green obfuscated by criticizing its proposed boundaries. Even though the western line had been moved eastward to the twenty-fifth meridian, Green insisted that not more than two-sevenths of the area included within them could be cultivated. He urged that thirty thousand square miles be taken from southern Nebraska and annexed to the proposed state. "Without this addition . . . ," he said, "Kansas must be weak, puerile, sickly, in debt, and at no time capable of sustaining herself."[18] Kansas's bid for statehood was postposed yet again.

PART II

THE SPY: SPENCER KELLOGG BROWN IN THE CIVIL WAR

★ ★ ★ ★

Chapter Nine

FLEEING FAMINE

"It seemed as if the gates of Hell . . . had been thrown open."
                    —Topeka State Record, July 14, 1860

MARY BROWN DESCRIBED THE YEAR 1860 AS ONE OF "death and famine."[1] It was closer to hell on earth. Since their arrival in 1854, farmers had been annually burning the hardy buffalo and blue grama grasses, unaware of their importance in holding the prairie soil in place. Within a year, settlers were complaining of a south wind that lasted several days and was "loaded with the black dust from the burnt prairie, which penetrates every corner of our houses, and makes everyone who is exposed to it as sooty as a collier."[2] Exacerbated by overgrazing and several years of low rainfall, the soot soon turned to dust that one settler said, "fills our eyes, ears, nose, and mouth; settles upon our broadcloth; turns black brown; seasons our victuals; and endows us with a little of the grit."[3]

The tipping point was the winter of 1859–1860, which brought no rain or snow and mostly mild weather. With nothing to hold the parched soil in place, dust blew constantly and was so thick at times as to reduce visibility to several yards. To add to the misery, a late frost on May 9, 1860, filled much of the fruit crop, including Orville's orchard. June brought terrific storms and tornados that leveled homes and picked up barrels, boxes, and bricks, tossing them like so much chaff in the prairie wind. With July came blazing furnaces of heat that reached 115 degrees Fahrenheit. Newspapers likened the conditions to the raging siroccos of North Africa. In some counties, crops that didn't wither in the field were devoured by grasshoppers. Despairing farmers tried sowing hardy buckwheat but that, too, was destroyed by grasshoppers. Others tried planting three or four crops in the vain hope that enough rain might fall to secure at least one of them. It didn't. Cattle that did not perish in the drought succumbed to a then-mysterious tick-borne illness called Spanish fever.

Settlers who had arrived from the East brimming with hope and optimism just a few years earlier were now facing starvation. In many counties people had neither food nor money and lived on buffalo meat—if they could hunt the treacherous beast—which became legal tender. Countless thousands were reduced to ragged beggars. Along the Missouri River, the only area of eastern Kansas that the drought had mercifully spared, dozens of emaciated men lined up with their wagons seeking handouts of free foodstuffs. One man drove his wagons two hundred miles to obtain food for his starving community. After a week of waiting he was given twelve sacks of meal and eight sacks of potatoes for four hundred people. Another was Abraham Huck who had come from Illinois the previous March. Huck had left his wife and eight children at home in Anderson County with some turnips and "a peck of meal" so he could look for food in Atchison. A *Chicago Tribune* correspondent described his ragged appearance:

> *He was literally clothed in rags. Such a tatterdemalion one can scarcely conceive of. His garments, originally home-spun, had*

been patched with so many different materials, mostly variet-
ies of bed-ticking and sacking, that the feeble threads would no
longer hold together, and the shreds were flopping about him
as he walked. His face was haggard and hunger-worn; cheek-
bones protruded; flesh had shrunk away, and his eyes were hol-
low and eager, and had the terrible starved look in them which
I saw once in a famine-stricken party of Irish, in '47, and which
I shall never forget.[4]

Many simply packed up and left. Along the roads was a constant stream of grim-faced returnees as if, one correspondent
wrote, "death were in the rear."[5]

In a letter written to family in New York, Orville described
conditions in Osawatomie in mid-July:

We have not had six hours of good rain in ten months. Winter
and spring wheat will yield less than the seed. Vegetables there
are none. Some corn may seed. The heat is 114 degrees in the
shade, the simoom drying and crisping vegetation in an hour.
The springs and streams are all dry; but, thank God, we have
plenty of good water from wells, in town. I have nothing in my
garden but a few small onions. Early corn, potatoes, peas, and
everything else, blasted, dried up. There can be no hay cut, as
my hill will burn like tinder. Money there is none. The biggest
oxen in Kansas, formerly worth one hundred and forty dollars,
now find no buyers at fifty to sixty dollars. . . . My own health,
as usual, bad.[6]

Worried for the family, Mary urged Orville to leave Osawatomie with the boys at once for a place where he could find temporary
work. "Go to Kansas City," she urged, "and if there is nothing there,

manage some way to get to St. Joe and bring Spencer."[7] Broke, without work, and in poor health, Orville nonetheless refused to quit Kansas or abandon his abolitionist mission. "Until I know how the war is to turn [I] hardly feel at liberty to leave for farther east," he wrote.[8] No longer able to care for his large family, he sent the girls back east to Mary. Before the drought was over, nearly a third of the territory's one hundred thousand white settlers would flee, prompting one newspaper to plead with settlers not to leave Kansas for the East or the mines in the West.[9]

As if Orville's own situation was not bleak enough, residents of the county were appealing to him for assistance. In April Dr. W. W. Updegraff, who had fought alongside John Brown in the Battle of Osawatomie, wrote Orville a letter describing the situation in southern Lykins County and pleading for food supplies. "Within the last ten days I saw a large number of teams returning with no more than two sacks of flour and two to five of meal," Updegraff wrote. "Some of them had travelled one hundred forty or one hundred fifty miles to reach that. Our animals, as you are well aware, are wholly unfit for food at this time; and consequently we are entirely without resources at home.... The young wheat promises an abundant harvest but this is in the future and we must have bready today." To add to their fears, the Kiowa, Comanche, and other tribes were organizing and making threatening moves on the southwestern frontier.[10]

In November 1860, Charles Robinson sent several letters to Orville to forward to Congress, saying "their presentation will result in good to Kansas."[11] The petitions pointed out that ever since establishing residency in the Territory, Kansans had paid taxes just like states, and now they requested famine aid. But apart from making a personal donation of one hundred dollars, President Buchanan could only authorize federal aid if Kansas had statehood.

With no help from Washington forthcoming, requests for relief went out to the Eastern cities. One request from the Kansas legislature to the New York legislature indicated that in 222 townships there were 47,000 destitute people. Petitions for donations in the newspapers led to large amounts of provisions for suffering Kansans in Leavenworth and Atchison. Utica organized a relief committee to solicit donations of food and clothing. Other Eastern cities came through as well, though aid would not arrive for some months. Since so much aid was being sent from Chicago, Mary suggested Orville appeal for assistance to a friend of theirs there, Tuthill King, a millionaire who had made his fortune in real estate. Too proud to beg, Orville set out for Kansas City with Rocky in the hope of finding work "so they could earn enough to eat."[12]

Not wishing to be a burden any longer, Spencer volunteered to go in search of employment elsewhere. He wrote to Colonel Boone, reminding him that he was "the little prisoner you had in Bull Creek camp in 1856," offering to perform any honest labor while expressing a preference for a business in which he could rise.[13]

Meanwhile, Orville had found a job for Rocky with the *Journal of Commerce* newspaper in Kansas City, a job Mary thought more suitable for Spencer who had demonstrated greater literary talent. "Spencer will die, mentally and mortally, if he does not soon have some incentive for living." she fretted.[14] Separately she wrote to Rocky and Orville, attempting to persuade them to let Spencer have the newspaper job. But Spencer was not about to usurp his brother's good fortune, nor continue to be a burden to his father in such hard times. With no word from Boone, on November 2, 1860, Spencer said goodbye to friends and family and set out for Hazel Glen, where Dr. Keith had once offered to find him a teaching job. Little did he know it would be the last time he would ever see his father.

True to his word, Dr. Keith found Spencer a teaching position in a small school near Hazel Glen. Strangely, he made no reference to seeing Molly again. Spencer had worked but a few days when news of Abraham Lincoln's election sent Missouri into paroxysms of rage. When word got around that "a Brown" from Kansas was in town—and from Osawatomie at that—an angry crowd descended on the school. They gave Spencer forty-eight hours to leave or his life would be in danger. Whether the Missourians believed he was John Brown's son or not, the very name had become so reviled that they could not tolerate a Brown in their midst. That he was a protégé of Dr. Keith had likely been the only thing that saved him from being killed. Later his father would pen a short end-rhyme about the stigma John Brown had laid upon the family name with his actions at Pottawatomie Creek:

> *The heavy blows of old John Brown*
> *Had roused the southern ire*
> *And no such name could stay in the town*
> *Without feeling southern fire.*[15]

Realizing that by staying he would put Dr. Keith and his family in jeopardy, not to mention his own life, Spencer decided to move on. With nothing more than the clothes on his back, he set out for St. Louis. Here and there he stopped to perform some menial labor in order to get by. To spare his family worry, he sent a letter to his sister Kitty in Utica claiming that his job prospects "were a little better."[16] He asked that in her reply that the name *Brown* not appear anywhere in the letter, inside or out. Since he could not use the Brown name on outgoing letters either, he wrote to his father by way of his family in Utica. He now expunged Brown from his formal name. Henceforth, he would go by the name "Spencer Kellogg."*

After weeks of drifting, he arrived in St. Louis homeless, friendless, and alone. Apart from the odd job here and there, he found no stable employment. He continued to drift eastward in search of work. By the time he reached Kentucky, he was sick with malaria topped with a cold, and he was losing weight. Feeling he had exhausted his options, he enlisted in the Union Army at Newport Barracks, Kentucky, under the name of Spencer Kellogg. Soon after, he went to the military hospital where he was given a heavy dose of syrup of ipecac (to induce vomiting) into which was stirred a cathartic of calomel. The harsh treatment left him bedridden for several days.

When he recovered, he was assigned as one of four company cooks in Newport Barracks, an unexciting job for a teenager on the cusp of manhood looking to test his mettle. "I do not object to the cooking so much," he wrote his father, "the great trouble is that while one is ten days in the kitchen, he aggregates considerable grease and his clothes are not quite as shiny when he comes out."[17] On a rotating basis two cooks served as nightly orderlies to ensure the kitchen was spotless, that no one spit on the floor, that nothing was stolen, that good fires were kept, and that all lights were extinguished at taps. Despite the tedious work, the job came with certain advantages: unlimited rations, no drills, and no roll calls to answer. Being cook also relieved him of onerous tasks assigned the rest of the company such as scrubbing floors, washing windows,

---

* Despite the danger the name posed, Orville was disappointed his son had dropped the family name, one he proudly felt had been "immortalized by the heroism of John Brown." Later, while descending the Missouri, he too was harassed by passengers who thought he was a relative of John Brown.

cleaning the mess-table and benches, and chopping extra wood on Sunday. Notwithstanding his special status, he was required to take target practice and stand guard three times a day, two hours on and four off. On days he was off from his post, he was excused from drill and fatigue duty.

Spencer quickly fell into the routines of army life. At first light, he was wakened by reveille and served a breakfast of a large square of bread with slices of pork or beef on tin plates with vinegar. Coffee was served in pint tin cups, sweetened but with no milk. After breakfast he turned to washing and packing clothes and polishing buttons and shoes for inspection. At 8:30 AM they paraded for inspection of their weapons while a band played. He particularly looked forward to Sunday, the day the entire garrison turned out with their arms for general inspection. Every button and shoe had to be in the highest state of polish and clothes brushed and free of lint. Personal appearance was scrutinized, and if any man's hair was too long he was ordered to cut it. The arms were then closely examined, and the iron ramrods were wrung through to the bottom to see if the barrel was clean inside. After parade the soldiers repaired to their quarters where the major and lieutenant made an inspection. In front of their bunks, enlistees spread their knapsacks on the floor with their overcoats neatly folded on one side and clothes on the other as they stood at attention behind. In the kitchen, Spencer was required to have every knife, fork, and spoon shining, the cups stacked up tightly, and the tin plates arranged neatly in cupboards. In his free time, he was usually perched upon his bunk on the third tier, twelve feet from the floor, reading or writing to his family.

It seemed a sad and frustrating turn of events for a boy who once aspired to literary pursuits. But on balance Spencer was satisfied with his decision to join the army. For the first time in his life he had gainful employment, and with his new identity he no longer feared retribution for being a Brown. In addition to his salary of $11 a month, he received an allowance for clothes—$43.97 the first year and $33 dollars each year after that. He intended to save $250 to start a cattle ranch in Kansas with Rocky. To this end, he monitored every expense, even the most trifling, as those who grow up in penury often do. But since he had to send money to help out at home, the dream of a ranch would not be realized anytime soon. Writing in his journal he tried to reassure himself that, in the grand scheme of life, five years was not such a long time.

Certainly, the camaraderie of army life helped pass the time. There was his "bunky" O'Connell, a hot-tempered, florid-faced, whiskey-drinking Irishman, who became Spencer's constant companion. Another enlistee, Crandale, had an ear for music and was much given to singing. Even Corporeal Grimes, another enlistee, liked to sing German opera, much to Spencer's amusement. Spencer played whist with a tall, lanky French-Canadian named Kalmart, a five-degree Freemason. Then there was the mysterious and withdrawn Second Sargent Irwin. Irwin's aloofness puzzled Spencer all the more since they had known each other since enlisting in Kentucky. One day they were sitting on a bench together when Spencer expressed a desire to transfer to the artillery regiment. When Irwin inquired as to his reasons, Spencer began speaking of a friend when Irwin abruptly interrupted him. "There is no such thing as a friend!" Irwin bellowed, as he struck the bench angrily with his fist. "You didn't always think so," Spencer retorted. At that Irwin rose and, with some half-spoken excuse, sauntered away. A few days later the men were divided into squads and Spencer fell into Irwin's. As Spencer was looking for a new place to bunk, Irwin said, "Why don't you like this place?" pointing to one nearer to him. "The bed was my bunky's. Oh, but it doesn't make any difference to me," Irwin said, "I just thought you would not like to sleep so near that man Beach." Despite Irwin's professed indifference, Spencer realized this lonely embittered man was making an enormous gesture toward him.[18]

In early January 1861, Spencer sent a letter to his father informing him of his new life in the military: "I am a soldier," he announced, "or rather a recruit, and wear Uncle Sam's livery with many other poor fellows driven, like myself, to this. But knowing that I could do no better, and being determined not to return to you and your hard times in Kansas, I chose this alternative."[19] As the son of an abolitionist, he was also proud to be serving in Mr. Lincoln's army (or would be when Lincoln officially took office in March 1861). Somewhat puffed up by his new job, Spencer was expecting his company of eighty enlistees to be ordered to Washington to "keep everything straight at the [Lincoln] inauguration." First, however, they would be sent to the arsenal at St. Louis to repel a threatened attack.

News of his enlistment came as a shock to his parents who feared for the boy's safety. Kitty thought it "dreadful." Mary urged Orville go to St. Louis and seek Spencer's discharge on the grounds that he was a minor and find "a proper situation for him."[20]

The family's fears for the boy were wholly justified. That Kansas had joined the Union as a free state had done nothing to settle the national conflict over slavery. Kansas had merely been the precursor of what was to be a far larger, national argument between North and South. Despite defeat in Kansas, the South maintained the federal government could not interfere in what was fundamentally a states' right issue. Southerners believed they had the Constitutional right—affirmed by the Dred Scott decision—to migrate to the territories with all their property, including slaves. Moreover, they asserted that property should be protected against men like John Brown who fomented unlawful insurrection and violence against slaveholders.

Nearly eighteen months earlier, John Brown and a group of men had raided the federal arsenal at Harpers Ferry, Virginia. When he seized the arsenal, Brown had announced to the startled watchmen, "I came here from Kansas, and this is a slave State; I want to free all the negroes in this State."[21] But Brown's force of twenty-two men was greatly outnumbered, and the next day a detachment of marines under the command of an army officer by the name of Robert E. Lee crushed the uprising. Brown was tried and found guilty of murder, inciting a slave rebellion, and treason against the state of Virginia. At his trial, Brown declared slavery un-Christian, and that he did not intend to harm anyone but only to liberate slaves. Pro-slavery Virginians found him guilty and he was hanged six weeks later.

Just as he had raised the stakes in bleeding Kansas, John Brown's actions at Harpers Ferry had the effect of polarizing national public opinion over slavery. Even though most Northerners rejected his violent methods, they applauded his commitment to end an odious institution. As Northerners mourned Brown's death, Southerners failed to distinguish between radicals and moderates. They assumed all Northerners were radicals like Brown. "It is useless to disguise the fact, that the entire North and Northwest are hopelessly abolitionized," one Southern newspaper wrote. "We want no better evidence than that presented to us by their course in this Harper's affair."[22] His violent life and tragic death led Northerners and Southerners to assume the worst about each other.[23]

But the tide was rapidly turning against the South. The election of Abraham Lincoln in 1860 showed that the majority of Americans were against the expansion of slavery into the territories. Just months after his election, Kansas finally gained admission to the Union as a free state on January 29, 1861.* Worse still, the new Republican president had expressed his intention to eradicate the moral evil entirely at some future time. Despite continued hopes for peace on both sides, the reality was that, with Lincoln's election, any hope for compromise had faded. By the time Lincoln entered the White House in March 1861, seven states had already seceded from the Union. Four more would soon follow, as cotton states began organizing their own forces to face the regulars and militias of the North. Of prime importance to the North was keeping Missouri in the Union.[24] It was not only a populous state of over one million people but an economic powerhouse with a major port city, St. Louis. Missourians who had fought in Kansas came from the western portion of the state. The majority of the state's population actually opposed secession, particularly the loyal German immigrants in and around St. Louis.

Even though in the minority, an influential group of secessionists were working arduously to break from the Union. Governor Claiborne Jackson was in secret correspondence with Confederate leaders in the expectation he could turn Missouri to the secessionist side. And in a complete reversal of its position on New Year's Eve 1860, the state's most influential newspaper, the *Daily Missouri Republican,* had published an editorial calling for secession if the South's grievances were not redressed by March 4, 1861.

As tensions heightened over the state's political direction, military units on both sides began conducting drills. At stake was the massive arsenal at Jefferson Barracks under the command of Major Peter V. Hagner. If war broke out, whoever controlled its

---

* On February 9, Charles Robinson took the oath of office as the state's first governor.

60,000 muskets, 90,000 pounds of powder, 1.5 million ball cartridges, and numerous field guns controlled the city. And whoever controlled St. Louis controlled the state. To protect the arsenal, two companies, including Spencer's 2nd Infantry under Captain Thomas Sweeney, were dispatched to the site in January 1861. In a letter to his mother, the boy described the scene: "We are confined as closely as convicts in a penitentiary, and a large number of guards [are] continually on post with the strictest orders. [On] Monday we threw up several earthen breastworks and yesterday some unfinished ones were completed."[25] Assigned to post, Spencer's unit stood guard for two hours and rotated back in every four hours. When fresh reliefs came in he and the guards in his unit were then ordered to "the shooting grounds" to practice firing at a target a hundred yards distant.

Such measures, however, were not enough to suit newly arrived Captain Nathaniel S. Lyon, a West Point graduate and veteran of the Mexican War. A short man with a short fuse, Lyon had arrived at Jefferson Barracks in February 1861 from Kansas where he had served at Fort Riley. Lyon had deep apprehensions about the vulnerability of the arsenal to attack and resolved to die before losing it to southerners. Having openly coveted command of Jefferson Barracks for himself, Lyon accused Major Hagner of "imbecility" in failing to take the secessionist threat more seriously. Shortly after Lincoln's inauguration in March, Lyon began maneuvering with Frank Blair, a colonel in the Missouri Volunteers, whose brother Montgomery was a close confidant of the president. On March 20, Lyon was given command of defense of the arsenal and line troops while Hagner maintained control of the ordnance troops and stores.

Meanwhile, a thousand miles away, at dawn on April 12, Confederate floating batteries under the command of Brigadier

General P.G.T. Beauregard opened fire on Fort Sumter, South Carolina. After thirty-four straight hours of firing, Sumter surrendered. The war both sides had hoped to avert had ineluctably begun. Many thought the war would be short-lived. Orville, the veteran of bleeding Kansas, said he was expecting "a vigorous and protracted war."[26]

With Spencer garrisoned in a Southern state, Mary was beside herself with worry. Soon after the attack on Sumter, she traveled to St. Louis in an attempt to convince her son to resign. She arrived on April 20, staying with a cousin, William Cozzens. Surprisingly, even William was under the impression Mary was John Brown's wife, saying it was only "Osawatomie Brown" he had any knowledge of. The next day William rode to Jefferson Barracks and informed Spencer his mother wished to see him. With some difficulty, he was able to finagle a brief leave of absence from Sweeney. The first meeting lasted an hour, during which Mary expressed concern about his decision to join the army and gently tried to coax him to return with her to Utica to find work. He admitted a preference to do something else if it were in view, but he lacked a trade or education. And with no money, an education was out of the question. He would leave the army but did not know where to go or what to do. Mary found him forlorn and anxious to get away. As the following day was Sunday she got permission from his commanding officer to allow Spencer to spend the day with her. Much of the time they shared news of the family—him from Kansas, her from Utica—and the devastating drought that had broken the family apart. Though she was unable to convince him to leave the army, she had been happy to see him after so long a separation.

From St. Louis, Mary traveled to Osawatomie. Since she had departed in haste from New York, she had not informed Orville who, it turned out, was on his way to Utica with little Fanny. By miscommunication Orville had assumed Spencer had come to his senses and was now safely in New York.

But Spencer was still in Missouri where secessionists were moving into high gear. Legislators had passed a law allowing the governor to name heads of the local militia, the sheriff, and the entire St. Louis police force. Governor Jackson promptly appointed secessionists to these positions, giving him a large force at his disposal to neutralize the loyal home guard and take Jefferson Barracks. With no authority to muster troops and the Jefferson Barracks lying vulnerably low and exposed to attack by land and river, Lyon decided to act to secure the arsenal. He had already been in contact with Illinois Governor Richard Yates, who requested a requisition from Secretary of War John B. Floyd for ten thousand muskets from the arsenal. On Wednesday night, April 24, the governor's representative, Captain James H. Stokes, arrived in St. Louis and worked out a plan with the arsenal command to load the arms on a steamboat and secret them away to Illinois. The following night the *City of Alton* moved quietly to the arsenal landing, where seven hundred men proceeded to load the arms and boxes of ammunition onto the steamer, which then returned to Alton.

Lyon's actions came none too soon, for the following week Missouri Governor Jackson had come out openly in support of the Confederacy, proclaiming to the legislature, "Our interests and sympathies are identical with those of the slaveholding States, and necessarily unite our destinies with those of theirs."[27] Another disturbing development was that on May 6, when several state militias under the command of General D. M. Frost began to gather in Lindell's Grove on the outskirts of St. Louis for training. A similar encampment had been held the previous year at Camp Lewis, and the governor now used this as his justification for holding the annual encampment for the militia at Lindell's Grove. Frost's intentions, however, were unclear. At seven hundred men, Frost's militia was far too weak to oppose Jefferson Barracks, now ten thousand strong. Lyon was nonetheless concerned and decided to seek more intelligence before acting. A story, probably apocryphal, claims Lyon infiltrated Frost's camp disguised in a black veil as the mother-in-law of Frank Blair![28] More likely, he dispatched spies to infiltrate the camp. Whatever the means, intelligence reports indicated the camp was heavily armed and rife with talk of secession. Even though Frost openly declared his neutrality, his sympathies appeared to lie with secessionists, for he had named his assemblage Camp Jackson after the governor. Even the streets of the camp were named after leading Confederates such as Davis and Beauregard, the latter having led the assault on Sumter. Of greater import, Lyon learned Frost was about to receive a massive load of two twelve-pound howitzers and two thirty-two-pound guns with ammunition for each, a gift of Jefferson Davis.[29] On May 8, the *J. C. Swan* pulled into St. Louis with the weapon and munition stores disguised as marble and ale.

Convinced of Frost's malevolent intentions, Lyon, who had just been promoted to brigadier general, was now bristling to attack the camp. His aides advised him not to act rashly. Not only were Frost's intentions still unclear, the camp would legally expire in a few days. Moreover, a federal marshal could recover the stolen weapons by a writ of replevin. Dismissing his subordinates' advice, Lyon ordered a call up of the troops.

On May 10 at 9:30 AM, Spencer's company received orders to fall in from Lyon's second in command, Captain Sweeny. By then, a rumor was already circulating among the men that they were to attack secessionists at Lindell's Grove, who had gathered under the guise of the regular annual state encampment. After a close inspection of arms and ammunition, three companies marched out the main gate of the arsenal. Just beyond the gate they halted, while the artillery came up with two twelve-pound brass howitzers followed by some seven thousand volunteers and home guards. After marching six miles, they arrived in the vicinity of the encampment in late afternoon. Locals greeted them with a barrage of insults directed mainly at the volunteers who were nearly all German and known for their unwavering loyalty to the Union.

When they reached within gunshot of Frost's men, the command was halted. Riding up to Sweeny, Lyon said: "Sweeny, if their batteries open on you, deploy your leading company as skirmishers, charge on the nearest battery, and take it."[30] With Sweeny's men on the right, the volunteer regiments immediately began to surround the camp from the left. Lyon then sent a message to Frost accusing him of treasonous activities and demanding his immediate surrender. According to Spencer:

> *There was no chance for refusal. The light field-pieces had already been planted on three neighboring heights, on as many different sides, loaded with grape and canister, with their round, black throats pointing so directly towards the Secessionists that they could see nothing but the muzzles.*[31]

Outnumbered and outgunned, Frost surrendered. In his message to Lyon, he denied having any intention of assaulting federal forces. Sweeny then turned to his men and ordered them to retire their cartridge boxes, which they did with undisguised disappointment.

A bizarre accident then happened to Lyon. He had dismounted from his horse when a major in one of the volunteer regiments rode up for an order, and, turning to go, his horse kicked the captain full in the stomach. While in this condition, Frost's adjutant general, William Wood, rode up and inquired for Lyon. Wishing to conceal Lyon's condition from the enemy, Sweeny replied that he would receive any message intended for the general. Wood then said: "General Frost sends his compliments to General Lyon, and wishes to know if the officers will be allowed to retain their side-arms, what disposition shall be made of government property, and if a guard will be sent to relieve his men now on post and take possession of everything when the camp shall be evacuated."[32] Sweeny replied they intended to confiscate everything.

That night Spencer's company was posted to guard the officers' and sutler's property at Camp Jackson. He spent the night with Captain Sweeny in Frost's tent under a heavy rain. In the morning he helped pack all of Frost's arms and supplies into wagons, which were brought back to the arsenal. When they arrived in the early afternoon, the volunteers began to help themselves to the spoils, including Spencer who, with Sweeny's approval, took two clean handkerchiefs, two blankets, and a heavy wool robe he used for his bed.

Inexplicably, rumors had been circulating that Spencer had deserted and the next day he wrote Kitty to set the record straight and to relate the exciting details of the assault on Camp Jackson. "Give yourself no fear about my desertion," he wrote, "I would never take a discharge, even, in a time like this."[33] For his part Orville had a sudden change of heart about his son's enlistment, even as he continued to worry for his safety. In a letter to Spencer in May, he wrote, "Of your standing truly and faithfully by your country's flag in this its hour of greatest peril I cannot doubt for a moment that God will protect your life and health is my daily prayer." He expressed the pride he felt that his son had participated in "so bold and important a move for disarming and disbanding state treason."[34]

Whether Lyon had acted recklessly in attacking the camp, as

one historian argues, will never be known with any certainty, as to this day Frost's actual intentions are unclear.[35] But that Lyon's next move was a colossal blunder there can be no doubt. Just before Spencer and the others seized possession of the weapons, Lyon ordered Sweeny to march into the encampment and take Frost's men prisoner. He then marched the prisoners humiliatingly through the streets of St. Louis trailed by a band playing "Yankee Doodle."

If this had been an attempt to dampen secessionist enthusiasm, it backfired wildly. Outraged Southern sympathizers poured into the streets and began hurling rocks, brickbats, and other objects at the soldiers. At places along the defile they tried to break the ranks of the guards by taunting the men and pressing against them. Some of the Germans, who did not understand what was being said, became angry. Suddenly the command, "Charge bayonets!" was sounded. As tensions increased, a man, possibly drunk, rode up on his horse and fired two shots into the ranks of the German guards who responded by firing indiscriminately into the crowd. When the shooting ended three minutes later, twenty-eight citizens, three militia members, and two federal troops lay dead. Scores were wounded. The next day Lyon sent a detailed report of the incident to Washington defending his actions. General Harney was horrified.

But worse fallout was yet to come. When news of the bloodshed in St. Louis reached the state capital in Jefferson City, legislators hurriedly passed a Military Bill to mobilize the state on the Confederate side and sent it to the governor for signature. Additional measures were passed appropriating $10,000 to secure the alliance of Indians along the state's borders. Responding to rumors that Lyon was marching on Jefferson City to subdue the legislature, Jackson ordered the members of his staff to seize a locomotive and hasten to St. Louis to reconnoiter the enemy's advance and, if necessary, to destroy the bridges over the

Gasconade and Osage Rivers to thwart the march. Other rumors that Lyon's men were roaming the countryside slaughtering men, women, and children prompted secessionist groups around the state to begin driving Unionists from their homes.

For a time, General Harney, had calmed the situation by striking a truce with Major General Sterling Price, the commander of the state militia. A former congressman and governor of Missouri, Price had been so appalled by Lyon's attack on Frost's camp that he had gone over to the secessionist side. By the terms of the truce, the state guard would control most of Missouri while federal troops would remain in St. Louis.

But radicals like Frank Blair were not interested in accommodation with secessionists. A formidable and influential politician, Blair began lobbying Washington for Harney's removal, intending to replace him with the more aggressive Lyon. Although Lincoln was opposed to removing Harney—not least because he thought Lyon rash—on May 30, after considerable pressure from Blair and others, the president finally gave in and named Lyon head of the western department.

With Lyon now in command, he and Blair intended to drive Governor Jackson and his secessionists from the state altogether. In early June, Jackson and Price asked to meet with Lyon and Blair in the hope of finding a solution to the domestic disturbances. On June 11, the two sides met at the Planter's House Hotel in St. Louis. The meeting, which lasted four hours, was contentious, with Jackson demanding that Union forces depart Missouri and Lyon demanding that Jackson nullify the Military Bill and disband the state militia. At the conclusion of the standoff, Lyon rose imperiously from his chair and bellowed, "Rather than concede to the State of Missouri for one single instant the right to dictate to my Government in any matter however unimportant, I would [pointing to everyone in the room] see you, and you, and you, and you, and every man, woman, and child in the State, dead and buried."[36] With these threatening words, the die was cast.

The next day Jackson called up fifty thousand militia troops to defend the state "against invasion." Spencer's unit, which had been stationed in St. Louis for the past month, was ordered to move on Jefferson City by way of steamboat up the Missouri River. As Lyon's forces approached the capital, Governor Jackson, who had thus far only been able to assemble 120 men, fell back to Boonville, some fifty miles upriver. Located strategically high atop wood bluffs along the Missouri River, Boonville would allow Jackson to maintain communication with secessionists north and south of the river and thus allow the concentration of the militia. Upon arrival Jackson telegraphed orders to his commanders to concentrate their men at Boonville and Lexington farther upriver. *

Lyon pressed on. Because the water was low, his forces had to periodically disembark to allow the boats to pass over the shoals, slowing their movement upriver. By the time they arrived, four thousand Confederate forces were assembled at Boonville.

In recent weeks, Spencer had so impressed Sweeny that he had made Spencer his adjutant general. The promotion, however, came as a disappointment. It proved to be a monotonous job he described as "half servant, half clerk."[37] Now the young soldier wanted to participate in the fighting but, whether because of his age or position, Sweeny refused.

Approaching to within three hundred yards from the crest

---

* In retaliation for Lyon's actions in St. Louis, irregular militias had sprung up all over the state, attacking unionist homes and stealing food and livestock. It was a situation not unlike the guerrilla war in Kansas in the summer of 1856.

where Confederate forces were dug in, Lyon gave the command to attack. The artillery began shelling the enemy's position as the German infantry advanced with the regulars, firing as they went. For several minutes the Confederates held their ground, but the steady advance of Union troops combined with the onslaught of the shells proved too much for them. Price began to retreat, but it soon degenerated into a rout as the undisciplined forces scattered. As he pushed forward into the enemy camp, Lyon seized over a thousand pairs of badly needed shoes, twenty to thirty tents, and a large quantity of arms and ammunition.

When Price learned two columns of Union forces were approaching—James Montgomery's forces from Leavenworth and another from the Iowa line—the Confederates fell back behind the Osage River. Lyon now had near complete control of the Missouri River, allowing him to cut off the Confederates of the north from those in the south. With the Confederates now holding behind the Osage, Lyon planned to drive them into Arkansas. To this end he sent Sweeny's column to Springfield to take the Osage from the rear and Colonel Franz Sigel's forces to occupy the southwestern part of the state.

As Sweeny approached Springfield, once again Spencer pleaded with his commander to participate in the fighting. This time Sweeny relented. Giving him several of the finest horses in the company, he detached Spencer with several men under his command to scout enemy positions. Seeing an opportunity to impress Sweeny with his acumen, Spencer wrote to his brother Rocky on July 3:

DEAR ROCK:

Please send me news in Osawatomie, particularly where [James] Montgomery is, and how many men he has. Be very careful to send as correct news as possible, something that can be relied upon, as it will be of great importance to me if correct. Please address me as dear brother, and do not speak of Father in your letter. Do not express any wonder at what I ask. To set your mind at rest about my safety, I am doing well, but can do still better if you can send me this information that I ask. If you know where Lane is, and how many men he has, it will be useful. Address "Spencer Kellogg," Springfield, Green County, Missouri, and write, sure, by return mail.

Love to Mother,
SPENCER*[38]

Altogether Spencer would log some nine hundred miles scouting enemy positions. Still, he was keen to see more action and frustrated at being a lowly adjutant. He planned to seek a discharge from the regular army and reenlist as an officer in one of the new companies springing up like mushrooms all over the state when the Battle of Springfield intervened.

As Sweeny advanced on Springfield, Colonel Franz Sigel's troops were coming up from St. Louis through Rolla. On July 5 Sigel clashed with the main body of Jackson's men at Carthage and was pushed back to Springfield. There Lyon joined him with his own troops and took command of the entire force, numbering about six thousand men.

---

* Mary was dismayed to hear of the letter exclaiming, "Poor Spencer! I tremble for him.... He is in General Lyon's army, at Springfield, Missouri, where they are waiting for accessions, to have, I suppose, the greatest battle they have had yet. If his life is only spared, let us be thankful for that; but I think he was never before so exposed."

Meanwhile, Jackson's forces had moved into Carthage. The next day they marched to Neosho where they were joined by Brigadier General Ben McCulloch's force of several thousand men who had come up from Texas, Louisiana, and Arkansas. Many of them were Texas Rangers, hard fighting men, who had served in the Mexican War. Price also came up with 1,700 mounted state guard troops. As Confederate forces were augmenting to some twenty-three thousand, Lyon's own soldiers—few of whom had any battle experience—were now dwindling, owing to the fact that many who had rushed to enlist in the spring had signed up for three months and were not returning.

On July 3 the government created the Western Department which included Lyon's old department, Illinois, Kentucky, and all the states and territories as far as the Rockies. Its new head was the daring explorer General John C. Frémont.

Despite his extensive forays as an explorer of the West, Frémont was nonetheless wholly unqualified for the military command. Once again Frank Blair had been behind the appointment to a post critical not only for its size but its political complexity, because the populations of Western states were bitterly divided.

Upon arrival in St. Louis on July 25, Frémont was besieged by requests by Lyon for more money, men, and supplies. But, consumed as it was with the war in the East after the demoralizing and surprising defeat at Bull Run, Washington had nothing to spare. With the more strategically important town of Cairo, Illinois, under immediate threat, Frémont decided to focus his limited resources on preventing Confederates from advancing there. With no resources to offer Lyon, he advised him that if he could not hold at Springfield, he should fall back to Rolla.

Despite being vastly outnumbered, the headstrong Lyon dismissed the advice of Frémont and his own advisers. At dawn on August 10, he launched a surprise attack on Confederate forces at Wilson's Creek twelve miles southwest of Springfield. Early on in the fighting, it appeared Lyon had the upper hand, having taken the hill overlooking the Confederate camps. But Lyon's hopes of an early rout were dashed when an Arkansas battery began unleashing a barrage of shells, giving Price's infantry time to organize lines on the south slope of the hill. Fighting raged on for several hours like an "encounter of two badly armed mobs."[39] Thousands of Union horsemen, completely unarmed, began riding amid the fighting, doing little but getting in the way. At one point, Lyon ordered one of his captains to open fire on a regiment fast advancing from two hundred yards. But as the regiment neared they noticed it was bearing both a Confederate and Union flag, forcing them to halt their fire until they could determine if it was the enemy. Another time, Sigel's men mistook the grey uniforms of the 3rd Louisiana for the 1st Iowa Infantry (which also wore gray uniforms) and withheld their fire until the Confederates were nearly upon them. His brigade was consequently routed and Sigel fled the field, leaving Lyon and Sweeny to hold out alone.

With musket balls falling as "thick as hailstones," Lyon rode gallantly among the ranks urging on his men.[40] A few hours into the fighting his horse was shot and he suffered wounds in the head and ankle. When Captain Sweeny called attention to his wounds, Lyon replied dismissively. "It is nothing."[41] Then, attempting to take over from a fallen colonel, Lyon was struck by a ball to the chest and died instantly. Ninety minutes later, Union forces, exhausted, demoralized, and low on ammunition, fell back to Rolla, leaving Lyon's body on the battlefield.[42] Sweeny was seriously wounded. In the first major Civil War battle west of the Mississippi, the defeat at Wilson's Creek was every bit as demoralizing for the Union as Bull Run had been. Indeed, it was sometimes called the "Bull Run of the West."

Spencer had not taken part in the disastrous battle, having been made commissary sergeant to Major Mudd just prior. After the battle he accompanied Sweeny to St. Louis where the latter was sent to recover from his wounds. There in May, Spencer chanced to meet a girl, Mary Manahan. A brief but aggressive courtship followed before he returned to duty. Before leaving he promised to marry her upon his return.

Chapter Ten

THE WESTERN FLOTILLA

*"The art of war is simple enough. Find out where your enemy is.
Get at him as soon as you can. Strike him as hard
as you can, and keep moving on."*
—General Ulysses S. Grant at the start of
the Tennessee River Campaign

SEPTEMBER 1861 MARKED NEARLY A YEAR THAT
Spencer had been in the army, most of it spent in garrison. During
that time, he had acquired some knowledge of military tactics and
led a team of scouts in battle. In doing so he had earned the respect
of fellow soldiers and officers alike. After the Battle of Springfield,
he was even promised a captain's commission. But when the promotion failed to materialize he took an honorable discharge in
order to become a first lieutenant under Frémont. His job was to
recruit for the Lyon Legion, a corps of scouts for the south and west
of the war theater named in honor of the fallen general. The scouts,
most of whom were refugees from secessionist communities in
Arkansas and Missouri, were to be attached to the 24th Regiment
of the Missouri Volunteers who had mustered in for service for
three years under the command of Colonel Sempronius Hamilton
Boyd.[1] In a letter to Kitty, Spencer shared the good news even as he
wondered what his life would have been like outside the military:

> *The war is fairly beginning. Lucky for me was the apparently
> untoward circumstance of my enlistment in the "regulars," for*

it fits me to fill the position I occupy, and, perhaps, for future advancement. Ah! your little, unpractical, theoretical brother has had many of the sharp, uncompromising corners rubbed from him, and is getting, more than ever he thought, a man of the world. I am sorry! Almost ashamed! When I look back it seems that if I had married happily, with the old notions and green-ness, and retired to some out-of-the-way town, life had been full of much keener enjoyment than can ever come to me as worldly as I have got to be. Yet I have friends—that is, acquaintances—now, that I had not then, and money, too—better, you see, in every worldly view; yet I am sorry for the exchange.[2]

But Spencer's future was inextricably linked to that of Frémont's, for whom things had gone from bad to worse after the Union defeat at Wilson's Creek. Frémont's pleas for more arms, supplies, wagons, and horses went virtually ignored by Washington. As a result, gue-rilla war raged across the northern and central parts of the state, a situation the embattled general described as "a tide of rebellion, rapine, and plunder which has literally swept over the state."[3] In desperation he declared martial law over the entire state on August 30. In his proclamation, citizens caught with arms in secessionist areas would be shot if found guilty, as would anyone caught destroy-ing bridges, telegraph lines, and railways. In addition, Missourians found aiding the enemy would have their slaves liberated.

While many supported the draconian measures, Lincoln opposed them, feeling the politically inexperienced Frémont had overstepped his bounds. Killing Confederates, Lincoln believed, would only invite retaliation against Union supporters. More important, by threatening to free slaves Frémont had crossed a sen-sitive political line that Lincoln had been careful not to breach. Until now the war had been about maintaining the Union, not emancipating slaves. By threatening to free slaves, Frémont's proclamation threatened to drive states like Kentucky, which had thus far been neutral, to the Confederate side.

Frémont might well have survived the blunder were it not for a number of critics intriguing for his removal. Frank Blair, once his chief supporter, had since turned against him, accusing him of incompetence and blaming him (unfairly) for Lyon's death. Jealous West Pointers who resented the explorer's appointment to the Western command were eager to find fault with him. Frémont also had enemies in the Cabinet. With so many working against him, Lincoln finally relieved him of command on October 24, the very day the Lyon Legion went into service.

With the removal of Frémont, Spencer failed to get confirmation for his commission. Feeling betrayed by the army, he began to cast about for a new opportunity, something in which he could advance quickly. After two months of weighing his rather limited options, he joined the US Navy aboard the gunboat *Essex*.

The navy might seem an unpromising move for a young enlistee seeking rapid advancement. But in fact, the navy was every bit as important—if not more important—than the army itself. Early on, both sides recognized that whoever controlled the Mississippi River would likely determine the outcome of the war. The mighty river coursed 2,300 miles through the heart of the country, providing access to thousands of miles of other strategic rivers such as the Ohio in the east and the Missouri in the west. Unlike the road networks that were inadequate and in poor condition, rivers provided ready-made highways for swiftly moving soldiers and equipment or conducting a surprise flank attack against the enemy. And because so many Southern states lay along the Mississippi, the river was critical to the Confederate economy and communications and transportation. Break its communication lines and you would break the Confederacy.

Although neither side had combat-ready ships at the outset of the war, the North's superior industrial base gave it a comparative advantage over the South. Within weeks of the surrender of Fort Sumter, Commander John Rodgers, assigned to command the Western Flotilla, scrambled to assemble a war fleet. In Cincinnati, Ohio, he purchased three river steamers that he altered into gunboats. Thick hulls of oak were raised, boilers were lowered into protective holds below, and large cannons were mounted on the broadsides and sterns. The tiny fleet was then sent down river to Cairo. A few months later the Department of War contracted James B. Eads for the construction of seven brand new gunboats, each with thirteen heavy guns, plated with iron two and a half inches thick. Working seven days a week with the new fleet commander, Admiral Andrew Hull Foote, Eads tackled the myriad problems of design and even invented new machinery for the construction of parts. With four thousand men working day and night, Eads delivered the boats in the astonishing time of three months.[4] When completed, the ships, with their flat bottoms, heavy Iron casement, and enormous paddle wheels, looked like no other vessels. They were nicknamed "Pook's Turtles" because the protective iron casement designed by Sam Pook resembled turtle shells.

In November an eighth boat, the *New Era,* was commissioned under the command of William D. Porter. Porter hailed from one of the most distinguished families in the US Navy. His father, Commodore David Porter, had served in the War of 1812 and later commanded the famous USS *Constitution,* famously known as Old Ironsides. William's brother, David Dixon Porter, was about to command a flotilla that would participate in the capture of New Orleans. The portly, bearded William had first entered the navy at the tender age of twelve after signing on to his uncle's naval war vessel. By the time the Civil War started, he had gained over ten years' experience overseeing the outfitting of steamships for the navy, experience that he was now about to draw on extensively.

As the *New Era* had been a St. Louis ferryboat, Foote had given Porter a mere eighteen days in which to convert her into an iron-clad gunboat. There being no naval yard, Porter took three large coal scows and converted them into a floating navy yard. He proceeded to ingeniously convert the boat while simultaneously plying the Mississippi on patrol. Of one scow he made a blacksmith's shop and iron-working shed, another a boat shed and carpenter's shop, the third a coal depot. He then divided his crew into gangs—woodchoppers, coalmen, carpenters, and caulkers—creating a thoroughly self-sufficient maritime workshop. When moving upstream or down, he towed the scows along as he worked. In some cases, he went into action, fighting at one end, while carpenters, caulkers, blacksmiths, and painters were working at the other.[5] When completed, the *New Era* boasted three nine-inch and one ten-inch Dahlgren guns (aptly nicknamed soda bottles for their tapered shape), two humongous fifty-pound rifled Dahlgrens, and two heavy howitzers.

In late November, Porter took his five-hundred-ton ship into dry dock at St. Louis for minor repairs. When he returned to the flotilla at Cairo the ship sported a new name, the *Essex,* in honor of the frigate *Essex* his father had commanded during the War of 1812. It was while the boat was in St. Louis that Spencer had come aboard as a common sailor.

Things were relatively calm on the Mississippi after Spencer's enlistment. The *Essex* reconnoitered the Mississippi and its eastern tributaries, and the fleet engaged in no major battles. While the *Essex* was docked at Cairo, Porter received word that several enemy vessels were towing a large floating battery upriver from Columbus, Kentucky. Four miles north of Columbus, the *Essex* and *St. Louis,* it will be recalled, had engaged the enemy at Lucas Bend, forcing three Confederate gunboats to retreat to Polk's impregnable iron batteries.[6] It was then, in January 1862, while Porter was reprovisioning in Cairo, that Spencer and Trussel contrived to pose as Union deserters in order to gather intelligence on Polk's batteries.

Shortly after the boys had jumped ship, Porter received orders to move up river. For some time, the Confederate Army had been busy establishing a fortified base of operations in Tennessee between the Tennessee and Cumberland Rivers. Until recently, no Union strategist had bothered to note that if there was a soft underbelly to the Confederacy, it lay not in the East but in Tennessee, where a vital communications and transportation line crossed the state. The Memphis and Charleston Railroad ran from the Mississippi River east through Corinth, Huntsville, and Chattanooga before forking north into Virginia and south into South Carolina. Tennessee also had seventeen pig iron furnaces, more than any state in the Confederacy, and was a major producer of grain, gunpowder, and mules and horses.

The western approach to the region was guarded by two forts— Fort Henry on the east bank of the Tennessee River and Fort Donelson on the south bank of the Cumberland River—at a point where the rivers drew to within twelve miles of one another near the Kentucky line. Of the two, Fort Henry was the more vulnerable, lying on low ground and subject to flooding. By early 1862, the Union realized that if they could conquer the forts they could penetrate the three-hundred-mile defensive line from Columbus, Kentucky, to Bowling Green and effectively cut the Confederacy in two.

On January 30, 1862, the Department of War issued orders to Ulysses Grant and Andrew Foote to undertake a joint expedition against the forts. Had the Union known of the conditions inside the forts, they might well have struck sooner. The 2,800 Confederates under Brigadier General Lloyd Tilghman were armed with ancient flintlock muskets and were sick from the winter's cold and damp. Heavy rains had left Fort Henry's parade ground submerged beneath two feet of water and dampened much of the powder in the magazines.

On February 2, Foote embarked from Cairo with a fleet of seven gunboats, including the *Essex,* arriving at Paducah, Kentucky, that same evening. The fleet commander had wanted four additional boats for the mission, but a shortage of men in Cairo made staffing them impossible. A few days later, Grant started from Cairo with seventeen thousand men. Upon learning of the size of Grant's force from scouts, Tighlman shifted the bulk of his forces at Fort Henry to the more defensible Fort Donelson. Yet he left a small force at Henry, intending to make a stand against the approaching gunboats. The fort had a commanding view two to three miles downstream and twenty mounted guns, twelve of which were trained on the ascending fleet.

Foote's plan was to approach the fort with four ships abreast, guns firing from the bow—the least vulnerable part of the boat—while Grant attacked from the rear. To confuse the enemy, he planned to advance and fall back so as to force the enemy to constantly adjust its firing range.

On the afternoon of February 5, Foote came on board the *Essex* and addressed the crew. He admonished them to be brave and courageous and above all to place their trust in Divine Providence. To one battery commander he stressed the importance of wasting no shots: Remember, he said, "that your greatest efforts should be to disable the enemy's guns, and be sure you do not throw any ammunition away. Every charge you fire from one of those guns cost the government about eight dollars. If your shots fall short you encourage the enemy. If they reach home you demoralize him, and get the worth of your money."[7]

The next day, Foote's fleet came up. Grant was still nowhere in sight, having been delayed by muddy roads and heavy rain the previous day. After waiting a half hour, Foote decided to attack without Grant. One mile from Fort Henry, the fleet began firing, and it fired more rapidly as it advanced upstream. The *Essex,* which until now had been advised to wait until Foote's boat had established the proper range of the fort, began advancing and firing with deadly accuracy. Thirty minutes into the action, Porter called his men below deck to congratulate them on their splendid execution. Just then, a thirty-two-pound ball struck the port bow of the *Essex,* killing in its flight a master's mate, S. B. Britton Jr., and piercing the boiler. High pressure steam shot in all directions, scalding nearly three dozen men. Several threw themselves in the river. Porter, who had been standing in front of the boiler, was seriously scalded. As the disabled ship drifted downstream to Cairo, the *John Ives* drew alongside and picked up the dead and wounded.

All this time the three remaining gunboats had been steadily raining shells on the fort, which had been reduced to a blazing inferno. By now Grant's troops had finally come up in the rear to prevent any retreat of the army. Judging the situation hopeless, Tighlman, exhausted and coated with soot, raised a white flag. When the defeated general came aboard Foote's boat, he wringed his hands in distress and moaned, "I am in despair; my reputation is gone forever."[8] In the Union's first major victory in the Western theater, two thousand Confederates lay dead and fourteen thousand were taken prisoner.

But the toll on the *Essex* had been costly. Three men were killed in the boiler room explosion and several had drowned jumping into the river. Four more died that night from burn wounds. Captain Porter was critically wounded.

As the *Essex* was limping back to Cairo, Spencer and Trussel were in Columbus gaining the confidence of Polk's men. Once aboard the steamer *Charm,* Captain Guthrie proceeded to grill them on Foote's activities on the Mississippi. Not wishing to divulge any real intelligence, the two "answered in a way that seemed remarkably like prevarication to each other." Guthrie then went to consult with Polk. When he returned, he put the two spies on a floating battery where they spent three days of idleness, all the while affecting "a cheerful countenance."9

On February 4, two days before Foote attacked Fort Henry, the two were transferred to the timberclad gunboat, the CSS *General Polk.* They were immediately sent below and placed under guard. Captain Guthrie then came down to say that since the boys expressed a desire to join the Confederate Army, it was decided that they would be taken to Captain Gray's company on Island Number Ten, so called because it was the tenth island in the Mississippi from the mouth of the Ohio. A few hours later, as the *General Polk* was descending to Island Number Ten, Spencer and Trussel were brought on deck. Their shabbily dressed shipmates were very solicitous toward the new recruits, offering everything but clothing, which was clearly in short supply. At noon they all partook of grog followed by an excellent supper, followed by more grog. Despite the growing rapport between the spies and the Confederates, doubts about the two lingered. In the morning, Spencer and Trussel were separated and subjected to an intense cross-examination. Having prepared for just such a grilling, the two passed with flying colors. They were finally in.

When they found time, the two spies walked about the deck,

examining the peculiar construction of the boat. Originally a side-wheel river steamer, when the war broke out the *General Polk* was purchased for $8,000 and converted into a timberclad gunboat. It was fitted with four rifled Parrott guns that were mounted on a carriage and slide of Southern invention. It was superior to any-thing the two had seen in the North. Having noticed the boys scrutinizing the boat, the second mate remarked half-jokingly that they appeared to be such "a couple of sharp-looking fellows" that he would send them on an information gathering mission.[10] The unintended irony of the remark prompted a nervous laugh from Spencer.

Over the next few days the *General Polk* steamed between Island Number Ten and New Madrid, Missouri, on business unknown to Spencer. The strategic importance of the two positions lay in the two severe oxbows at these sites that forced ships to slow in order to turn, making them easy marks for Confederate batteries. Island Number Ten was a particularly strong defensive position. It stood about ten feet above the low water mark and featured seven guns.

On February 6, Spencer and Trussel were finally sent ashore on Island Number Ten where Captain Gray of the Confeder-ate Corps of Engineers immediately set them to work building a house. For the first time since their defection, they had an oppor-tunity to speak in total privacy. They used it to compare notes. Afterward, Gray ordered them to clean a sixty-eight-pound gun that had just been mounted. After putting it in perfect order, they moved it a couple miles on a boat and guarded it until they were relieved by soldiers.

By now the two boys had been gone nearly a week. Even though Captain William D. Porter had approved an absence of ten days, Spencer was feeling anxious and decided he had enough informa-tion to return to the Union side. Trussel, however, convinced him to linger a few days longer in the hope of gathering more intelligence. That opportunity came the very next day when Captain Gray took Trussel along to Columbus, Kentucky, where they spent most of the time getting drunk. When Gray returned alone, Trussel stayed nearly a week gathered information on fortifications, guns, and torpedoes before returning with an assistant engineer.

Yet Trussel's efforts came too late to be of use, for word had begun to circulate that Fort Donelson had fallen on February 15 and Columbus would soon be abandoned. To avoid being cut off from the Confederacy, on March 1, General P.G.T. Beauregard, who had taken command of Polk's forces at Columbus, decided to fall back to Island Number Ten, located about sixty miles below Columbus. From Bowling Green, General Albert Sidney Johnston moved back to the capital at Nashville.

A few days later Spencer and Trussel were surveying with their new boss, Pattison,* on Island Number Ten, when boatload after boatload of Confederate soldiers began arriving from Columbus with large quantities of ammunition and commissary stores. At the time of the evacuation there were only seven guns mounted on Island Number Ten, prompting Spencer to remark that if Union gunboats had attacked, "t'would have been a take worth having."[11] Yet Beauregard would soon rectify the weakness by mounting some 150 pieces of artillery in and around the island.

Amid the flurry of Confederate activity, Spencer and Trussel continued to survey, sometimes on the island or the opposite shore, though mostly onshore where they now lived. When Spencer had volunteered for the assignment, he had not anticipated the backbreaking work he would be required to perform in order

---

* Most likely William Patterson, third assistant engineer whose state of origin is unknown.

to maintain his cover. Fortunately, a break came when Pattison made Trussel a flag bearer and Spencer was put in charge of two "lusty negroes" who carried the heavy chain used to measure distances, distances that Spencer committed to memory. All the while, Spencer and Trussel anxiously awaited the Union attack on New Madrid twenty miles down river so they could make their escape.

They would not have to wait long. On February 28, Brigadier General John Pope, commander of the Union Army of the Mississippi, began marching on New Madrid from Commerce, Missouri. Pope had selected Commerce as his base of operations because it was the low point in an otherwise mass of high bluffs along the river. But the location came with a serious impediment, for the entire way to New Madrid lay through the Great Mingo Swamp, a dismal morass of mud and muck. As Pope's men lugged supplies and artillery through the swamp, snow and rain began to fall, making it nearly impassable.

Despite the all-but-impossible conditions, Pope's doughty force reached the outskirts of New Madrid on March 3 and laid siege to the city. Union gunboats still had not come up and so Pope ordered heavy artillery brought in from Cairo. In the meantime, he began to infiltrate the town to cut off its access to Island Number Ten, which every day was sending supplies and reinforcements. By this time, the Confederates had amassed some nine thousand men. That very evening Pope's artillery arrived—four 128-pound siege guns. At daybreak he unleashed his guns on the forts and the gunboats at New Madrid. Despite having thirty-two guns in and around New Madrid, the Confederates were all but powerless in the face of Pope's heavier guns. The next day, Confederate gunboats and troops fell back to Island Number Ten and Tiptonville, Tennessee.

On March 14, Pope moved in to occupy New Madrid—

unfortunately for Spencer and Trussel. For on that day the boys were eleven miles away surveying at the foot of Reelfoot Lake to see if there was any passage by which Union soldiers could enter. After confirming that there was none, they returned to Island Number Ten to hear that New Madrid had been evacuated. Just then, Spencer noticed five Union gunboats and a few mortar vessels approaching and firing on the island. Suddenly he realized his moment to escape had arrived. Alas, Trussel was in bed sick with dysentery. Even though Trussel urged him to flee, Spencer refused. To do so would certainly put his comrade's life in jeopardy. As shells exploded all around them, Spencer instead went to Trussel's bedside to minister to his suffering friend. Several times a day he would go down to the riverbank in the hope of getting the attention of one of the Union gunboats. One evening he went to the river when, unbeknownst to him, a Confederate soldier spotted him waving to a Union ship. In the morning Spencer was outside preparing tea for Trussel when he was suddenly arrested and whisked off by an Irish lieutenant of the sappers. Spencer was prohibited from having any contact with Trussel, who, still bedridden, had no idea what had happened to his mate.

Spencer was taken before General W. W. Mackall, commander of Island Number Ten. "This young man, General, was standing on the bank yesterday all day, and we suspect him of being a spy, and about to give information to the enemy," the Irishman said.[12] Spencer made no effort to refute the charge and stood silent before his accuser. Mackall immediately put him in the custody of Colonel Thomas Scott of the 12th Louisiana Volunteers.

On March 17, Foote attacked Island Number Ten with six ironclads and ten mortar boats. Because the water was high and the boats were difficult to control, the gunboats had to fire from a distance of more than a mile away lest they take a hit and drift helplessly into the enemy's hands. To approach any closer would expose the unarmored sides of the vessels to the Confederate batteries. But from such a distance the bombing was ineffective. As a result, it continued for weeks. Foote knew he needed a means to cut off the island from the rear to prevent reinforcements and supplies from reaching it. Yet to run the ironclads past the batteries would be tantamount to suicide. The only effective way of taking the island, Foote concluded, was to send boats to General Pope so that he might cross the river from below and attack the rebel works from the Tennessee shore. But how to do this was the question. Finally, General Schuyler Hamilton suggested they circumvent the island by digging a shallow canal on the Missouri side at the hairpin curve of the river. Though a wild proposition, the canal would allow Foote to bypass the batteries and come out just east of New Madrid. To accommodate small boats, the canal had to be fifty feet wide. It would have to run twelve miles, with six miles cut through heavy timber where every tree had to be sawed off four and a half feet below the waterline. For nineteen days, soldiers and sailors labored in the muck and mud felling trees with saws and axes and hauling them out with rope and capstans.

Meanwhile, on April 4, after nineteen days of digging, Pope's men miraculously completed the canal and shallow-draft boats began transporting rejoicing troops down to New Madrid. By this time, a number of Confederate batteries had been taken out, as the ironclad *Carondelet* had successfully run past the Confederates with a coal barge lashed to its port side for protection. Two days later the *Pittsburg* also ran the island, shelling batteries as it went along. With Pope's men now approaching from the Tennessee side, Mackall surrendered the island that evening. Several thousand Confederates attempted to retreat to Tiptonville where, caught between the swamps and the river, they laid down their arms and surrendered.*

But Spencer was not among the captives. For soon after being paced in Scott's charge, the 12th Louisiana Volunteers had embarked for Tiptonville. As they were marching into town, Spencer took the opportunity to help one of the men with his bags, thereby gaining a measure of goodwill and a pair of blankets to sleep under for the rest of the time that he was under guard there. At Tiptonville they camped in the mud. Spencer sat all day under guard and slept fitfully at night.

Although he was five miles away, Spencer could distinctly see Foote's mortar shells bursting in the air all through the day and into the night over the island. About midnight his regiment retreated from Tiptonville on a boat that started south. All night he stood by the furnace door under guard, trying in vain to warm himself. In the morning, having not been given any breakfast, he cheekily demanded to speak with Colonel Scott. He then asked Scott if he had orders to starve him, to which Scott responded by taking him upstairs and giving him a hearty breakfast. When one of the soldiers later insulted him, Spencer shot back that he would not dare do so if he were not a prisoner. Having practiced with a bayonet in the army, Spencer then challenged him to duel with a sword or bayonet, which the guards refused to allow.

Later he was taken up the hill and placed upon the side of a bank where he slept in the warm March sun nearly the entire day.

---

* With the Tennessee River now open to Foote's gunboats, an important communications line from Memphis to Chattanooga was now exposed. So vulnerable was it that Confederate Secretary of War Judah P. Benjamin told General Robert E. Lee that he should defend it at all costs—even if it meant abandoning Richmond.

After a late supper (he had once again been neglected), he was given a small blanket to sleep on in the open air. Late at night it began raining and, after considerable pleading with the guard, he was allowed to sleep on the covered commissary porch.

The next day Spencer was lying in a tent when Sergeant Dan Hickman of the 12th Louisiana Volunteers came in "pretty tight, but in a good-natured way," with a canteen full of whiskey.[13] Sitting down by his side, the inebriated Hickman began to brush Spencer's hair back affectionately.

"You're a pretty good-looking feller," he said. "What's your name?"

"Kellogg. Spencer Kellogg, all the world over, and in the Southern Confederacy to boot!"

"Well, Kellogg," Hickman said, still fumbling around the boy's head, "they say you're a spy, but I reckin it's all right. You've got a good for'ed, and a fine open countenance. Will you have a drink?"[14] By now the son of a temperance leader had partaken of a lot of whiskey and grog on the *General Polk* and on Island Number Ten as a way of promoting good fellowship with the Confederates, and Spencer threw back a healthy swig.

The next day the 12th Louisiana Volunteers continued south with their captive. They soon arrived at Fort Pillow, Tennessee, where Spencer's situation was about to take a bizarre turn.

Chapter Eleven

RETURN AT SHILOH

"Take your damned regiment back to Ohio.
There is no enemy closer than Corinth."
—General William T. Sherman to a subordinate

FORT PILLOW IN TENNESSEE HAD RECENTLY BEEN built on the Mississippi by Major General Gideon J. Pillow. Spencer remained under guard there for the rest of March 1862. At least his captors here treated him with greater kindness, thanks to his youth and the naive innocence he deliberately affected. In time he won the confidence of the officers and men to such a degree that he was invited to join his captors in games of whist and ball. He was even permitted to teach the officers sword practice and bayonet exercise to the enlisted men. So complete had been the trust Spencer earned that he was able to enter the commanding officer's guarded tent and, from his trunk, take plans, instructions, and maps, which he then forwarded to his Union commanding officer, Captain Porter.* With the arrival of spring, Spencer was actually enjoying his captivity and claimed, with all the hubris of youth, to have "no apprehensions for the future."[1]

---

* Spencer's early biographer speculates the documents were probably sent by a black messenger who was all too willing to betray his master.

One day, Spencer inveigled one of the officers to speak on his behalf with Brigadier General John Villepigue, the commanding officer. Upon hearing of the young captive, Villepigue immediately sent for him. In a brief discussion, the general inquired as to his intentions. Having heard of a massive Confederate recruitment effort underway at Corinth, Mississippi, Spencer replied "with all the earnestness he could muster" that, having been so warmly treated by the men he had had undergone a change of heart.[2] He now wanted to enlist in the Confederate Army. Just how long it took the young captive to convince Villepigue of his intentions is unclear. What is clear is that at the end of the conversation, Villepigue not only released him, but gave him a pass, transportation, and five days' provisions. Spencer repaid the general by delaying his departure three days in order to make note of every aspect of Fort Pillow.

Just why Villepigue released him had little to do with gullibility and everything with the massive buildup of troops the Confederate Army was planning in order to halt the devastating Union advance. Having been routed from their strategic positions in Kentucky and most of Tennessee, Johnston and Beauregard realized that to repel the Union advance they needed to reconstitute a larger, more powerful army. While Polk was collecting those who had been dispersed in from Columbus, New Madrid, and Fort Pillow, an urgent call went out to Pensacola, Mobile, New Orleans, and other cities for thousands of men. The Pensacola-Mobile area alone sent ten thousand recruits. Companies in other states responded to the call, and by the end of March, Johnston had assembled a force of over forty thousand men. Corinth was chosen as the rendezvous point as it was strategically located at the junction of two vital rail lines, the Mobile and Ohio and the Memphis and Charleston, "the vertebrae of the Confederacy" according to LeRoy Pope Walker, the first Confederate Secretary of War.[3]

Among the new recruits, of course, was Spencer, who had started for Corinth via Memphis in early April. In Memphis, he got his pass stamped at the provost marshal's office after which he toured the city to study fortifications and other strategic points. In the evening he departed for Corinth by train. By sheer happenstance a Confederate officer, James de Berty Trudeau and his aide were in the car on their way to the Confederate confab. An artillery specialist, Trudeau had laid out the fortifications at Columbus for Polk and was chief of artillery there. He had also commanded the batteries at Island Number Ten before the Confederate withdrawal. Securing a seat near them, Spencer was able to obtain valuable information from their conversation. The next day, as he was about to leave for Corinth, he ran into a soldier belonging to the 1st Louisiana Cavalry Volunteers, who, much to his satisfaction, picked Spencer up as a recruit to his company.

After a day together in Corinth, the two proceeded to Iuka, Mississippi, some twenty-five miles farther on, where his regiment was expected to report that night. In the evening the regiment came in but refused to officially swear in Spencer and the other enlistees until they could give him the fifty dollars in bounty for enlisting.

Meanwhile, Union forces were preparing to deal a final death blow to the beleaguered Confederates—or thought they were. General Grant had chosen Pittsburg Landing, Tennessee, a small trading post on the west bank of the Tennessee River twenty miles from Corinth as the place to unite with Major General Don Carlos's Army of Ohio, which was still in Nashville. The site had been recommended two weeks earlier by his subordinate, Major General William T. Sherman.

By early April 1862, five of Grant's divisions were camped on the tablelands west of the river near a log meetinghouse named Shiloh. Grant had set up headquarters nine miles upriver in Cherry

Mansion at Savannah, Tennessee. So confident was Grant of Confederate disarray that he failed to conduct a reconnaissance of the rendezvous point. Nor did he bother to dig entrenchments when he arrived or send scouts forward to study Confederate positions. Although aware Johnston was reconstituting his force, Grant did not believe they were in any position to launch an offensive. On the day before Johnston attacked, a Union soldier reported having seen enemy cavalry in the woods, but officers dismissed it as a reconnaissance party.[4] So when Johnston attacked Pittsburg Landing at dawn on April 6, Grant's men were taken completely by surprise. Union soldiers, who had just woken and were half-clothed, scattered in panic as hordes of Confederates sounding their eerie cry came at them. "My God, we are attacked!" Sherman was famously known to have uttered.[5] Among the rebels charging through the woods was the future African explorer, Henry M. Stanley, a private in the 6th Arkansas Infantry. In the half-light of the morning, Stanley described the furor with which the rebels attacked:

> *I tried hard to see some living thing to shoot at, for it seemed absurd to be blazing away at shadows . . . at last I saw a row of little globes of pearly smoke streaked with crimson, breaking out . . . from a long line of bluey figures in front. . . . After a steady exchange of musketry, which lasted some time, we heard the order: "Fix bayonets! On the double-quick!" . . . The Federals appeared inclined to await us; but, at this juncture, our men raised a yell. . . . It drove all sanity and order from among us.*[6]

Spencer had just emerged from eating breakfast in one of the mess tents when he suddenly heard the sound of fighting in the distance. At eleven o'clock all available men in the regiment were ordered to

report for service. Spencer was given an old double-barreled shotgun, ten cartridges, and an emaciated horse "that was never out of
a perpetual jiggle."[7] Soon after they left camp for the Tennessee
River, passing "many fine houses from which came ladies of various degrees of comeliness, wearing innumerable white and bandana
handkerchiefs."[8] From Iuka the river was only eight miles away, but
the weather was unseasonably hot and they had to pass over moun-
tains a good part of the way. As the men marched, Spencer now
became anxious at the prospect of shooting at Union soldiers. "The
sound of the battle in progress raging with a continual roar," he said,
"caused anxiety to us all, but to me of a peculiar kind. I expected
every moment to be brought into a fight against my friends, and you
may imagine it caused me trouble."[9]

Amid clouds of dust they rode quietly along at a trot, swelter-
ing in the heat of the sun. After a few miles the road came to run
along a beautiful valley in the midst of which flowed a meandering
stream, which they crossed repeatedly in their advance. Few knew
where they were headed, and to allay the anxiety "jokes were current, and merriment and good-humor pervaded all."[10] When they
were within a mile of the river, a halt was ordered, and the colonel
and a detachment went forward to reconnoiter. Upon their return,
the colonel issued orders to fall back. They began to retrace their
march, leaving pickets at strategic places. Striking a crossroad running along the river, they followed it toward the scene of action. By
this time, darkness had fallen and the roar of the smaller cannons
had ceased. Occasionally there came, wafted on the breeze, a sullen
boom that Spencer knew to be the heavy Dahlgren guns of the
Union boats. They continued to travel by moonlight until the men
grew fatigued. Fearing he would be called upon to engage in battle,
Spencer's "every nerve seemed pounded to a jelly."[11] He now began
to look for the first opportunity to escape. As they continued

their march along the river, a distant storm approached and every moment the sky grew darker. Long after midnight, they halted and made camp in a pasture. Spencer received a few ears of corn and a little water for his feeble horse. He lay down on his blanket, having not eaten since morning, and quickly fell into a sound sleep. In the morning, they learned from the sons of the landowner that the Tennessee River was about a mile and a half distance.

It was then that Spencer decided to make a break for the Union side. Sauntering back to camp nonchalantly, he casually fed and watered his horse, all the while looking around to assess the situation. Seeing that no camp guard had been posted, he left his coat hanging on a fence and strolled off into the brush. Once out of sight of the camp, he launched into a full sprint. Within fifteen minutes he reached the Tennessee River. Such was his natural curiosity that upon seeing the Tennessee for the first time he paused to gaze at it. Wet with perspiration from his mad dash, he approached the water's edge, and tearing off his shoes, trousers, and overshirt, plunged in. The intensity of the cold water caused him to gasp for breath. Realizing he needed to swim fast if he was to make it across the frigid river, he returned to shore and this time stripped down completely naked with the exception of his cap. It was a secesh cap that he had been given at Fort Pillow. Plunging in, he swam to an island in the middle of the river. There he frantically combed the brush for some means of conveyance. Miraculously, he found an old, leaky dugout canoe. He dragged it through the brush, taking care not to further damage the fragile vessel. Pushing off, he jumped in and allowed the current to carry him, nearly knee-deep in water, downstream. After drifting two miles he saw a man ploughing and hailed him. Upon seeing a naked boy in the rotten canoe who was waving frenziedly, the farmer thought he was a wild man and became frightened. With no help forthcoming, Spencer continued five miles farther. He encountered a man along the shore who gave him some shabby clothes and a piece of bread and bacon, the first food he had eaten since breakfast the previous day. From there he took off barefoot inland. For several miles he walked gingerly over a sharp, flinty road that lacerated his feet. At last, he found a Union man who put him upon a mule and took him thirteen miles up to Savannah where Grant was encamped.

"I was, at last, home," he sighed with relief.

The battle was in its second day and still raging when Spencer arrived. The first day Confederate forces, surging through the woods with wild abandon, had overwhelmed Grant's men. By midmorning Union soldiers had rallied, establishing a powerful defensive line called the Hornet's Nest that the Confederates were unable to break. The fighting had been vicious with heavy casualties on both sides. Almost every house in town was filled with wounded men, and hundreds more lay upon the ground crying and moaning in pain. General Albert Johnston himself had died on the battlefield when a ball severed an artery in his leg.

It wasn't until evening that Buell's men finally began arriving from Savannah. At the same time two Union gunboats came up and began bombarding Confederate positions. According to Grant, his forces had suddenly "nearly doubled in numbers and efficiency."[12]

On the second day of the battle, Grant launched a counterattack and began pushing the rebels back. Grant was in the field giving directions to his division commanders when Spencer came into his headquarters at Pittsburg Landing. Anxious to convey the strength and position of the enemy, Spencer loudly requested to be taken to Grant. But instead of being taken to the great general, he was placed under some trees and left to stand scantily clad shivering in the rain. Expecting a hero's welcome, he had been taken for a rebel spy instead.

By now the tide had turned, and Union forces were driving the Confederates back. At last Grant returned to his tent. Having stood in the rain for more than two hours, Spencer was finally taken into his tent under heavy guard. When given an opportunity to speak, Spencer explained he was a sailor assigned to the *Essex* when Captain Porter approved his scheme to infiltrate the Confederates at Columbus, Kentucky. He then assured Grant that, as he had been in the rear of the enemy's army for days closely observing their movements, no reinforcement of the Confederate force engaged in the battle was possible. The intelligence most likely confirmed what Grant had already concluded: that the Confederate attack had been more a mad dash than a sustainable military offensive. On April 8, the Confederates began to retreat, demoralized and in disarray, abandoning much of their equipment in the intractable mud as they withdrew. Shiloh would prove to be the costliest battle of the Western theater, with more than ten thousand killed on each side. But for Grant's failure to pursue the ragtag Confederate army, historians believe the war might have well ended there.[13]

Later, Spencer provided details of the rebel strongholds at Columbus, Island Number Ten, Fort Pillow, and other towns. Much of what he provided was no longer relevant except to demonstrate the veracity of his claims. Finally convinced he was no longer a rebel spy, Spencer was given "an awkwardly large but warm suit of clothes."[14] For the first night in a long time he slept in a warm bed. As he lay down to sleep, he thought of all that had transpired since he had jumped the *Essex* four months earlier. Though it seemed like a dream, his odyssey behind enemy lines was only just beginning.

Chapter Twelve
VICKSBURG

"When Vicksburg falls, with it falls the whole South West."
—Flag Officer Charles Henry Davis

IN MID-APRIL 1862, SPENCER RETURNED TO NAVAL duty in St. Louis where the *Essex* was undergoing repairs. So, too, was Captain Porter whose wounds turned out to be far more severe than first thought. For weeks his vision was so impaired it was feared he would be permanently blind. Nevertheless, he insisted on recuperating on board the gunboat so he could direct repairs of the ship from his sick bed. While surgeon Thomas Rice tended to Porter, his executive officer Robert Riley supervised the repair work of the ship.[1]

This time Porter sought to create an indestructible vessel. He lengthened the ship by forty feet to two hundred five feet, rebuilt the three boilers, and placed them below the waterline. He also raised her casemates from six and a half feet to a towering seventeen and a half feet in height, the highest of any Union vessel in Western waters. The forward casemate was rebuilt with wood thirty inches thick, covered with India rubber one inch thick, and plated with iron plating nearly an inch thick. The roof was bombproofed and the conically shaped pilothouse buttressed with wood eighteen inches thick topped with one-inch India rubber and one-

and-three-quarter-inch iron plating. With false sides, no steam ram could harm her, and with forty-two watertight compartments she was virtually unsinkable. Finally, the ship was armed with three nine-inch Dahlgren guns, one ten-inch Dahlgren, two fifty-pound rifled Dahlgrens, one long-range thirty-two-pound gun, and one twenty-four-pound howitzer. Low, squat, and massively bulwarked, the *Essex* wasn't pretty but it was formidable. A floating fortress.

Spencer had high expectations that his valorous service behind enemy lines would be rewarded with a promotion. As anticipated, on April 28, a recovered Porter signed a commission making Spencer a master's mate (petty officer) at a salary of $40 a month, twice his former pay. Until the ship returned to service, Spencer served as an amanuensis to Porter who had recognized the boy's literary talents. In the morning Spencer picked up and delivered the commander's mail and handled all his correspondence. In his spare time, he wrote a short history of the Porter family that he later published in the *St. Louis Democrat*. Once the ship embarked, Spencer would report directly to first master and executive officer, Robert Riley, who navigated the ship. Normally, a mate ensured the ship was properly outfitted for the voyage. He hoisted and lowered the anchor and docked and undocked the ship. He also examined the ship's rigging daily, notifying the master if there were problems with the sails, masts, ropes, or pulleys. But in Spencer's case, as the lowest ranked of the master's mates, he became one of four assistants to Riley.

As he had not been paid since the previous September, Spencer was also expecting a windfall in back pay. All of this good news, as well as his remarkable journey as a spy in Secessia,* he recounted in

---

* The term "Secessia" was a pejorative for the Confederacy.

a long letter to Kitty, along with some money. "Never *again* doubt your brother," he admonished.[2] To his father, now bedridden with the rheumatism that had so long afflicted him, he sent what money he could, assuring him of more when his back pay came through. To his mother, Mary, in Utica he sent an invitation to visit in St. Louis. She accepted, bringing Freddy and Lilly with her the first week of June. A week later his pay came through in the form of gold. After sending some money to his father, he married Mary Manahan on June 14. The newlyweds spent a few days in the city on a quick honeymoon before Spencer reported back to duty.

While the *Essex* was still in dry dock, events on the ground were conspiring to dictate her next engagement in battle. Upon learning of the retreat of Beauregard from Corinth, the Confederates retreated from Fort Pillow to Memphis on June 4. At dawn the next day, Union Flag Officer Charles H. Davis, who had replaced a wounded Admiral Foote, took possession of Fort Pillow and pursued the fleeing Confederates up the Mississippi to Memphis. As Davis approached the city, his gunboats were met with heavy fire from the Confederate flotilla. The sound of booming cannons and whizzing shells drew thousands of nearby residents to the edge of the bluffs above the river. As gunships exchanged volleys and rams rushed at one another like wild beasts, the residents cheered the rebels on. Ninety minutes later, however, the Confederate fleet was destroyed, including one of two rams under construction, the *Tennessee*. The other, the *Arkansas*, was towed out of harm's way up the Yazoo River to Yazoo City, Mississippi. There Commander Isaac Brown, a thirty-year veteran of the US Navy, oversaw the completion of its construction. Over the next five weeks Brown proceeded to make the *Arkansas* the most formidable naval weapon in the Confederate fleet. Using local craftsmen and two hundred soldiers he placed thirty-six-foot, three-inch-thick dovetailed railroad ties on its sides, backed by heavy timber. With its battery of ten heavy guns—fore, aft, and sides—the ironclad ram became the most feared vessel on the Mississippi.

Meanwhile on June 27 the *Essex* was ready to be put into service and her trial trip went without a hitch. Having fully recovered, Porter was now itching to return to battle. He would not have to wait long. On July 5 he and his crew of 145 men received orders to join Commodore Davis's fleet of rams and gunboats in an attack on Vicksburg, Mississippi, the last obstacle to Union control of the entire Mississippi River Valley. The following day the *Essex* left St. Louis, stopping at Cairo, Illinois, to take on ammunition and stores. On the evening of the ninth, it steamed down the Mississippi, arriving four days later at the anchorage ground of Davis's fleet above Vicksburg. Also joining Davis was Flag Officer David G. Farragut, who had just swept victoriously up the Mississippi in a whirlwind, wresting New Orleans, Baton Rouge, and Natchez from Confederate control.

But heavily fortified Vicksburg would not fall as easily. Sixteen thousand rebel soldiers under Earl Van Dorn precluded an assault by the infantry. A naval attack faced a no less daunting battery of two hundred guns placed on the sides and top of the bluff for three miles overlooking the river. What the Union needed was a combined assault from land and sea but Major General Benjamin Butler insisted on the need to keep his troops in New Orleans and was only willing to spare three thousand—hardly enough to attack the town.

On the evening of the fourteenth, Porter and one of his officers went ashore directly opposite Vicksburg to reconnoiter the city's batteries. On his reconnaissance he took two enemy prisoners who provided information that the dreaded *Arkansas* was on its way down the Yazoo River and would arrive the following day to attack Davis's fleet.

Armed with the intelligence, at dawn the next day Farragut sent the gunboats *Tyler* and *Carondelet* up the Yazoo to reconnoiter. Six miles upstream the ships encountered the *Arkansas*. Having no armor whatever, the *Tyler* quickly withdrew, leaving the *Carondelet* to engage the Confederate ironclad. After an hour of firing, the *Arkansas* attempted to ram her but abandoned the attempt after finding the water too shallow. Now the *Arkansas* passed boldly through Farragut's fleet, firing and receiving fire as she passed. So protected was she, it was said that shells "fell as harmless from her sides and deck as hail from the walls of a fortress."[3] In the running battle several ships were seriously damaged including the *Tyler* and the *Carondelet,* which limped back to Cairo for repairs. The *Arkansas* then turned its guns on the *Essex.* But the attack had little effect, thanks to heavy bulwarks Porter had installed. The *Essex* answered with a thirty-two-pound steel plug that struck the *Arkansas* stack and a ten-inch shell that exploded on her quarter, causing some damage and wounding Commander Brown. Just as the *Essex* attempted to get up the steam to finish off the Confederate ram, its boiler malfunctioned, forcing it to dock under the cover of two batteries for repairs and ammunition.

Over the next several days, Davis and Farragut rained mortar on Vicksburg at a rate of three thousand shells a day. While this bombardment reduced the town to rubble, it had little effect against the Confederate batteries.[4] Farragut even attempted to cut off the city's batteries by digging a canal at an oxbow of the river in the hope the river would be diverted to a new channel, but his efforts were thwarted by a summer drought that caused the river to drop precipitously.

As the stalemate dragged on, Commander Charles Ellet Jr. of the *Queen of the West* proposed a bold plan to Davis: because of its invincibility, the *Essex* would attack the *Arkansas* at close quarters while Davis's fleet attacked the upper forts and Farragut the lower forts to draw some of the heavy fire from the *Essex*. Just before dawn on July 22, Porter lifted anchor and steamed slowly downriver past Davis's fleet with the *Queen of the West* in the rear. Above Vicksburg he turned the bend of the river and came within range of the city's upper batteries. According to Spencer:

> *The Essex, unassisted, ran the blockade within musket-shot of batteries mounting seventy-two guns and an almost impregnable gun-boat of heavier battery than our own, carrying ten guns. We got up anchor at four A. M. 22d of July . . . steaming down towards the point above Vicksburg, off which lay the Western flotilla, Flag-Officer Davis. The rebel boat (the Arkansas) lay under the upper batteries, and, together with them, opened fire upon us as soon as we came in range. Our ship, meanwhile, had been thoroughly prepared for action, every port being closed, every man and officer at his station, all ready.*[5]

Beneath a storm of shells, the *Essex* made straight for the *Arkansas,* which remained moored, reserving the fire of her own guns for closer quarters. As the *Essex* neared, the *Arkansas* unleashed her forward battery of nine-inch guns. Confident in his redesign of the ship to withstand the pounding, Porter pressed forward with all speed intending to ram her with his prow. Moments before impact, however, the *Arkansas* released her bow line and swung out into the stream causing the *Essex* to glance off the ship and careen headlong into an embankment where her engines sputtered and died. Fortunately, just seconds before, the *Essex* had gotten off three rounds from her nine-inch bow guns. This volley ripped apart the iron plating of the *Arkansas,* injuring and killing eight of Brown's men and injuring several more. Some men of the *Arkansas* could be seen fleeing a fire on board, and its guns went silent. The *Queen of the West* had been delayed in the encounter, Ellet having misinterpreted a hand signal from Davis as an order to withdraw. As the *Arkansas* began to slip way downstream, the *Queen of the West* finally came up and attempted to ram her but managed only to deliver a glancing blow that did little damage to the rebel ram.

Meanwhile, the *Essex* lay helplessly ashore midway between the upper and lower batteries as the Confederates unleashed a merciless barrage, striking the casemates. The shells exploded so near the ports, in the words of Spencer, so "as to throw a continual lurid glare upon the darkened decks."[6] Shards of wood and pieces of broken shells flew in every direction, becoming deadly projectiles.

All this time, much to the exasperation of Porter and his crew, Davis's fleet had inexplicably remained in anchorage above Vicksburg. Farragut, too, was nowhere to be seen. With little support to divert the heavy shelling, the *Essex* and its crew lay exposed to thunderous fire for ten terrifying minutes. Porter ordered his men to lay down on the deck for cover. He had to think fast. To remain in his present position amounted to suicide, as one hundred siege guns were mercilessly bearing down on them. Just then the ship's engines revived and, with no other option, Porter resolved to run the two-mile gauntlet past the lower Confederate batteries, hugging the shoreline for protection. Miraculously, the vessel passed through with little damage or loss of life. Once beyond the batteries, to the crew's frustration, they spotted the Union fleet, according to Spencer, "lying quietly at anchor, tranquil spectators of the fiery gauntlet we had run."[7] The *Arkansas* had quietly slipped upstream, damaged but not destroyed.

So thoroughly had Porter reinforced his craft that the *Essex* had sustained little damage despite having taken an astonishing five thousand shells and shot. However, the wheelhouse and chimney, as well as all the vessel's iron plating, were pockmarked with shell explosions and cannon shot of every caliber. One shell had lodged in her side and exploded, killing one and wounding several of the crew. Another, a sixty-eight-pound cannon ball, had struck the port-quarter aft, penetrating the iron casing to the executive officer's cabin where it demolished the wardroom and wheelhouse before finally lodging in the starboard side under the iron plating.

The Union's failure to destroy the *Arkansas* sparked bitter recriminations among the fleet commanders. Charles Ellet, the commander of the *Queen of the West*, blamed Davis, who in turn faulted Farragut for not lending support striking the upper batteries.[8] Whoever was to blame, the second attempt to take Vicksburg had been an utter failure.

With the river level continuing to fall and many of his men sick with malaria, Farragut gave up on taking Vicksburg. In a letter to the Secretary of War, Farragut wrote that to attack the *Arkansas* again "would be madness."[9] Upon hearing the Union army was abandoning its mission, Porter, probably miffed to say the least in having risked so much for nothing, wrote Commodore Davis for clarification. In reply, Davis ordered him to cruise between Vicksburg and New Orleans and make the latter his headquarters. As Farragut's war ships descended toward New Orleans, the *Essex* guarded the rear against a possible attack from the *Arkansas* that was lurking, like an angry beast, four miles away. Brigadier General Thomas R. Williams was ordered to return with his men— also suffering from malaria—to Baton Rouge.

Over the next two weeks, the *Essex* quietly patrolled the river with the gunboats *Cayuga*, *Kineo*, and *Katahdin*, and the paddle-wheel steamer *Sumter*, which had been captured from the Confederates at the Battle of Memphis in June. Just before dawn on August 5, the crew heard firing in the direction of General William's garrison at Baton Rouge. Confederate General John C. Breckinridge was attempting to regain the city by attacking the arsenal with fifteen thousand men. Porter was not at all surprised, having earlier expressed to Williams his concern that the city was vulnerable and in need of fortification, advice that had gone ignored. With only 2,600 men to defend the city, Union forces were forced to fall back from the town. During the retreat, Williams was killed.

Upon learning of the enemy advance, Porter unleashed his heavy guns on the city, forcing the rebels to retreat. Just then a heavy column of smoke upriver gave Porter notice of the approach of his old antagonist, the *Arkansas,* which had been delayed by engine malfunction. While at Vicksburg, the deck of the *Arkansas* had been plated with iron and covered with cotton bales, making her even less vulnerable than before. Porter had been keeping a wary eye out for the ram, knowing full well that if the rebel behemoth struck the *Essex,* he would certainly be sunk. Determined to strike first, Porter proceeded upstream where he found the *Arkansas* moored to the shore undergoing yet another engine repair. As Porter approached, the engines of the *Arkansas* suddenly sprang to life. She streamed straight toward the *Essex* intending to ram her. Porter ordered his gunners to take good aim and, with the heavy shells from his nine-inch bow guns, struck the rudder engines squarely, forcing the *Arkansas* to spin out of control and retreat into a small bayou. Porter continued to fire, eventually striking the *Arkansas*'s ports, where it ignited some cotton and wool. The ship was soon ablaze, sending plumes of smoke and flames high into the air as her crew fled for land. As the *Arkansas* lit up, the fire reached her magazine of eighteen thousand pounds of powder, touching off an explosion that resounded throughout the valley like a thunder clap. "Such a sight! It was the grandest I ever beheld," Porter's acting first mate exclaimed.[10] Triumphant at last over the *Arkansas,* Porter and his jubilant crew turned and headed downstream.

The withdrawal of Davis and Farragut's fleet from Vicksburg had essentially left the Confederates in undisputed control of a four-hundred-mile stretch of the Mississippi River from Helena, Arkansas, to Port Hudson, Louisiana. Confederates were now busy digging defenses to maintain their communication with the Western states and access supplies coming down the Red River, which emptied into the rebel-controlled section of the Mississippi River fifty miles above Port Hudson.

After making repairs and taking on stores at Baton Rouge on August 9, 1862, the *Essex* went up to procure coal at Bayou Sara, Louisiana, the only place Porter could obtain any coal outside New Orleans. Ever since the fall of New Orleans, towns along the river were seething with hostility toward the Union. The presence of the *Essex* caused considerable grumbling among inhabitants, especially since supplies, which had just arrived from western Louisiana, were on the levee awaiting shipment to Generals Daniel Ruggles and Breckinridge in the interior. To quell the unrest, Porter sent for the Mayor of Bayou Sara, to whom Porter proposed a reciprocal arrangement: he would guarantee the personal safety of the city's inhabitants and respect for their property in return for the coal lying at the wharf, which would be supplied to the *Essex.* In addition, all Union prisoners held by the municipal authorities would be turned over to Porter. In return, Porter pledged to obtain a cessation of Union attacks on the Confederate population in Baton Rouge, which had done so much to sour residents toward Union soldiers. Reluctantly, the mayor agreed. After the prisoners were delivered, Porter took on fuel and descended to Baton Rouge to urge its commander to desist from attacks on the local population, leaving the *Sumter* to protect the remaining coal.

As soon as Porter departed Bayou Sara, inhabitants began agitating for an attack on the *Sumter*. While at anchor, the *Sumter* somehow ran aground. Fearing an attack by the townsmen, officers and crew abandoned ship. When news of the abandonment of the *Sumter* reached Porter, he hastened back to find the steamer in flames. Rebel guerillas had shot and wounded several of the fleeing crew and burned the coal on the wharf to prevent it from falling into Union hands.

While in Bayou Sara, Porter learned Union forces had begun to withdraw from Baton Rouge. He immediately dispatched a message to Colonel Paine, the commander at Baton Rouge, urging him to delay his evacuation of the city. Porter then requested the commander at New Orleans send gunboats to prevent the erection of the batteries and to take out the ferries bringing supplies from Texas and the Red River Valley to rebels on the east side of the Mississippi. With no gunboats forthcoming and Paine continuing with his withdrawal, Porter took the *Essex* up to Port Hudson where he found the reported earthworks in the process of construction. As Porter began firing on the earthworks, the heavy ten-inch gun burst.

Spencer now saw an opportunity to distinguish himself. He approached Porter and asked for permission to slip ashore and destroy one of the main Red River ferries that was furnishing supplies to the garrison at Port Hudson. This time, however, Porter nixed the idea as too dangerous. Spencer replied, "You know, Captain, I have been in many a tight place and yet have always got away. Let me try."[11] Against his better instincts, Porter acquiesced, giving Spencer forty armed men and a small boat for the mission.

On the morning of August 15, 1862, Spencer and the men set out in the small boat with a dinghy in tow. When they neared the ferry, he and four men jumped into the dinghy and rowed her alongside the ferry. No crew was aboard and, according to Porter, they set her ablaze.[12] Brimming with hubris from their triumph, they then did something rash. Continuing in their dinghy the five rowed ashore—most likely at Spencer's urging. For what purpose is not clear, though perhaps it was to gather intelligence on the batteries. A few paces from the boat they encountered two men who professed to be Unionists. While they talked, a company of rebels suddenly burst from the bushes and seized Spencer and his companions. His capture occurred just a week after his twenty-first birthday.

Chapter Thirteen
A SPY AND DESERTER

"The Reb authorities scared up this greatest wonder,
Made it a prison, and named it Castle Thunder."
—From *Castle Thunder*, Anonymous

IT WAS JUST AFTER MIDNIGHT WHEN PORTER learned his men had been captured. The thirty-five other men, who had been waiting in the boat off shore to provide protection, had cowardly retreated out of fear the rebels would make good on their threat to hang any member of the *Essex* they captured. Porter immediately dispatched a gunboat from Baton Rouge to secure their release. The next day he dispatched a message to General Ruggles, the commander of the rebel army at Port Hudson, requesting a prisoner exchange. But having been assigned there for just two weeks to supervise the building of fortifications, Ruggles was uninterested in getting embroiled in negotiations over a prisoner.

On September 7, 1862, Porter steamed to New Orleans to seek assistance from Major General Benjamin Butler, the commander of Union forces in the city. Two days later Butler met with former Louisiana Governor Robert C. Wickliffe under a flag of truce to discuss a prisoner exchange. Wickliffe assured Porter that "his [Spencer's] person was sacred" and that an exchange was forthcoming. In the meantime, he said, Spencer was being held at Camp Moore, the main base of Confederate operations in eastern

Louisiana where 'he would receive all the considerations afforded to the most favored prisoners of war.'[1]

On the surface at least, prospects for Spencer's release looked promising. At the outset of the war, Lincoln had been adamantly opposed to prisoner exchanges, concerned it would imply de facto recognition of the Confederacy. For this reason, captured rebel soldiers were treated as pirates rather than prisoners of war. But as more and more reports of wretched conditions in Southern prisons reached Union prisoners' families, a public outcry arose for prisoner exchange. Faced with growing pressure, in July 1862 an agreement had been reached, the Dix-Hill Cartel that established the protocols for exchange of prisoners. By the time Spencer was captured, prisoner exchanges had become so common that prison camps on both sides were largely empty.

A week passed with no progress on his release. Little did Porter know that shortly after Spencer's imprisonment, he had been released on parole.[*] But when one of the engineers with whom he had worked on Island Number Ten recognized him, he was rearrested, this time on the far more serious charge of spying. This time he was sent to Pearl River prison in Jackson, Mississippi. Located in the ruins of a rickety covered bridge on stilts over the Pearl River, the prison was crowded, damp, and miserable. Because of its wood construction, Confederates would not allow any fires to be built for warmth. Not surprisingly, many prisoners became ill and died from exposure.

When he learned Spencer was in the notorious Pearl River prison charged with spying, Porter realized negotiations needed to

---

[*] Based on an arrangement used during the War of 1812, prisoners of war were often paroled but prohibited from taking up arms until properly exchanged.

be elevated to the highest level. Traveling overland with his personal secretary, J. Harry Wyatt, he arrived in New York where he briefed Secretary of the Navy Gideon Welles on Spencer's case. He also met with General Henry W. Halleck, head of the Department of the Mississippi, who took a keen interest in the case when he learned of Spencer's meritorious service. In dealing with numerous espionage cases that year, Halleck was of the firm opinion that a spy who had succeeded in escaping to the unit that employed him is not liable to punishment for that offense if subsequently captured by the enemy."[2*] In other words, while Spencer had indeed conducted espionage—something Halleck had readily acknowledged—he was captured as a soldier on the battlefield, not as a spy. In Halleck's logic, Spencer was not a spy—which was punishable by hanging—but a prisoner of war and thus subject to prisoner exchange.

Buoyed by the meeting with Halleck, Wyatt wrote Orville with comforting news: "The department have had full and explicit information of his services and noble character," he wrote. "I would not like to raise false hopes, yet I have still the conviction, from the inquiry made by the heads of the departments, that had he been sentenced by a court-martial the Confederate Government would have at once communicated the fact to our Government in reply to their interrogatories."[3]

Weeks passed and Spencer's parents still had no idea he was in prison, because the jailers were intercepting mail to and from his family.

While in prison, Spencer made a valuable ally in a Baptist pastor, Reverend William Crane, the rector of the St. Andrews church,

---

[*] Halleck's opinion was later adopted at The Hague Peace Conference in 1899.

who performed religious services every Sunday for the prisoners. By sheer happenstance, Crane was a nephew of Levi Cozzens, a cousin of Spencer's mother, though it is unclear if he was aware of their distant relations at the time. In any case, Crane developed a great liking for Spencer whom he found to be, in addition to intelligent and well-read, "a devoted Christian."[4] Three times a week Crane visited Spencer for two or three hours at a time, sometimes bringing his daughter along for the visit. He also furnished the young captive everything he requested from food to clothing and books. Among the books he brought were *John Bunyan's Complete Works* and a Greek grammar so Spencer could read the New Testament in the original. Crane's wife also paid regular visits to Spencer, bringing him bouquets of flowers on occasion. "[They] fill my eyes with pleasure," he rhapsodized, "for I have not seen any green plants for nearly eight months—not even a blade of grass—and they fill my cell with perfume." Through the minister's influence, Spencer hoped he would eventually be set free.

Crane also lent Spencer a prayer book bound in black muslin. On the blank pages Spencer began making short entries each day. One such entry read, "In close confinement eight weeks today. How well God has taught me what it means to 'glory in tribulation!'" And a week later: "Let me write it now—whether, at some future time, when free, I live to read it, or for some loved one— that through Christ's love there is no more fear in death, but an earnest hope that, if it please God, I may soon be free from this terrible warfare."[5] Strong though his faith was, with the threat of execution looming his mood swung wildly from feelings of inner calm one day to abject despondency the next. Although deeply depressed, outwardly he feigned cheerfulness and gratitude toward the numerous ministers and chaplains who visited him. During his long and lonely months of incarceration in

Jackson, Spencer never once uttered words of bitterness toward his captors.

In late September, Crane attempted to slip a letter from Spencer to his wife past the prison guards but was unsuccessful. That his parents were still in the dark as to his whereabouts four months later is evidenced by a letter his mother wrote to Porter in January of 1863:

Captain Porter,

Information is desired of Spencer Kellogg, fourth master of the *Essex*. We have not heard from him since the 9th of August. If anything has befallen him will you please direct information to his grandfather, L[evi]. Cozzens, Esq., Utica, New York, and greatly oblige his anxious mother and friends.[6]

Soon after, she received the devastating news: Spencer was being held in a Confederate jail charged with spying. Immediately, she wrote to Orville informing him of Spencer's dire situation, "with no gleam of hope for his life."[7] In contrast to Mary's grim pessimism, Orville was confident that Porter's close attention to the matter would result in a positive outcome. "Let us not despair of our noble boy," he admonished.[8] Orville turned to influential friends and colleagues in Kansas to intercede on his son's behalf. When Samuel Pomeroy, who was now the US senator from Kansas, learned of Spencer's plight, he contacted Lincoln and urged him to take action to secure his release. Since Lincoln had long been opposed to prisoner exchanges, it is unlikely he gave Pomeroy's request any consideration.

With no regular means of communication with their son, the family was now at the mercy of every bit of news and hearsay that

came their way. In late January one of the men who had been captured with Spencer was released on parole. He told William Cozzens that he had learned from a jailer in Jackson that Spencer had
already been hanged as a spy. Even though it was thirdhand news,
Mary and Orville took the news at face value and wrote to President Lincoln and Major General Nathaniel Banks, commander
of the Department of the Gulf, in the hope of obtaining details of
his trial and execution. Still Orville could not give up on his son
entirely. "I have some hope that he still lives and may be saved,"
Orville said.[9]

In late January an aide-de-camp of the prison commandant
informed Spencer that his trial would take place within ten
days. Two men were expected to testify against him, most likely
engineers with whom he had worked on the Mississippi islands.
Spencer knew that if this were the case then the weight of the tes-
timonies with regard to the charge of espionage would be damn-
ing. He now fully expected to be executed. He calmly began to
organize his affairs, sending his father instructions on the distri-
bution of his meager estate and ensuring arrangements were made
for his pension to go to his wife, Mary, in St. Louis. He even issued
instruction to settle outstanding minor debts to his *Essex* mates.
"My hope of seeing you [his parents] again is gone," he lamented.
"Yet God in kindness to you and in great and unmerited mercy
to me will not, I hope and trust, separate us forever."[10] The letter,
however, did not reach his parents who assumed, by now, their son
was dead.

As news of Spencer's incarceration spread, the extended Brown
family now rallied around Mary and Orville. A slew of letters came
pouring into Utica and Osawatomie offering moral support and
prayers. But in a letter to Mary in March, her sister, Cornelia, could
not refrain from questioning Spencer's judgment. "Poor boy," she

wrote. "It was bad enough to know he was suffering in the hands of the rebels in prison. . . . How can he so go among them a second time? It seems to me rather rash."[11] However true her observation, to a mother despairing over the fate of her eldest son, it must have come as a particularly insensitive rebuke.

Months passed and no trial came. At night Spencer slept fitfully in a vermin-infested cell and woke exhausted and despondent. When his boots wore out from pacing to and fro in his cell, a prisoner on death row bequeathed Spencer his pair. Father Crane sent two pairs of socks and some clothes to replace his worn-out ones—and more books. Spencer passed the time reading the books Crane brought and exercising a few minutes each hour to maintain his health in the damp quarters. He prayed to Jesus Christ to give him strength and hear his prayers. That other prisoners were being tried and executed was a disquieting reminder of the likely fate that awaited him. His mood continued to oscillate between hope one day and despair the next. "Last night, thank God, He gave me rest and this morning I enter fresh upon the duties of the day. My days of greatest darkness almost always follow feverish nights," he wrote.[12] Confined in squalid quarters and doomed to an almost certain death was at times too much to bear. "If God ever sets me free to live in the world," he wrote, "I hope and pray He will make me remember, every Sunday afternoon at least, to visit those in prison. If Christians but knew, as Paul did, the feelings of those shut up in prison, they would remember more often those 'in bonds.' There is no such commentary upon those words as the actual bitterness of confinement."[13]

On Tuesday, March 31, 1863, one of the prisoners was taken out and shot. "I know not how soon that, or a worse fate, may be my own," he fretted.[14] In spring the superintendent of the prison gave him permission to spend two hours a day walking in the courtyard outside his cell. To his dismay, he found his body had been greatly weakened by confinement.

In April his family received fresh hopes when one of the master's mates of the *Essex,* Matthew Snyder, told Orville he believed Spencer was still alive and in Jackson. At once Orville wrote Porter for more information. However, Porter could offer no encouragement but instead provided something of a consoling eulogy:

> *Mr. Kellogg was a most excellent officer and a brave man. I was assured on the word of honor of ex-Governor Wycliffe, of Louisiana, that he would be exchanged, but I have no doubt he has been most cruelly murdered by the rebels. I am now urging an investigation of the matter.*[15]

Despite believing the boy was dead, Porter nonetheless instructed his personal secretary to look further into his case. Having been good friends with Spencer both on (as a master's mate) and off the ship, Wyatt was only too happy to oblige.

In late May, Wyatt unearthed good news: After speaking with the former paymaster of the USS *Indianola,* C. Storrs, he was able to confirm that, as of March 15, Spencer was still alive. In February 1862, Storrs had been taken prisoner when the *Indianola* was destroyed on the Red River. He had recently been freed in a prisoner exchange. Just before his release from Jackson, Storrs had exchanged a few words with Spencer who had asked that some arrangement be made to provide for his wife who was in St. Louis. Storrs subsequently contacted the paymaster of the *Essex* to have his account forwarded to him so he could arrange to have Spencer's pay sent to his wife.

Wyatt immediately informed Porter of the news so that negotiations for his release could be resumed. William Cozzens wrote David D. Porter, William Porter's father, who had succeeded Davis as commander of the Western Flotilla, to urge an exchange. Yet Storrs simply had been a prisoner of war; Spencer by contrast was being charged with spying, a charge of which he would almost certainly be found guilty.

In May the family followed Grant's western campaign with baited breath. As part of his strategy to take Vicksburg, Grant first planned to eliminate the threat posed by General Joseph Johnston's six thousand greycoats at Jackson. Johnston had arrived on May 13 to counter the threat posed by Union forces gathering in the area. The very next day, however, twenty-five thousand Yankees under Major-General William T. Sherman and Major-General James M. McPherson launched a vicious attack and sent Johnston's men reeling in all directions.* When Union forces arrived at Pearl River prison, it was empty. But tantalizing traces of Spencer's presence there soon began to emerge. One of Grant's officers in the 2nd Brigade, General Joseph A. Mower, was given a packet of letters by a Catholic priest who had received them from Father Crane. These were the very first ones Spencer had written to William Cozzens and Mary Kellogg. There were also several pages of foolscap written in the form of a diary. Virtually every bit of space on the sheets was covered in Spencer's hand. In some cases, he wrote from top to bottom, then from bottom to top between the lines, and then by crossing the pages with lines that

---

* Sherman then began to do something for which he later became infamous: He set about systematically destroying all the infrastructure and factories in Vicksburg, as well as many homes and stores. (The St. Andrews church was completely destroyed in the conflagration.)

reached from end to end, evidence that it was not easy to obtain all the paper he needed. His letter to Mary read:

DEAR WIFE:

Through the kindness of Mr. Wheat, a minister, I am enabled to send you word where I am, and explain the meaning of my long silence.*

I could not write to you before, for I have been a prisoner over a month, and I am yet one, and, darling, may never see you again. Charged with being a spy, and without aid of any kind (except from God), it is not likely that I can escape a court-martial's usual sentence—'Guilty.'

Yet, darling, hope for the best, and remember, "He doeth all things well," and if I die here you may meet me in heaven. I have often gone to meet you, pet; could you not try to meet me there?

When you see Jack, tell him where I am, and ask him, for me, to tell my uncle also. Tell him he can get the Masonic jewels from my aunt, with whom I left them for safe-keeping. Give him my kind remembrances, and tell Mr. Cozzens that I recollect his kindness in days past....

And now, dear one, what can I say to comfort you? I long to see you so much, and think of you and pray for you very often. But our Father in heaven bless and care for and comfort you, since He leaves me no longer with you. He is both able and willing and has promised. Do not mourn for me too much; and remember, if we do not meet here we may in heaven....

---

* The name Wheat was a cover to protect Crane.

Do not grieve after me, but remember I am under the care of One who died for me, and that all things will work together for good to those that love Him.

Good-bye, darling! May God bless you and comfort you!

SPENCER [16]

By the time the letters reached William Cozzens in August 1863, he had already received fresh intelligence from an informant on a secret mission in the South regarding Spencer. Whether this is a cryptic reference to one of Pinkerton's agents in unclear. As Grant was marching on Jackson, the prisoners were secreted from Jackson to Montgomery, Alabama, and then to Cahaba Prison, an unsanitary former cotton warehouse near Selma, Alabama. In Selma, Cozzen's informant had spoken directly with Spencer whom he described as looking well but "in close confinement."[17] Spencer told him that he had repeatedly asked for a trial but as yet had none. Spencer handed him a letter to carry, but the informant later got into a "tight place" and was forced to destroy it.[18]

A week later Orville received a cryptic letter from Cozzens saying that he had received a letter from Spencer indicating that while he was still in prison he was "much nearer to home" than before and being well treated. Cozzens was reluctant to relay further details because the letter contained sensitive information that if divulged could "destroy his chances of ever being released and implicate others mentioned in the letter." Because the local newspapers were referring to Spencer as "one of the Yankee Hostages," Cozzens took this to mean he was not a prisoner. "I now have strong hopes of his speedy release from prison," he added jubilantly.[19]

But Cozzen's optimism was unjustified, for two weeks later William Porter received notice from the commissioner general of prisoners that Spencer was being held at Castle Thunder prison in Richmond, Virginia, awaiting trial on charges of espionage. The news couldn't have been worse. A former tobacco warehouse, Castle Thunder had been converted to a prison for deserters, spies, political prisoners, and those charged with treason—in short, the Confederacy's worst offenders, most of whom were on death row. There were also escaped slaves whom the Confederates were trying to return to their masters, and over a hundred women charged with treason or disloyalty.

Castle Thunder opened in August 1862 to absorb the overflow from nearby Castle Godwin. At the time of its opening, the prisoner exchange system had collapsed over Confederate anger at Lincoln's Emancipation Proclamation, causing prison populations to surge. At Castle Thunder, three thousand inmates lived in a facility designed for half that number. Not surprisingly, the facility was foul-smelling and unsanitary. Cells were cramped, about fifteen feet square, with boarded up windows. Prisoners slept on blankets or straw.

Castle Thunder acquired an ominous reputation early on as a dungeon of horrors. According to one local newspaper, the prison's name had been devised to instill a fear in prisoners, to denote an "Olympian vengeance upon offenders against her laws, and one which, in a point of sound, is as good as any that could be chosen."[20] Its commandant, Captain George W. Alexander, had been an engineer in the US Navy. When the war broke out, he resigned his position to join the Confederacy. As a volunteer in the army, Alexander led groups of other volunteers to capture Union boats around Baltimore. In 1861 he was captured while fighting near Baltimore. While awaiting execution by the Union Army, he escaped from prison by disguising as a Union soldier in a uniform smuggled in by his wife. He fled to Richmond where he served briefly as the city's assistant marshal before becoming commandant of the prison.

Bald with a trim beard and a stern gaze, Alexander was a complex man, a kind of Dr. Jekyll and Mr. Hyde. He ran the prison with an iron fist yet had the artistic sensitivity of the most refined aesthete. He was a poet, playwright, music composer, and dramatic actor in the Richmond theaters.[21] But in prison, Alexander was a stern disciplinarian who believed that the prison rules he laid out be strictly obeyed—and woe betide those who didn't. Overseeing the enforcement of his rules was chief detective John Capehart, an enormous man known as the "anti-Christ" because of the heavy club he regularly used on prisoners. Unruly prisoners were routinely subjected to physical punishment of varying degrees often carried out by Capehart. The most common form of punishment was flogging. A more severe punitive measure was being forced to wear, for days at a time, the barrel shirt, which consisted of a large, heavy flour barrel with apertures cut for the head and arms. Another was the sweat box, an enclosure in which prisoners were forced to stand in the hot sun. In winter they were forced to stand in the courtyard outside, with no sleep, for up to three days—sometimes in driving rain or snow. Not surprisingly, some died of pneumonia. Bucking, a type of hog tying, and stocking were also practiced, as was confinement in impossibly small cells where the prisoner could neither stand nor sit. Some were branded with hot irons. The worst offenders were hung from their thumbs for the better part of a day. By the time Spencer arrived, Alexander had already been investigated by a Confederate congressional committee for prisoner abuse. He was eventually acquitted, though not before many witnesses had testified as to the harsh nature of life at Alexander's prison.*

---

* After the war Alexander became a wanted man. He fled to Canada where he taught French to children. He returned to the United States after the general amnesty in 1872 and died in Laurel, Maryland, in 1895.

Despite Alexander's unsavory reputation as a commandant, Spencer got on well with him. It may have been because Spencer did not flout the rules—though he privately contemplated escape. Perhaps, too, the cultivated commandant saw in Spencer a refined and educated man like himself. Whatever the reasons, Alexander allowed him many privileges, such as giving him access to the daily papers and books.

When he first arrived in May, Spencer and three other prisoners were put into a large room with ninety inmates. One of them, also charged with spying, was James H. Sherman. Sherman had been an investigator in the National Detective Bureau, the Union's covert intelligence gathering agency, when he was captured and charged with being a spy. Sherman described the newly arrived Spencer as "a pale, careworn, reserved man heavily ironed."[22] Sherman gave him blankets for bedding and a large cavalry overcoat, and the two former spies quickly became friends.

Because the room was large, Spencer was able to exercise regularly and soon regained his spirits and strength.* He and other prisoners in good standing were also permitted access to tools with which they made combs, rings, and other trinkets they were permitted to sell. Spencer excelled so much at producing trinkets that he was able to convert them into hard cash, which he used to supplement his prison diet. He exhorted his fellow inmates to be of good cheer and enjoyed their pastimes of game and sport.

Within days of Spencer's incarceration at Castle Thunder, hope reemerged that he would be rescued. As part of his plan to take Richmond, Major General George B. McClellan had swept up the Virginia Peninsula and driven back General Joseph John-

---

* Sherman escaped in February 1865, "broken down and used" from his ordeal at Castle Thunder.

ston's seventy-five-thousand-man Army of Northern Virginia. By late May 1863, Johnston's men had fallen back behind the Chickahominy River into defensive positions north and east of Richmond. With McClellan's army looming on the outskirts of the city, it looked as if the Confederate capital might fall. Fortunately for the Confederates, heavy rains had made the Chickahominy passable only at the bridges. Knowing he could not endure a prolonged siege, Johnston decided to attack an exposed flank on the south bank before Union reinforcements could arrive from Fredericksburg. At daybreak on May 31, Johnston attacked. McClellan's men would have been "torn to pieces" in one historian's estimation, but for the fact that Johnston had failed to give his generals written orders, creating delays and confusion among Confederates.[23] The fighting was fierce with heavy losses on both sides. By afternoon of the second day, the Confederates managed to thwart McClellan's advance on Richmond. Although the Battle of Seven Pines, as it was called, was inconclusive, eleven thousand men died in the fighting, second only to Shiloh in the number of casualties. When news of McClellan's retreat reached Castle Thunder, Spencer came to the grim realization that his last hope of being rescued had evaporated.

During his entire time in Confederate prisons, Spencer had not received a single letter from his wife, Mary. He had only received one that was sent shortly after he left St. Louis to return to duty more than a year earlier. He found her silence inexplicable, yet he continued to write or send messages to her through others. Shortly after arriving at Castle Thunder, Spencer now sent Mary a final farewell, saying he fully expected to be executed and would not see her again.

Oh! my darling, do not grieve for me as one that is lost, but think often of me and try to meet me above. We had happy

hours together, darling; God grant they not be the last.... I
have asked my father or my uncle to see to the money that I left
for you. I hope you will be pleased ... I know how bad—how
hard—will be your grief; but, darling remember what I tell
you; when your heart seems bowed and broken, when you have
not a friend left in the world, then pray to Christ, who is a kind
and good Friend..... If you love me, darling, try to come to
me. Good-bye! God bless you! Your Husband.[24]

Mary would not receive the message, written on a leaf of the
Bible, until 1867.

As the months passed, Spencer once again entertained renewed
hope he might be spared. After all, he reasoned, he had been in
Confederate prisons for over a year and was still alive. Commandant Alexander, moreover, showed him every kindness and seemed
well disposed to the young man from Kansas. One day, however,
he and James Sherman were walking for exercise when Spencer
noticed a man observing him through a window. At sight of the
man he instantly became agitated, for it was one of the engineers
with whom he had worked on Island Number Ten. Noticing his
unease, Sherman led him out of sight of the stranger. "If that man
has recognized me," Spencer said, "my days are numbered." Not
long after, a lawyer met with Spencer and bluntly told him that
after studying the case against him, there was no use in making
any defense because he would unequivocally be found guilty
and hanged.

On September 24, 1863, Reverend William Scandlin, an
agent with the US Sanitary Commission, a relief agency that supported sick and wounded Union soldiers, sent a telegram to Utica
stating that Spencer had been tried and found guilty of spying
and desertion. According to Scandlin, the trial had taken place

on September 18. Two men had testified against Spencer, eliminating any possibility of doubt as to his guilt as a spy. His sentence: death by hanging with no possibility for remission. As if Spencer were already dead, Scandlin insensitively forwarded the gold ring his wife Mary had given him as well as some handiwork he had made while in prison. "I can see little for him," he closed with grim finality.[25]

Refusing to give up on Spencer, Orville and Levi fired off a frenzy of telegrams and letters—to William Porter, Halleck, and Secretary of War Edwin Stanton—requesting their intervention in a desperate last ditch attempt to save Spencer. He had also appealed to Roscoe Conkling, US senator from New York, to write to Secretary Stanton on Spencer's behalf. Using Halleck's argument, Orville maintained that Spencer was not a spy and should be treated as a prisoner of war. In response Stanton sent an immediate telegram to General S. A. Meredith, agent for the Exchange of Prisoners, ordering him to seek a suspension of the execution until the facts of the case could be established. "There must be some mistake in the matter," he added.[26] As the final hours drew near, Orville rushed off a letter to Spencer reassuring him that the family was doing all it could to save him.

Meanwhile, Spencer was preparing for his last days at Castle Thunder. Since his trial he still had not heard of the sentence but nonetheless expected his time on earth to be short. Most of the time, he immersed himself in Scripture, often reading aloud and marking notable passages. Entire afternoons were spent in prayer. In late September he finalized his last will and testament, first drafted while in the Jackson prison. He sent a letter to his father asking him to draw his pay from the government and invest it in US bonds, the interest of which was to be paid semiannually to his wife. Upon Mary's death, the principal was to go to Freddy.

He also asked J. Harry Wyatt to direct his remaining possessions to Levi Cozzens and to use his back pay to reimburse shipmates of the *Essex* for loans outstanding. To Kitty went his prayer book, and to his wife Mary his Bible, which he had arranged a fellow prisoner to deliver upon his release. On Sunday he attended church services with his fellow prisoners. His only desire to continue living was so that he might be able to tell his family and wife how he had wronged them and to seek their forgiveness. When Spencer told his fellow inmate he expected to be executed, many began to weep. Yet he himself remained stoic. "I look past the gloom of the dark valley," he wrote, "and find cheer in the hope of the better world."[27]

Tuesday, September 21, was the day of his sentencing. Commandant Alexander sentenced him to death by hanging on Friday, September 25. On the day of his sentencing, Reverend Scandlin arrived at the prison, it seems, in a last-minute attempt to obtain a reduced sentence for the boy. If such was his intention, nothing came of it, though the reverend was permitted to hold a service for Spencer and a hundred prisoners in the attic of Castle Thunder. After the service, Spencer expressed to Scandlin his conviction; he would receive the death penalty, adding stoically, "My peace is made with God. I yield my life a willing, cheerful sacrifice upon the altar of the nation. The risk I knew; the responsibility I took; I will not shrink from the result."[28] By a strange mistake, the next day he was taken into town to testify as a witness in a trial. He was grateful for the error, for the trip to town gave him some fresh air and a brief respite from the depressing confines of his cell.

In his last days, Commandant Alexander showed Spencer every kindness. He allowed him to eat at his table and gave him a large, well-lit room where he was permitted to read books and the daily papers. He also allowed him to send two final telegrams. To Mary he bid farewell and urged her to correspond with Kitty. To his father he wrote:

Dear Father:

God bless and comfort you. Remember me kindly and respectfully to all my dear friends and relations. Tell Kitty I hope to meet her again. Take care of Freddy for me. Put him often in remembrance of me.

Dear Mother, good-bye! God comfort you, my Mother, and bless you with the love of happy children.

Farewell, my Father! We meet again by God's mercy.

Spencer Kellogg[29]

On September 26, Orville and Levi traveled to Washington in the hope they could induce Stanton to save the boy. They went by way of New York where they were joined by William Porter who intended to go directly to Lincoln to intervene in the case based on the valuable service Spencer had rendered the Union. Wyatt was somewhere in the South, attempting, by some means, to save Spencer "if it cost him his life."[30]

On Monday, September 28, Orville and Porter arrived at the office of General Halleck, now General-in-Chief of the Union army. Halleck told them that Spencer was still alive and that the rebels would not dare execute him. "Mr. Brown, your son is safe," he said. "All the power of this Government will be employed to protect him."[31] Halleck told them that they had imprisoned a rebel and threatened to retaliate if Spencer was hanged. Orville then attempted to send a telegram to his son but was so distraught he was unable to put words to paper and gave up.

Halleck was as far as the two men took their case. If Porter requested an audience with Lincoln, there is no indication the two ever met to discuss the matter. Having done all they could in Washington and being reassured by the government, Porter and Orville returned by train to New York. Over dinner together, Porter said he was planning to promote Spencer. Pointing to Spencer's naval cap at his side, he said affectionately, "That was your son's cap. Before he left me, I proposed to exchange with him because his cap had a nice oil-cloth cover; so the insignia of rank were changed and I took his cap and he mine."[32] Porter then went on to relate to Orville an example of Spencer's courageous indifference to danger, telling him of the time when the *Essex* was disabled and lying under the pounding of the Vicksburg batteries and receiving no support from the fleet above, Spencer volunteered to go on deck and learn where Davis's squadron was. By Porter's permission he went and, while shells rained down on the ship, took a calm survey of the river and saw that no assistance was forthcoming. It was his brave action that led Porter to decide to run the gauntlet of batteries that saved his own vessel.

After dinner the two parted ways. Orville went to see William Cozzens. Upon arrival Cozzens asked, "Have you seen the *Evening Post*?"[33]

Little did Orville and Porter know that while they were on their way to Washington, Spencer was on his way to the gallows at Camp Lee on the west side of Richmond. On September 25, at eleven o'clock, a detail of one hundred men under Captain Potts from the City Battalion marched from Castle Thunder with Spencer in custody. Union style to the last, Spencer was clad in the dark blue coat with brass buttons that James Sherman had given him, a blue checkered shirt, light blue pants, and a black wool cap. He was placed in a carriage with Dr. J. L. Burrows of the local Baptist Church, the prison chaplain J. T. Carpenter, Detective John Capehart, and another officer. According to Sherman, at the last minute, Carpenter, who looked up to Spencer, offered to take his place on the gallows. Guarded front and rear by mounted soldiers from the City Battalion, the cortege moved up Main Street with the drum corps on the right followed by two companies of infantry. Behind them was a crowd of men, women, and children eager to see the execution of the Union spy. Little did Spencer know that in the crowd was forty-five-year-old Elizabeth "Crazy Bet" Van Lew, a Union spy who had helped prisoners escape from Richmond's Libby Prison. As they neared the scaffold, Van Lew heard Spencer say to one of his minders, "Did you ever pass through a tunnel under a mountain? My passage, my death, is dark, but beyond all in light and bright."[34]

At 12:30 PM the procession reached the gallows where a large crowd of men women had already gathered. When the carriage halted about a hundred yards from the scaffold, the crowd rushed up, hoping to get a glimpse of the young spy as he sat with his head resting on his hand. After ten minutes all was ready and the party proceeded to the scaffold. Commandant Alexander read the charges against the accused and the sentence of the court-martial: "to be hanged by the neck until dead."[35] Dr. Burrows then offered a short prayer at the conclusion of which a visibly shaken Spencer mounted the scaffold. Behind him was John Capehart. So that Capehart could admit the noose over his head, Spencer took off his hat and threw it aside. As the hat fell off the scaffold, it struck a gentleman standing below. Turning quickly, Spencer bowed and said, "Excuse me, sir." After the rope was arranged around his neck, Capehart began tying his arms behind his back to which Spencer calmly remarked, "Isn't this hard, captain?" His ankles were then tied together and his hat

---

* Although Confederates were suspicious of Van Lew, she was never discovered and operated a successful espionage network until the end of the war.

given back to him. Capehart then bid farewell to Spencer and left. A black man then mounted the scaffold with a ladder and proceeded to fasten the rope to the upper beam, Spencer looking on, now with the greatest composure. After the rope was fastened, the man was coming down when Spencer looked up at it and remarked, "This won't break my neck. Tisn't more than a foot fall. Doctor, I wish you would come up and arrange this thing. I don't want to have a botched job of it." The rope was rearranged and the cap placed over his head. Spencer then bowed his head and engaged a few seconds in prayer. At the conclusion he raised himself, and, standing perfectly erect, announced in a clear voice, "All ready!"[36]

Just before one o'clock, the drop opened and Spencer was launched into oblivion. For a few seconds he struggled, his body twitching and jerking spasmodically. Then all went still. In the eerie silence his lifeless body now swayed to and fro as the rope creaked on the post above. After thirty minutes the rope was cut and his body was examined by a physician who pronounced him dead. His body was placed in a plain coffin and laid to rest at Oakwood Cemetery in Richmond.

On Sunday, October 18, a funeral service was held for Spencer in Adams, New York. Apart from Rocky, who was serving in the Union Army in Pine Bluff, Arkansas, Spencer's entire family was there including his wife, Mary, now with a child Spencer never knew.* Mary Kellogg would die before receiving his final letters addressed to her.

---

* Rocky had enlisted in the cavalry in Kansas soon after Sumter. After serving three years, he was injured and reenlisted in Winfield Scott Hancock's 1st Veteran Corp that allowed partially disabled soldiers to continue to perform light duties. He retired in a soldiers' home in Bath, New Mexico.

EPILOGUE

IN THE DAYS FOLLOWING SPENCER'S DEATH, ORVILLE wandered the streets of New York City distraught and in anguish. "I am suffering very much," he wrote his family, "and go about groaning aloud when alone."[1] Hoping to retrieve his son's body, he had written the Commissary General of Prisoners but to no avail. A recently released Richmond prisoner told him that Spencer had given Reverend Scandlin a ring and a message for his family but feared the rebels would callously withhold even this consolation. Each day Orville visited a Protestant church on Fulton Street for a noon prayer meeting seeking relief from the burden of his grief and meaning in the loss of his eldest son. "He put down his life for the cause," became his common refrain when referring to Spencer.[2] If Orville had ever experienced any remorse for his abolitionist beliefs, beliefs that indirectly led to Spencer's demise, he never expressed them to friends or in his writings.

As public interest in Spencer's life grew, Orville soon found a way to turn his son's loss into something positive. In the months after Spencer's execution requests for information about his contribution to the war effort began pouring in from journalists and writers around the country, including the popular histo-rian Benson J. Lossing. When the New York State Legislature requested that Orville prepare a biography of his son for the state archives, Orville responded by offering to compile biographical sketches not only of Spencer but of all New York natives who had fallen in the war, including New Yorkers who had found their way into the military from other states.

Orville had quit Kansas in April 1861, "thoroughly exhausted in resources and health."[3] Ironically, he never returned to live in the place he had poured so much of his heart and soul or the town he had created from prairie dust. Friends near and far tried to comfort him by praising his work in Kansas. From Litchfield, his brother Henry Wood wrote: "You can look back to the days of your youth when in Litchfield your whole soul seemed engaged in saving men and when your work seemed greatly blest and can but think that souls are saved through your instrumentality."[4] Referring to the abolitionists in Kansas, Wood continued in language laced with biblical allusions, "Let the professors of religion awake to the all absorbing theme of saving the immortal spirits of their fellow men. Then shall their light break forth as the morning, and their health shall spring forth speedily and their righteousness shall go before them. The glory of the Lord shall be their reward."[5] Since Kansas had achieved statehood, he continued to travel throughout the Northeast to raise money for the state. He always believed Stephen Douglas was a great man, his one mistake having been to pass the Kansas-Nebraska Act out of a desire to win the presidency.

In 1867, James Sherman sent Orville the letters that Spencer had sent to his sister Kitty. He also sent the prayer book that Spen-cer had given to him for safekeeping before his death. Spencer had written a diary in it. Just why it took Sherman so long to forward them to the bereft family is unclear. Two years later, Sherman began a correspondence with Orville in which he shared memories of his time with Spencer at Castle Thunder. Using the information furnished by Sherman, in addition to Spencer's diary and letters culled from former shipmates on the *Essex* and cellmates at the Jackson and Castle Thunder prisons, Orville began to compile a biography of his son titled *Union Spy and Scout*. He spent several years seeking a publisher but found no takers.

Orville dedicated the final years of his life to memorializing those antislave fighters who had fallen in Kansas and the Civil War. He had kept up a running correspondence with some of the early pioneers who felt themselves privileged to have been part of a turbulent, watershed period in the country's history. Their letters kept the memories of those early days alive and provided information for his work. In August 1877, Orville presided over a ceremony to commemorate the old man, John Brown, and those who had died in the Battle of Osawatomie. He also became a member of the Kansas Historical Society to which he sent letters, documents, photos, and likenesses of himself, Spencer, and John Brown to preserve the memory of those early struggles in Kansas. He also sent materials he considered sacrosanct, relics of those early years of struggle, such as the remains of his iron safe and the tuning fork for his piano that had been destroyed in the attack on Osawatomie.

In 1876 he and his wife moved to Adams, New York. Mary died two weeks after the move. In 1886 he was invited to attend the quarter centennial celebration of the admission of Kansas to the Union. "Nothing could give me more pleasure than again to see my adopted state, in modern dress of prosperity, and talk over some of the early scenes." he replied.[6] It was held on January 29 in Topeka. In addition to an address by ex-governor Robinson, many of his old fellow pioneers gave talks on various aspects of pioneer life in early Kansas. Two years later Orville married Eliza Ann Bushnell.

Despite the passing of time, he never recovered from the loss of Spencer whom he sadly called his "noble son."[7] Long after Spencer's death, when bleeding Kansas had become a distant memory, Orville would still receive inquiries from the early pioneers wishing to learn more about Spencer and his life in the military. Orville always responded with alacrity, proud of his son's courage and bravery. As late as 1893, he wrote to a friend: "Today Spencer Kellogg Brown sleeps in an unknown grave—no costly monument of marble marks the place where a hero fell. But the government lives, because they were heroes willing to lay down their lives upon the altar of the country in its direst need. And while he sleeps a sleep that knows no making, the living should ever cherish his memory as one of the martyred saints . . . if it is true that a country without heroes dies, it is equally true, with such heroes as America has produced, she will never die."[8]

In his final years, Orville began to succumb to the bronchitis and rheumatism that had plagued him his entire life. More and more, he was forced to take to his bed. Yet his interest in Kansas affairs never waned and he took pride in his involvement in the struggle for a free Kansas. As the light of his life grew dim, he lamented he no longer saw on the Board of Trustees of the Kansas Historical Society the familiar names of the early pioneers. In 1903, he finally witnessed the publication of his biography of Spencer by a reputable New York publisher.*

He died the following year in Leonardo, New Jersey.

---

* *Spencer Kellogg Brown: His Life in Kansas and His Death as a Spy, 1842–1863.*

BIBLIOGRAPHY

MANUSCRIPT COLLECTIONS

NEWSPAPERS

Boston Daily Advertiser
Daily Richmond Enquirer
Kansas Daily Tribune
Kansas Free State
Kansas Weekly Herald
The Leavenworth Herald
Lynchburg Republican
The New York Times
The New-York Tribune
The Republican-Citizen (Atwood, Kansas)

PRIMARY SOURCES

BOOKS

Ainsworth, Fred, and Joseph Kirkley. *The War of the Rebellion: A Compilation of Official Records of the Union and Confederate Armies.* Vol. 6. Washington: Government Printing Office, 1899.

Brewerton, George D. *Wars of the Western Border, or New Homes and a Strange People*. New York: Derby and Jackson, 1860.

Brown, George W. *The Truth at Last: Reminiscences of Old John Brown*. Rockford, IL: A. E. Smith, 1880.

Grant, Ulysses S. *Personal Memoirs of U. S. Grant*. Vol. 1. New York: C. L. Webster, 1885.

Holloway, J. N. *History of Kansas: From the First Exploration of the Mississippi Valley, to Its Admission into the Union*. Lafayette, IN: James, Emmons, 1868.

"Letters of John and Sarah Everett, 1854–1864." *Kansas Historical Review* 8, No. 1, (1939), 3–34.

New York Anti-Slavery Society. *Proceedings of the New York Anti-Slavery Convention*. Utica, NY: Standard and Democrat Office, 1835.

Phillips, William. *The Conquest of Kansas by Missouri and Her Allies*. Boston: Phillips, Sampson, 1856.

Porter, David D. *The Naval History of the Civil War*. New York: Sherman, 1886.

Redpath, James. *The Public Life of Captain John Brown*. Boston: Thayer and Eldridge, 1860.

Richardson, Albert D. *Beyond the Mississippi*. Hartford, CT: American Publishing, 1867.

Robinson, Sara. *Kansas: Its Interior and Exterior Life*. Boston: Crosby, Nichols, 1856.

Thayer, Eli. *A History of the Kansas Crusade, Its Friends and Its Foes*. New York: Harper and Brothers, 1889.

US Congress. *Report of the Special Committee Appointed to Investigate the Troubles in Kansas*. Washington, D.C.: Cornelius Wendell, 1856.

ARTICLES

Halleck, Henry Wager, and George D. Davis. "Military Espionage." *The American Journal of International Law*, 5, No. 3 (July 1911), 590–603.

Lester, C. E. "The Gun-Boat Essex." *Harper's New Monthly Magazine*. February 1863.

Moore, Ely Jr. "The Naming of Osawatomie and Some Experiences with John Brown." *Kansas Historical Collection 1911–1912,* 12 (1912), 338–46.

Walker, Lois H. "Reminiscences of Early Times in Kansas." *Transactions of the Kansas State Historical Society,* 5 (Topeka, 1896), 74–76.

SECONDARY SOURCES

ARTICLES

Epps, Kristin K. "Before the Border War: Slavery and the Settlement of the Western Frontier, 1825–1845." In *Bleeding Kansas, Bleeding Missouri: The Long Civil War on the Border,* edited by Jonathan Earle and Diane Burke, 29–46. Lawrence: University Press of Kansas, 2013.

Isley, W. H. "The Sharps Rifle Episode in Kansas History." *The American Historical Review,* 12, no. 3 (April 1907), 546–66.

Klem, Mary. "Missouri in the Kansas Struggle." *Proceedings of the Mississippi Valley Historical Association,* 9, Part 3 (1917–1918), 394–402.

Muller, H. N., and John Duffy. "Jedidiah Burchard and Vermont's 'New Measure' Revivals: Social Adjustment and the Quest for Unity." *Vermont History* 46, no. 1 (Winter 1978), 5–20.

Rosenberg, Morton M. "The Kansas-Nebraska Act in Iowa: A Case Study." *Annals of Iowa,* 37, no. 6. State Historical Society of Iowa (Fall 1964), 436–57.

Russel, Robert R. "The Issues in the Congressional Struggle over the Kansas-Nebraska Bill, 1854." *Journal of Southern History* 29, no. 2 (May 1963), 187–210.

BOOKS

Blackmar, Frank Wilson. *The Life of Charles Robinson: The First State Governor of Kansas.* Topeka, KS: Crane and Co., 1902.

Casstevens, Frances H. *George W. Alexander and Castle Thunder: A Confederate Prison and Its Commandant.* Jefferson, NC: McFarland and Company, 2006.

Coe, Noah. *A Narrative of the Revival of Religion in the County of Oneida.* Utica, NY: Hastings and Tracy, 1826.

Cozzens, Peter. *The Darkest Days of the War: The Battles of Luka & Corinth.* North Carolina: University of North Carolina Press, 1997.

Cross, Whitney. *The Burned-Over District: The Social and Intellectual History of Enthusiastic Religion in Western New York, 1800–1850.* Ithaca, NY: Cornell University Press, 1950.

Etcheson, Nicole. *Bleeding Kansas: Contested Liberty in the Civil War Era.* Lawrence: University Press of Kansas, 2004.

Foner, Eric. *Gateway to Freedom: The Hidden History of the Underground Railroad.* New York: W. W. Norton, 2016.

Frothingham, Octavius Brooks. *Gerrit Smith: A Biography.* New York, G. Putman's Sons, 1878.

Gihon, John H. *Geary and Kansas.* Philadelphia: King and Baird, 1866.

Hambrick-Stowe, Charles E. *Charles G. Finney and the Spirit of American Evangelism.* Cambridge: William Eerdmans, 1996.

Lee, Guy Carlton. *The True History of the Civil War.* Philadelphia: J. B. Lippincott, 1903.

Leverett, Wilson Spring. *Kansas: The Prelude to War for the Union.* New York: Houghton Mifflin, 1885.

Mahan, A. T. *The Gulf and Inland Waters.* New York, Charles Scribner's Sons, 1883.

McElroy, John. *The Struggle for Missouri.* Washington, D.C., The National Tribune, 1909.

McPherson, James. *Battle Cry of Freedom: The Civil War Era.* New York: Oxford University Press, 2003.

Nevins, Allan. *War for the Union: The Improvised War 1861–1862, Vol. 1,* and *War for the Union: War Becomes Revolution 1862–1863, Vol 2.* New York: Charles Scribner's Sons, 1959.

Nichols, Alice. *Bleeding Kansas.* London: Oxford University Press, 1954.

Nicolay, John C., and John Hay. *Abraham Lincoln: A History.* New York: Century, 1890.

Potter, David M. *The Impending Crisis: 1848–1861.* New York: Harper & Row, 1976.

Seibert, Wilbur H. *The Underground Railroad from Slavery to Freedom.* London: Macmillan, 1898.

Trollope, Frances M. *The Domestic Manners of Americans.* New York: Dodd, Mead, 1901.

Tyler, Alice. *Freedom's Ferment: Phases of American Social History to 1860.* Minneapolis: University of Minnesota Press, 1944.

US Congress. *The Congressional Globe: First Session, Thirty-Third Congress,* Vol. 31. Washington, D.C.: John Rives, 1854.

Villard, Oswald Garrison. *John Brown 1850–1859: A Biography Fifty Years After.* New York: Houghton Mifflin, 1910.

Wilder, Daniel W. *Annals of Kansas.* Topeka: George Martin, 1875.

ENDNOTES

Preface

1. William Porter, "The Campaign in Kentucky: Capt. W. D. Porter's Official Report of the Battle at Lucas's Bend," *The New York Times,* January 20, 1862.

Part I. The Abolitionist: Orville Brown in Bleeding Kansas

Chapter One

1. Spencer Kellogg Brown, *Spencer Kellogg Brown: His Life in Kansas and His Death as a Spy,* 1842-1863, ed. George Gardner Smith (New York: D. Appleton, 1903), 232.
2. Alice Tyler, *Freedom's Ferment: Phases of American Social History to 1860* (Minneapolis: University of Minnesota Press, 1944), 69.
3. Frances M. Trollope, *The Domestic Manners of Americans* (New York: Dodd, Mead, 1901), 79–80.
4. The Burned-Over District was considerably broader geographically than early historians had believed. See Judith Wellman, *Grassroots Reform in the Burned-over District of Upstate New York: Religion, Abolitionism, and Democracy* (New York: Garland Press, 2000), xii.
5. Tyler, *Freedom's Ferment,* 71.
6. Whitney Cross, *The Burned-over District: The Social and Intellectual History of Enthusiastic Religion in Western New York, 1800–1850* (Ithaca, NY: Cornell University Press, 1950), 287.

7. Tyler, *Freedom's Ferment*, 75.

8. Ibid.

9. Ibid., 307.

10. O. C. Brown, "Autobiography, 1894," folder 43, series B, Orville Chester Brown Papers, Kansas State Historical Society, microfilm MS-1293.

11. H. N. Muller and John Duffy, "Jedidiah Burchard and Vermont's 'New Measure' Revivals: Social Adjustment and the Quest for Unity," *Vermont History*, 46, no. 1 (Winter 1978), 5.

12. Charles E. Hambrick-Stowe, *Charles G. Finney and the Spirit of American Evangelism* (Grand Rapids, MI: William Eerdmans, 1996), 141.

13. Noah Coe, *Narrative of the Revival of Religion in the County of Oneida* (Utica, NY: Hastings and Tracy, 1826), 78.

14. O. C. Brown, "Pioneer Life in Kansas, 1854–1861," series C, folder 44, Orville Chester Brown Papers, Kansas State Historical Society microfilm MS-1294.

15. O. C. Brown, "Autobiography," 1894, microfilm MS-1293.

16. O. C. Brown, "Pioneer Life in Kansas," microfilm MS-1294.

17. Ibid.

18. O. C. Brown, "Undated Essays and Other Papers, file unit 2, n.d. folder 2, microfilm MS-1293.

19. Published in the Richfield Springs (NY) *The Mercury*, which is still in existence.

20. Brown, "Pioneer Life in Kansas," microfilm MS-1294.

21. Octavius Brooks Frothingham, *Gerrit Smith: A Biography* (New York: G. Putman's Sons, 1878), 164.

22. O. C. Brown, "Pioneer Life in Kansas," MS-1294.

23. O. C. Brown, "Autobiography," 1894, microfilm MS-1293.

24. Ibid.

25. New York Anti-Slavery Society, "Proceedings of the New York Anti-Slavery Convention," (Utica, NY: Standard and Democrat Office, 1835), 22–23.

26. O. C. Brown, "Pioneer Life in Kansas, 1854–1861," microfilm MS-1294.

27. Ibid.

28. O. C. Brown, "Correspondence and Other Papers, 1834–1904," folders 3–42, Orville Chester Brown Papers, Kansas State Historical Society microfilm MS-1294.

29. Eric Foner, *Gateway to Freedom: The Hidden History of the Underground Railroad* (New York: W. W. Norton, 2016), 30.

30. Ibid., 15.

31. O. C. Brown, "Pioneer Life in Kansas, 1854–1861," microfilm MS-1294.

32. Ibid.

33. Wilbur H. Seibert, *The Underground Railroad from Slavery to Freedom* (London: Macmillan, 1898), 56.

34. Ibid., 64.
35. John McElroy, *The Struggle for Missouri* (Washington, D.C.: National Tribune, 1909), 68.
36. O .C. Brown, "Correspondence and Other Papers, 1834–1904," folders 1–42, microfilm MS-1293.
37. O. C. Brown, "Pioneer Life in Kansas, 1854–1861," microfilm MS-1293.

Chapter Two

1. Morton M. Rosenberg, "The Kansas-Nebraska Act in Iowa: A Case Study," *Annals of Iowa*. State Historical Society of Iowa, 37, no. 6 (1964), 436.
2. Robert R. Russel, "The Issues in the Congressional Struggle over the Kansas-Nebraska Bill, 1854," *Journal of Southern History*, 29, no 2 (May 1963), 188.
3. Ibid., 160.
4. Speech in Springfield quoted in John C. Nicolay and John Hay, *Abraham Lincoln: A History*, vol. 1 (New York: Century, 1890), 335.
5. David R. Potter, *The Impending Crisis: 1848–1861* (New York, Harper & Row, 1976), 155.
6. *Boston Daily Advertiser*, January 31, 1854.
7. Russel, "The Issues in the Congressional Struggle," 207.
8. Ibid., 197.
9. Kristin K. Epps, "Before the Border War: Slavery and the Settlement of the Western Frontier, 1825–1845," in *Bleeding Kansas, Bleeding Missouri: The Long Civil War on the Border*, ed. Jonathan Earle and Diane Burke (Lawrence: University Press of Kansas, 2013), 31–32.
10. Potter, 163.
11. Eli Thayer, *A History of the Kansas Crusade, Its Friends and Its Foes* (New York: Harper and Brothers, 1889), 133.
12. Ibid., 225.
13. See David S. Reynolds, *John Brown, Abolitionist: The Man Who Killed Slavery, Sparked The Civil War and Seeded Civil Rights* (New York: Alfred Knopf, 2005).
14. Nicole Etcheson, *Bleeding Kansas: Contested Liberty in the Civil War Era* (Lawrence: University Press of Kansas, 2004), 20.
15. *New-York Tribune*, May 24, 1854.
16. U. S. Congress, *The Congressional Globe, First Session, Thirty-Third Congress*, vol. 31 (Washington, D.C.: John Rives, 1854), 769.
17. Thayer, *Kansas Crusade*, 98.
18. *Lynchburg Republican*, July 1, 1854.
19. Thayer, *Kansas Crusade*, 65.

20. *The Democratic Platform*, Liberty, Missouri, June 15, 1856.

21. William Phillips, *The Conquest of Kansas by Missouri and Her Allies* (Boston: Phillips, Sampson, 1856), 28–29.

22. J. N. Holloway, *History of Kansas: From the First Exploration of the Mississippi Valley to Its Admission into the Union* (Lafayette, IN: James, Emmons, 1868), 106.

23. "Election of Territorial Legislators," *Squatter Soverign*, March 6, 1855.

24. Quoted in Samuel A. Johnson, "The Emigrant Aid Company in the Kansas Conflict," *Kansas Historical Quarterly*, Vol. 6, no. 1 (1937), 23.

25. Ibid., 124.

26. Etcheson, *Bleeding Kansas*, 31.

27. Alice Nichols, *Bleeding Kansas* (London: Oxford University Press, 1954), 10.

28. Ibid., 130.

Chapter Three

1. Ely Moore Jr., "The Naming of Osawatomie and Some Experiences with John Brown," *Kansas Historical Collection, 1911–1912,* 12 (Topeka: 1912), 339.

2. Ibid., 346.

3. John and Sarah Everett, "Letters of John and Sarah Everett," *Kansas Historical Society,* 8, no 4 (1939), 5.

4. O. C. Brown, "Pioneer Life in Kansas, 1854-1861," microfilm MS-1293.

5. Holloway, *History of Kansas*, 136.

6. *New York Times,* December 26, 1854.

7. Sara Robinson, *Kansas: Its Interior and Exterior Life* (Boston: Crosby Nichols, 1857), 15.

8. Ibid., 16.

9. Ibid., 20.

10. *The Leavenworth Herald*, April 5, 1855.

11. O. C. Brown, "Pioneer Life in Kansas, 1854–1861," microfilm MS-1294.

12. Nichols, *Bleeding Kansas*, 29.

13. Frank Wilson Blackmar, *The Life of Charles Robinson, The First State Governor of Kansas* (Topeka, KS: Crane, 1902), 133.

14. *Kansas Daily Tribune*, July 14, 1855.

15. Etcheson, *Bleeding Kansas*, 71.

16. Nichols, *Bleeding Kansas*, 42.

17. Leverett W. Spring, *Kansas: The Prelude for the War for the Union* (New York: Houghton Mifflin, 1880), 65.

18. Etcheson, *Bleeding Kansas*, 71.

19. C. Stearns to Editor, *Herald of Freedom*, September 22, 1855.

20. Spring, *Kansas,* 66.

21. Etcheson, *Bleeding Kansas*, 72.
22. Holloway, *History of Kansas,* 196.

Chapter Four

1. O. C. Brown, "Correspondence and Other Papers," 1834–1904, microfilm MS-1293.
2. O. C. Brown, "Undated Essays and Other Papers," microfilm MS-1293.
3. Ibid.
4. O. C. Brown, "Pioneer Life in Kansas, 1854–1861," microfilm 1294.
5. George W. Brown, *The Truth at Last: Reminiscences of Old John Brown* (Rockford, IL: A. E. Smith, 1880), 5.
6. O. C. Brown, "Pioneer Life in Kansas, 1854–1861," microfilm 1293.
7. Ibid..
8. *New-York Tribune,* February 8, 1856.
9. Mary Klem, "Missouri in the Kansas Struggle," *Proceedings of the Mississippi Valley Historical Association,* 9, no. 3 (1917–1918), 407.
10. William Phillips, *The Conquest of Kansas by Missouri and Her Allies* (Boston: Phillip Sampson, 1856), 154.
11. George D. Brewerton, *Wars of the Western Border, or New Homes and a Strange People* (New York: Derby and Jackson, 1860), 154.
12. Holloway, *History of Kansas*, 216.
13. Ibid., 220–221.
14. Ibid., 221–222.
15. Daniel Wilder, *Annals of Kansas*, (Topeka: T. D. Thatcher, 1886), 88.
16. Holloway, *History of Kansas*, 224.
17. Charles Robinson, *The Kansas Conflict*, (Lawrence: Journal Publishing, 1898), 194.
18. Lois H. Walker, "Reminiscences of Early Times in Kansas," *Transactions of the Kansas State Historical Society* 5 (Topeka, 1896): 74–76.
19. Nichols, *Bleeding Kansas*, 65.
20. Wilder, *Annals of Kansas*, 89.
21. Ibid., 235.
22. William A. Phillips, 189.
23. Robinson, *The Kansas Conflict*, 199.
24. Brewerton, *Wars of the Western Border*, 182.
25. Ibid., 194.
26. Phillips, *The Conquest of Kansas*, 227.
27. Nichols, *Bleeding Kansas*, 75.
28. Ibid., 197.
29. Etcheson, *Bleeding Kansas*, 86.
30. James Redpath, *The Public Life of Captain John Brown* (Boston: Thayer and Eldridge, 1860), 92.

Chapter Five

1. Brewerton, *Wars of the Western Border*, 204.
2. Holloway, *History of Kansas*, 278.
3. Nichols, *Bleeding Kansas*, 85.
4. Etcheson, *Bleeding Kansas*, 95.
5. Brewerton, *Wars of the Western Border*, 210.
6. Spring, *Kansas,* 105.
7. Etcheson, *Bleeding Kansas*, 96.
8. Spring, *Kansas* 104.
9. Holloway, *History of Kansas*, 288.
10. W. H. Isley, "The Sharps Rifle Episode in Kansas History," *The American Historical Review*, 12, No. 3 (April 1907), 560.
11. O. C. Brown, "Pioneer Life in Kansas, 1854–1861," microfilm, MS-1294.
12. Ibid.
13. Ibid.
14. Ibid.
15. Ibid.
16. Ibid.
17. Brown, *Spencer Kellogg Brown*, 64.
18. Sara Robinson, *Kansas,* 191.
19. O. C. Brown, "Correspondence and Other Papers, 1834–1904," microfilm, MS-1293.
20. Ibid.
21. US District Court, Lykens County, Kansas Territory, "Indictment of Orville Chester Brown, John Brown Sr., John Brown Jr., Et Al," May 1856.
22. O. C. Brown, "Pioneer Life in Kansas, 1854–1861," microfilm MS-1294.
23. Spring, *Kansas,* 110.
24. Sara Robinson, *Kansas,* 235.
25. Charles Sumner, *The Crime against Kansas* (Boston: Jewett, 1856), 9.
26. Eric H. Walther, *The Fire Eaters* (Baton Rouge: Louisiana State University Press, 1992), 178.
27. Guy Carlton Lee, *The True History of the Civil War* (Philadelphia: J. B. Lippincott, 1903), 117.
28. Alfred Theodore Andres, *History of the State of Kansas* (Chicago: Western Historical Co., 1883), 130.
29. Quoted in Nichols, *Bleeding Kansas*, 112–113.
30. Letter, Salmon Brown to William E. Connelley, May 28, 1913.
31. US Congress, Report of the Special Committee Appointed to Investigate the Troubles in Kansas (1856), 107.
32. *Republican Citizen, December 20, 1879.*

33. US Congress, Report of the Special Committee, 107.
34. John Brown, *The Life and Letter of John Brown, Liberator of Kansas and Martyr of Virginia*, ed. F. B. Sanborn (Boston, Roberts Brothers, 1885), 250.
35. Sara Robinson, *Kansas,* 305.
36. Phillips, *The Conquest of Kansas*, 372.
37. Ibid., 373.

Chapter Six

1. Sara Robinson, *Kansas,* 313–14.
2. Ibid., 315.
3. Spring, *Kansas,* 184–85.
4. Nichols, *Bleeding Kansas*, 139.
5. O. C. Brown, "Pioneer Life in Kansas, 1854–1861," microfilm MS-1294.
6. Oswald Garrison Villard, *John Brown 1850–1859: A Biography Fifty Years After* (New York: Houghton Mifflin, 1910), 245.
7. Brown, *Spencer Kellogg Brown*, 68.
8. Ibid., 244.
9. Ibid., 69.
10. Ibid., 71.
11. Ibid., 73.
12. Ibid.
13. Ibid., 74.
14. Ibid., 75.
15. Ibid., 76-77.
16. Ibid., 173.
17. O. C. Brown, Pioneer Life in Kansas, 1854–1861," microfilm, MS-1294.
18. Brown, *Spencer Kellogg Brown*, 77.
19. Ibid., 79.
20. Ibid., 89.
21. Ibid., 82.
22. Ibid., 82.
23. Ibid.
24. Ibid., 83–84.
25. Ibid., 86.
26. Ibid.
27. Ibid., 91.
28. Ibid., 93–94.
29. Ibid.
30. Ibid
31. Ibid.

32. Ibid.

33. Villard, *John Brown*, 274.

34. Brown, *Spencer Kellogg Brown*, 111.

35. Ibid., 121.

36. Ibid., 120.

37. Ibid., 118.

38. John H. Gihon, *Geary and Kansas* (Philadelphia: King and Baird, 1866), 104.

39. Gihon, *Geary and Kansas*, 154.

40. Etcheson, *Bleeding Kansas,* 141.

41. Gihon, *Geary and Kansas*, 296.

42. O. C. Brown, "Correspondence and Other Papers, 1834–1904, microfilm MS-1293.

43. Ibid.

44. Nichols, *Bleeding Kansas*, 194.

45. Ibid., 212.

46. Spring, *Kansas,* 223.

47. Etcheson, *Bleeding Kansas,* 158.

48. Spring, *Kansas,* 239–40.

49. Ibid., 240.

50. Spring, *Kansas,* 238.

51. Spring, *Kansas,* 245–246.

52. Spring, *Kansas,* 247.

53. Ibid., 248.

54. Etcheson, *Bleeding Kansas,* 195.

55. Spring, *Kansas,* 251.

56. Ibid., 252.

57. Donald Gilmore, *Civil War on the Missouri-Kansas Border* (Gretna, LA: Pelican, 2005), 96.

58. Albert D. Richardson, *Beyond the Mississippi* (Hartford, CT: American Publishing, 1867), 296.

59. "Letter to President Buchanan from J. P. Jones," *Transactions of the Kansas State Historical Society,* Kansas State Historical Society, Vol. 5, 585–87.

60. Letter from James H. Lane to Governor Medary," January 9, 1859, *Transactions of the Kansas State Historical Society,* Kansas State Historical Society, Vol. 5, 588.

61. O. C. Brown, "Correspondence and Other Papers, 1834–1904," microfilm, MS-1293.

62. Ibid.

63. Ibid.

64. Ibid.

65. Perl Wilbur Morgan, ed., *History of Wyandotte County, Kansas and Its People,* Vol. 1 (Chicago: Lewis Publishing, 1911), 178.

66. O. C. Brown, "Correspondence and Other Papers, 1834–1904," microfilm MS-1293.
67. *Kansas Free State,* January 31, 1855.
68. *Weekly Kansas Herald,* October 9, 1858.
69. Ibid.
70. *New York Times,* November 1, 1860.
71. Brown, *Spencer Kellogg Brown,* 156.
72. O. C. Brown, "Correspondence and Other Papers, 1834–1904," MS-1293.
73. Ibid.
74. *Republican,* May 17, 1860.
75. O. C. Brown, "Correspondence and Other Papers, 1834–1904," MS-1293.
76. O. C. Brown, "Correspondence and Other Papers, 1834–1904," MS-1293.
77. Ibid.
78. Brown, *Spencer Kellogg Brown,* 160.
79. Ibid., 161.
80. O. C. Brown, "Pioneer Life in Kansas 1854–1861," MS-1294.
81. O. C. Brown, "Correspondence and Other Papers, 18341834–1904," 1904," MS-1293.
82. Ibid.
83. Ibid.
84. O. C. Brown, "Correspondence and Other Papers 1834–1904," MS-1293.
85. O. C. Brown, "Correspondence and Other Papers, 1834–1904," MS-1293.
86. Etcheson, *Bleeding Kansas,* 209.
87. Wilmington, *Daily Herald,* December 5, 1859.
88. Michael E. Woods, *Bleeding Kansas: Slavery, Sectionalism, and Civil War on the Missouri-Kansas Border* (New York: Routledge, 2017), 100.
89. Allan Nevins, *War for the Union 1861–1862, Vol. 1, The Improvised War* (New York: Scribner, 1959), 120.
90. O. C. Brown, "Correspondence and Other Papers, 183–1904,"MS-1293.
91. Ibid.
92. *Journal of the Missouri State Convention* (St. Louis: George Knapp, 1863), 241.
93. John McElroy, *The Struggle for Missouri* (Washington, D.C.: National Tribune, 1909), 72.
94. Ibid., 69.
95. James Peckham, *Gen. Nathaniel Lyon and Missouri in 1861: A Monograph of the Great Rebellion* (New York: American News, 1866), 150.
96. Brown, *Spencer Kellogg Brown,* 199.
97. Peckham, *Gen. Nathaniel Lyon,* 152.
98. Brown, *Spencer Kellogg Brown,* 202.
99. Ibid., 204.

100. Allan Nevins, *The Improvised War*, Vol. 1, 124–25.
101. McElroy, *The Struggle for Missouri*, 117–18.
102. Brown,, *Spencer Kellogg Brown*, 362.
103. Ibid., 208.
104. Nevins, *The Improvised War*, 316.
105. McElroy, *The Struggle for Missouri*, 181.
106. Ibid., 171.
107. Ibid,, 186.

Chapter Seven

1. J. Randall Houp, The 24th Missouri Volunteer Infantry, "Lyon Legion," (Alma, AR: J. R. Houp, 1997).
2. Brown, *Spencer Kellogg Brown*, 213.
3. Nevins, *The Improvised War*, 331.
4. A. T. Mahan, *The Gulf and Inland Waters* (New York: Scribner, 1883), 15.
5. C. E. Lester, "The Gun-Boat Essex," *Harper's New Monthly Magazine,* February 1863.
6. William Porter, "The Campaign in Kentucky," January 20, 1862.
7. David D. Porter, *The Naval History of the Civil War* (New York: Sherman, 1886), 145.
8. James A. Raab, *Confederate General Lloyd Tilghman: A Biography* (Jefferson, N.C.: McFarland and Co., 2004), 82.
9. Brown, *Spencer Kellogg Brown*, 234.
10. Ibid., 236.
11. Ibid., 237.
12. Ibid., 239–240.
13. Ibid., 241.
14. Ibid., 242.
15. Ibid., 243.
16. Ibid.

Chapter Eight

1. Peter Cozzens, *The Darkest Days of the War: The Battles of Iuka & Corinth* (Chapel Hill: University of North Carolina Press, 1997), 18–19.
2. Nevins, *The War for the Union*, 82.
3. Timothy T. Isbell, *Shiloh and Corinth: Sentinels of Stone* (Jackson: University of Mississippi Press, 2007), 20.
4. Tim Jeal, *Stanley: The Impossible Life of Africa's Greatest Explorer* (New Haven: Yale University Press, 2007), 45.

5. Brown, *Spencer Kellogg Brown*, 245.
6. Ibid.
7. Ibid.
8. Ibid.
9. Ibid., 246.
10. Ulysses S. Grant, *Personal Memoirs of Ulysses S. Grant*, 1 (New York: C. L. Webster, 1885), 154.
11. Ibid., 85.

Part II. The Spy: Spencer Kellogg Brown in the Civil War

Chapter Nine

1. Smith, ed., *Spencer Kellogg Brown*, 257.
2. C. E. Lester, "The Gun-boat Essex," *Harper's New Monthly Magazine,* February 1863.
3. Brown, *Spencer Kellogg Brown*, 255.
4. Ibid.
5. James McPherson, *Battle Cry of Freedom: The Civil War Era* (New York: Oxford University Press, 2003), 419.
6. Brown, *Spencer Kellogg Brown*, 281–282.
7. Ibid., 282.
8. Ibid., 283.
9. Barbara Brooks Tomblin, *The Civil War on the Mississippi: Union Sailors, Gunboat Captains, and the Campaign to Control the River* (Lexington: University Press of Kentucky, 2016), 162.
10. Ibid., 163.
11. "Lancaster at War," www.lancasteratwar.com/search/label/Rosenmiller_DP . Accessed October 4, 2018.

Chapter Ten

1. Brown, *Spencer Kellogg Brown*, 290.
2. Ibid., 290.
3. Ibid., 298.
4. See Henry Wager Halleck and George D. Davis, "Military Espionage," *The American Journal of International Law* 5, no. 3 (July 1911): 509–603.
5. Brown, *Spencer Kellogg Brown*, 298.
6. Ibid., 307.

7. Ibid., 321–322.

8. Ibid., 292.

9. Ibid., 292.

10. Ibid., 293.

11. Ibid.

12. Ibid., 328.

13. O. C. Brown, "Correspondence and Other Papers, 1834–1904," MS-1293.

14. Smith, *Spencer Kellogg Brown*, 338.

15. Ibid., 337–38.

16. Ibid., 338.

17. Ibid., 295.

18. Ibid., 320–21.

19. Ibid., 304.

20. Ibid.

21. Ibid., 306-307.

22. *Daily Richmond Enquirer,* August 12, 1862.

23. Frances H. Casstevens, *George W. Alexander and Castle Thunder: A Confederate Prison and Its Commandant* (Jefferson, NC: McFarland, 2006), 3.

24. Brown, *Spencer Kellogg Brown*, 350.

25. See Allan Nevins, *The War for the Union: War Becomes Revolution,* Vol. 2 122.

26. Smith, ed., *Spencer Kellogg Brown*, 357–360.

27. Brown, *Spencer Kellogg Brown*, 311.

28. Fred Ainsworth and Joseph Kirkley, *The War of the Rebellion: A Compilation of Official Records of the Union and Confederate Armies,* 6 (Washington: Government Printing Office, 1899), 321.

29. Brown,, Spencer Kellogg Brown, 366.

30. Ibid., 377.

31. Ibid., 371.

32. Ibid., 314.

33. Ibid., 315.

34. Ibid.

35. Ibid., 316.

36. Elizabeth R. Varon, *Southern Lady, Union Spy: The True Story of Elizabeth Van Lew, A Union Agent at the Heart of the Confederacy* (New York: Oxford University Press, 2003), 101.

37. Brown, *Spencer Kellogg Brown*, 377.

38. Ibid., 378–379.

39. O. C. Brown, "Correspondence and Other Papers, 1834–1904," MS-1293.

40. Ibid.

41. O. C. Brown, "Pioneer Life in Kansas, 1854–1861," MS-1294.

42. Ibid.

43. Ibid.

44. O. C. Brown, "Correspondence and Other Papers, 1834–1904," MS-1293.

45. Ibid.

Epilogue

1. O. C. Brown, "Correspondence and Other Papers, 1834–1904," MS-1293.

INDEX